AGGRESSION AND VIOLENCE IN ADOLESCENCE

Using data sets consisting of cross-sectional surveys drawn from nationally representative samples of adolescents in the United States and official sources of crime statistics, a portrait of aggression and violence among adolescents is presented. Fluctuations in self-reported and official sources of data are examined by year, gender, grade, and race. Both distal and contemporary risk factors for aggression and violence are discussed. Distal risk factors for violence in adolescence are presented using longitudinal studies. The General Aggression Model provides the framework for exploring which contemporary personal and situational factors increase or decrease risk for aggression and violence. Dating aggression in adolescence is placed in the context of normal development and varies according to individual partner and relationship factors. This book presents rigorously tested scientific prevention programs for adolescents with violent and aggressive behavior.

Since joining the faculty at the Institute for Child Study, Department of Human Development, at the University of Maryland in 1973, Dr. Robert F. Marcus has balanced his academic duties with his work in the community. Dr. Marcus holds a Ph.D. in human development and family studies from the Pennsylvania State University. Completion of his dissertation was supported by a grant from the National Science Foundation. Dr. Marcus has authored more than forty articles and presented more than fifty of his works at professional and scientific meetings around the country. Interested in counseling children and adolescents early in his career as a Psychology Junior Fellow for the New Jersey Department of Institutions and Agencies and as a school psychologist in New Jersey, Dr. Marcus became a licensed psychologist in Maryland in 1979. A clinical practice working with aggressive children and adolescents complemented his academic interests. Since developing the course "Adolescent Violence" in 1993, his interests started forming into this book. Currently, Dr. Marcus is a Practice Associate of Sheppard Pratt Hospital in Baltimore, Maryland, with an assignment at their satellite clinic in Columbia, Maryland.

Aggression and Violence in Adolescence

ROBERT F. MARCUS

Department of Human Development
University of Maryland

CAMBRIDGE
UNIVERSITY PRESS

Dedication

To my parents, Gilbert and Hannah Marcus

To my wife, Betsy Singer Marcus

CAMBRIDGE UNIVERSITY PRESS
Cambridge, New York, Melbourne, Madrid, Cape Town, Singapore, São Paulo, Delhi

Cambridge University Press
32 Avenue of the Americas, New York, NY 10013-2473, USA

www.cambridge.org
Information on this title: www.cambridge.org/9780521868815

First published 2007

Printed in the United States of America

A catalog record for this publication is available from the British Library.

Library of Congress Cataloging in Publication Data

Marcus, Robert F., 1943–
Aggression and violence in adolescence / Robert F. Marcus.
    p.   cm.
Includes bibliographical references and index.
ISBN 978-0-521-86881-5 (hardback) – ISBN 978-0-521-68891-8 (pbk.)
1. Aggressiveness in adolescence.   2. Violence in adolescence.   3. Aggressiveness in adolescence –
Cross sectional studies.   4. Violence in adolescence – Longitudinal studies.   I. Title.
BF724.3.A34M37   2007
155.5'18232 – dc22   2007005153

ISBN   978-0-521-86881-5 hardback
ISBN   978-0-521-68891-8 paperback

Contents

Acknowledgments

I gratefully acknowledge the assistance of Nicole Fowler and Sarah Knighton-Wisor for their help in gathering many important studies, and for providing a student's perspective on chapter content. My clinic colleagues, Dr. Karen Alleyne and Dr. V. Nia Shell, provided important psychiatric perspectives on key issues. Jared Marcus and Meredith Marcus provided technical assistance at various points in the preparation of this volume.

Introduction

Public attention to youth violence is typically brief, stimulated by dramatic events such as school shootings, followed by much blaming, but is rarely followed by sustained examination of etiology, cost, and prevention. Public concern about the association between media violence and children's aggression has actually waned with time, despite considerable concern in the 1970s. Public belief in the association between media (i.e., TV, movies) violence and aggressive behavior by children and adolescents, as reflected in magazine and popular press articles, was more certain in the mid-1970s than today, despite both experimental and correlational studies confirming a moderate association between the two, a linkage about as strong as that between smoking and lung cancer (Bushman & Anderson, 2001).

More surprising, a recent behavioral science text expressed doubt about any relation between video violence and aggression in adolescence. Meanwhile, increasing public acceptance of more graphic forms of media violence, and an insatiable hunger for novel forms of violence, perhaps best seen in the sales and enthusiasm generated over mature-rated video games, may reflect a fascination for actions far beyond the experience of everyday life. Gradual acceptance of media violence may be similar to gradual adaptation to the danger of violence in countries at war, or acceptance of violence in war zones that are present in some dangerous cities; there each act of violence is followed by a quick recovery and return to "normalcy."

Public attention to media or rarely occurring dramatic violent acts appears sustained by fearfulness, the great sentinel of attention processes. But fear is also likely to wane, carrying with it interest in repairing the situation. A dramatic increase in school violence often leads to increased parental protectiveness, modifications in school emergency plans, including lock-downs, metal detectors, and drive-by shooting drills. Perhaps our perceived helplessness in the face of predatory advertisers, environmental dangers such as lead-based paints or mercury in fish, as in the case of those seriously affecting adolescents, such as drugs, alcohol, and gun violence, has led to short bursts of effort by individuals and communities to take some immediate protective action. But fear of violence subsides, later to be replaced by yet newer fears of avian flu, killer bees, identity theft, or invasion by illegal immigration. Attention spans are short, but social and behavioral scientists also have been unable to promote the sense that both short- and long-term solutions are achievable.

What has become clearer, with the accumulation of improved methods of monitoring the impact of violence on individuals, families, communities, and nations, is that violence is costly in many ways. Each violent act, whether it is the case of an individual child who is bullied in middle school, or a high school shooting involving many individuals within a particular school and community, sends ripples of misery throughout the immediate and greater context. A bullied middle schooler may experience the lasting sense of humiliation among peers, personal shame for not responding at all, and fantasies of retaliation. Bystanders of bullying also may experience a greater sense of vulnerability to harm (i.e., "it could happen to me"), and all are inclined to feel a loss of faith in the abilities of adults to protect them; these emotional responses may endure well beyond the point where their bruises have disappeared. Two such bullied and bullying adolescents, Dylan Klebold and Eric Harris of Columbine High School, succeeded in having a much greater impact. On a much larger scale, their murders of 12 high school students and one teacher at Columbine High School on April 20, 1999, and their suicide led many students to suffer symptoms of post traumatic stress disorder (e.g., hyper-alertness, flashbacks, vivid recollections, persistent sense of vulnerability, and mistrust of others), and disruptions in their lives for months afterward. Suffering witnesses may have come to more closely approximate the beliefs held by those in very different circumstances, as noted by Garbarino (1997) who described the secrets learned by adolescents in toxic environments swamped by violence: that when it comes to violence anything is possible; you are not as invulnerable to harm as you thought; life is more fragile than you thought; and others cannot be trusted to protect you. Whereas the cost in 1994 dollars of a single gunshot wound has been estimated at $17,000 (Cook, 1999), the lifetime medical costs for the Columbine survivors, the police and legal costs, cost of school repair and increased safety measures, and lost productivity and wages, will be far greater.

There were much more poignant aftershocks within the society following Columbine. There was the story of a mother of one of the wheelchair-bound survivors who went shopping for a gun in a local pawnshop. When the store owner turned his back, she loaded the gun and killed herself with it. In addition, the friend of one of the students killed at Columbine High School committed suicide later that year. Hundreds of copycat attempts throughout the United States later that year, and websites set up in praise of school violence perpetrators, suggest that for each of the horrified witnesses to those events, there were many adolescents who thought the killings were attractive, justifiable, and perhaps even noble acts. Not only do violent acts promote greater acceptance of future violence among some adolescents, but they also generate motivation for further violent behavior.

Harder to calculate is the damage to a nation's psyche resulting from acts of mass murder by its young. A survey in 2005 of 17,000 adults in sixteen different countries around the world asked respondents what their opinions were about the character of Americans as a people (PEW Global Attitudes Project, 2005). The answers were shocking. Whereas the majority of respondents around the world agreed that Americans were "inventive" and "hard working," a majority also said that Americans were a "violent" people; 64% of Canadians and 49% of Americans agreed. Was the international perception of Americans as a violent people colored by highly visible school shootings, its exports of violent movies, or attempted or completed assassinations of U.S. leaders, such as John F. Kennedy, Martin Luther King, Jr., Robert F. Kennedy, Gerald Ford, Ronald Reagan, and many others? Or was it the prominence of gun violence in the United States as compared with other countries. According to a 1997 study of gun violence in 26 industrialized countries by the U.S. Centers for Disease Control, 86% of firearm-related homicides of children and adolescents occurred in the United States, and the rate (per 100,000 population) of firearm deaths of children in the United States was 16 times greater than the average for all of the other 25 countries combined (USDHHS, 1997). Loss of positive regard and deterioration of reputation among nations and its causes may be difficult to estimate, but a national disgrace nevertheless.

Violence among adolescents in the United States has also been the most prominent symptom of a national violence problem. The risk for intentional, life-threatening violent behavior is greater during adolescence than at any other time in the human lifespan. As one example, data on the causes of death among adolescents, as collected by the National Center for Health Statistics, for the years 1999 through 2002, have shown that for no other age group was homicide (ranked two), or suicide (ranked three) as prominent a killer as in adolescence. Among African-American adolescents, homicide has consistently ranked as the number one cause of death. Something dramatic happens during adolescence that requires careful scrutiny. A new report issued by the U.S. Federal Bureau of Investigation's Incident-Based Reporting System, for the years 2000–2004, showed that the greatest percentage (i.e., 38%) of offenders in schools were those ages 13 through 15, and 95% of arrests at schools were because of some form of physical assault (USDJ, 2006). Data derived from the National Crime Victimization Survey, for the years 1993 through 2004, have shown that adolescents ages 12 to 15 and 16 to 19 have remained the most victimized of all age groups (Snyder, 2004). Surges of violence among adolescents also demand very careful scrutiny as to what, where, when, and why. Violence is so emblematic of any society's problems with violence in general that epidemiologists use the proportion of adolescents in a society as a short hand, reliable index of a society's problem with violence as a whole.

The specific forms and problems of aggression and violence by adolescents had not previously been apparent because prior to 1980 in the United States we did not have the instruments with which to study its ebb and flow in the country over time, or variability within groups (e.g., age, gender, race). Nor could we estimate its prevalence in a way that was representative of the general population. Nor did we have both cross-sectional and longitudinal research data describing the linkages between and the sequential development of both. That deficiency has largely been remedied. Research over the past twenty years has greatly enhanced our ability to monitor adolescent aggression and violence, in many different forms (e.g., bullying, weapons use, criminal violence), and data have shown us that aggression and violence is startlingly common in the lives of U.S. adolescents (Marcus, 2005). In the United States, for example, the U.S. Federal Bureau of Investigation (in 1994) has said that arrests of juveniles for violent crime had reached "epidemic" and "unprecedented" levels. Whereas there was abundant evidence, from both police reports and confidential surveys of adolescents, that we also witnessed a decline in the most serious forms of criminal violence during the 1990s, it was also clear that not all forms of violence receded to the level of the 1980s. According to a report on youth violence, completed under the auspices of the Surgeon General of the United States (USDHHS, 2001), police reports of arrests for some gun crimes had shown declines, but for arrests in the case of aggravated assault (i.e., causing injury or using a weapon), elevations did not recede back to the levels of the 1980s. In addition, during the 1993–2002 period there had been a 29% decrease in the arrest of males for aggravated assault, but an increase of 7% among females during the same period (Snyder, 2002).

The results from surveys of nationally representative samples of adolescents, grades 9 through 12, and other confidential self-report data noted in the Surgeon General's Report on Youth Violence were more unsettling, and showed a more complex picture of declines and increases. Declines in some violent behaviors, no change in some, and increases in others clouded the picture of declines in aggressive and violent behavior among adolescents. Some self-report data in that report had shown changes among high school seniors, namely a monotonic increase in the prevalence of violent behaviors for each of the years during the 1990s and for each of the last thirty years (see Monitoring the Future cited in USDHHS, 2001). Other research using confidential interviews of high school and middle school youth in the mid-1990s also had shown that the risk for boys of having had a physical fight in the past year was very high in absolute terms; 40% of boys had reported having had a physical fight and 7.5% had suffered an injury as a result (Marcus, 2005). Whereas in the 1990s there was a decline in self-reported violent and violence-related behaviors for adolescents according to national surveys by the Centers for Disease Control, the declines were noted in some violent behaviors, but not others; and some violent or violence-related behaviors (e.g., injury resulting from physical fighting) actually increased (Brenner, Simon, Lowry, & Krug, 1999). Those same national surveys showed a decline from an average of 137 violent incidents per 100 adolescents in 1991 to 116 incidents per 100 adolescents in 1997 (Brenner et al., 1999), again suggesting that absolute levels of violence remained a serious problem. Unfortunately, many surveyed violent and violence-related behaviors have shown an upturn in prevalence in the most recent reported data in 2005, after having leveled off in 2001 and 2003.

With access to firearms by about 30% of adolescents, the potential for disaster – an adolescent who takes a dispute with a teacher or peer to the "next step" – is always present. Just as increases in aggressive and violent behavior had increased in the early 1990s, a new trend upwards could again threaten to overwhelm much of the successful efforts by professional organizations, schools, and state, local, and federal efforts to reduce violence by adolescents.

The Current Volume

The focus of this volume is both broad and narrow in scope. Throughout the volume, there is an attempt to collate evidence in order to describe, and where possible, explain the prevalence of aggressive and violent behaviors among adolescents in the United States over the past twenty years. Aggression and violence are the sole focus, rather than all antisocial behaviors, such as substance abuse and delinquency, even though these and many other behaviors may positively correlate with aggressive and violent behavior. The current view is that aggression and violence are related to one another, and unique, despite positive correlations with other antisocial behaviors. Second, every effort is made to martial empirical evidence coming from a variety of data sources about behavior in natural settings, including self-report surveys, interviews, observations by teachers and parents, and clinical case studies in order to construct a valid portrait.

In Chapter 1, there is reliance on large data sets from nationally representative studies of adolescents that are now available. These data can sensitively be used to describe changes over the last twenty years and to characterize differences among various subgroups by age, gender, and race. Confirmation of trends over the years and individual differences among adolescents can also be found in multiple survey sets generated at similar points in time. Both self-report data and official data sources addressing the same differences are compared. When available, comparable research findings from other countries are used to address individual differences among groups. Wherever possible, and in most chapters, meta-analytic studies are used to enable generalizations according to the "weight" of the evidence and to identify important correlates and effective prevention efforts. The primary focus in all chapters will be on adolescence, roughly defined as the period between the beginning of middle school and the end of the high school years, and ages 11 through 18. Research in developmental psychology has consistently shown this period in human development to be unique with regard to family and peer relationships, and personality, physical, and cognitive development.

Development from early childhood to early adolescence, in Chapter 2, will shed light on theoretical and research models articulating the paths of the early development of aggression and violent behavior. Sometimes referred to as distal influences on violence, Chapter 2 describes the course of important individual differences in physical, social, emotional, and cognitive development that help to define a trajectory toward violence in adolescence. Important models of the early influences on the development of aggression and violence are described. The relative influence of each formative influence and individual risk factor relating to aggression and violence will be summarized in an important meta-analytic study of longitudinal studies predicting violence in adolescence.

Chapters 3 and 4 provide a current look at proximal, or contemporary risk and protective factors for the development of aggression and violence. Chapter 3 reviews what is known about key personality traits serving to motivate aggression and violence, those that mediate (i.e., modify or alter) the direction or strength of individual dispositions, and that moderate (i.e., delimit) the expression of aggression and violence. Chapter 4 is a review of situational risk and protective factors that increase or decrease the likelihood of both behaviors. Chapter 4 makes use of a recently proposed model of situational influences based on both laboratory and naturalistic studies, although the current review of situational influences in adolescence will focus on risk factors in natural settings.

Chapter 5 reviews a body of research concerning relationships with romantic partners, and the appearance of aggression directed toward partners during the middle and high school years. Here, as in earlier chapters, aggression toward dating partners is discussed in the context of the normal development of romantic relationships, and the individual social and emotional development of boys and girls.

Chapter 6 is a discussion of important primary, secondary, and tertiary prevention programs designed to thwart the appearance of aggression and violence. After first discussing scientific standards for quality programs developed over the last twenty years, variations on three kinds of prevention programs that have met these standards are presented. Specifically, programs directed at younger children prior to the appearance of aggression, those directed at children at risk (e.g., individually handicapped, reared in violent neighborhoods), and those directed at the adolescents who already are violent will be examined for their content and effectiveness. Whereas space did not allow for the presentation of all effective and exemplary prevention programs, those that specifically address risk factors noted in preceding chapters were given priority. The result was a sampling of a variety of effective programs developed over the last twenty years.

Chapter 7 offers a recapitulation of major themes presented in this volume and offers suggestions for furthering our understanding and prevention of aggression and violence in adolescence.

1

Prevalence of Aggression and Violence in Adolescence

Adolescence, as a stage of human development, has always been regarded as a time in which risk-taking behaviors are common. The likelihood that an individual will engage in aggressive or violent behaviors during the middle school and high school years is illustrated when we take a broad view of data that has emerged about adolescent aggressive and violent behaviors over the past fifteen years. Currently for adolescents the ages 14 to 18 is a period when 42% of boys and 28% of girls in the United States acknowledge having had a physical fight in the past year (USDHHS, 2006a). Death as a result of homicide consistently ranks second among the causes of death among 15 to 24 year olds, the highest ranking for homicide of any age group across the lifespan (NCHS, 2004). Crime surveys have consistently shown that 12 to 19 year olds have the highest rates of victimization by violent crime of any age group (Snyder, 2004; Snyder & Sickmund, 1999). Exploration of variation over time in prevalence rates for aggressive and violent behaviors during adolescence, and variations with grade, gender, and race, will tell us what is happening in the real world and who is at greatest risk. This macro-examination of relatively fixed and key markers will be followed by narrower focus on the early development of aggression and violence (in Chapter 2), and by discussion of more malleable personality and situational risk factors (in Chapters 3 and 4).

Research over the past twenty years has given us an increasingly complete picture of adolescents at greatest risk for aggression and violence, gained primarily through two available measurement tools: (a) survey and interview responses from nationally representative samples of adolescents (e.g., the Centers for Disease Control and Prevention's Youth Risk Behavior Survey), in which students are asked about their participation in easily recognized forms of aggression and violence such as physical fighting and weapon carrying; and (b) serious forms of criminal violence reported to police headquarters around the United States, such as homicide and simple assault (e.g., the Federal Bureau of Investigation's Uniform Crime Reports). Both self-reports and "official" reports are essential to a more complete understanding of which adolescents are in greatest danger for the most serious forms of violence (USDHHS, 2001; Snyder & Sickmund, 1999). Self-report data is essential because of its usefulness in describing prevalence in the population and individual differences, and "official" reports because of their focus on more serious criminally violent behaviors.

Definitions of Aggression and Violence

As a clinician working for more than 30 years with middle and high school students, I found two counseling cases that typified the many cases of violence seen over three decades of work. The first was a 15-year-old male, brought by his mother and referred by the courts for counseling. This very large and friendly young man bragged about his involvement in fighting, drug sales, and many other anti-social behaviors, both locally and in a nearby city. He spoke proudly of the many violent and non-violent crimes he had engaged in, taking care not to be too specific about the details. The list was a long one, and his violence was motivated by thrill seeking in teen clubs, and a few incidents were punctuated by various stages of continuing police and court involvement. He bragged about how his father taught him to box, typically knocking him down, until he knocked his father off his feet, thus ending his fight training. After many weeks of counseling, he abruptly stopped coming for counseling, with no apparent reason given. Shortly afterward, he was arrested. According to newspaper reports, he was accused of robbing a student at gunpoint when the student left the high school my client used to intermittently attend.

Perhaps more typical of the everyday violence, as reported by youths on self-report measures, was a middle schooler who was 12 years old when I began seeing him. His history included child neglect, which caused him to live with his grandmother; and years of poor schoolwork. At the time I first saw him, he was uncooperative with teachers, and had conflict with, and rejection by, peers. One day, he appeared for counseling with a swollen, bruised, and bleeding lip, looking disheveled and physically trembling, having come directly from school. Shaken and exhausted, he told of another boy, one who had bullied him for many months. The middle school classmate had unleashed a furious assault on him in school, within sight of teachers and students, none of whom responded to his distress. He was later transferred to a special school better equipped to monitor both his safety and academic work.

Both are examples of violent behaviors. The first is less common than the second, but both are not rare occurrences in the lives of adolescents. The second case is actually very common among middle school students, more so among males, and increasingly more common among females. What makes these two instances of violence both similar to, and different from, instances of aggression is important to understanding the prevalence of both, and the origins of both as discussed in subsequent chapters.

The current focus will be on interpersonal aggression and violence because they share important and distinctive features, and because they are relatively distinct from other antisocial behaviors (e.g., stealing, substance abuse, vandalism). At the very least, both aggression and violence involve interpersonal confrontations, whereas stealing, vandalism, and substance abuse do not confront victims. Distinctions made between interpersonal aggression and violence at times appear more like discipline preferences, the former by psychologists, and the latter by criminologists, but others have differentiated the behaviors based on intentions, intensity, the presence or absence of injury, and probable illegality. A psychological dictionary defines aggression as "behavior . . . that results in harm to or destruction or defeat of others . . ." (VandenBos, 2007, p. 30). The definition of violence is "the expression of hostility and rage with the intent to injure or damage people or property through physical force . . . passion or intensity of emotions . . ." (VandenBos, p. 982). The greater intensity of emotional arousal in the case of violence, is consistent with dictionary adjectives describing violence such as "extreme," "severe," or "harsh" (Webster, p. 773). Aggression and violence, therefore, appear to lie on a continuum of severity or intensity, both with the goal of harm to another. Slapping one's romantic partner or pushing someone into a hallway wall at the aggression end, and gang fights and assault with a deadly weapon at the violence end.

Aggression and violence also differ from other antisocial behavior because they are intended to harm another. While it is clearly difficult to decide whether a behavior is intended to harm another person, many of the behaviors described in this chapter will be listed because they appear to be intentional, not because they have been vetted as such. That doesn't mean that intentionality is unimportant. Recently, some have argued that determining intentionality is not a definitional problem, but a measurement problem. Moreover, it is insufficient to define aggression as an outcome alone (e.g., a bruised lip); it is a social construction applied by the perpetrator or observers to "a heterogeneous category of human behavior . . . a judgment (made) . . . that relies on cues to intent, outcome potential, biological arousal, and social context . . . a 'fuzzy set'" (Dodge, Coie, & Lyman, 2006, p. 722). For example, differentiating "horseplay" from true aggression among middle school students had required addressing the behavior and its impact, the distress or annoyance of the target, and whether the perpetrator showed surprise or regret after the behavior caused distress (Boulton, 1991). Using these criteria for intentionality, acts would be judged aggressive, and intentional, if a slap had reddened the face of an opponent, the opponent became upset as a result, and the perpetrator was unfazed by the victim's upset. Another example of observing intentionality in an entirely different real-life, adult setting (a barroom) reliably assessed aggression when the following were seen by trained observers: (a) the person was angry and their actions were likely to affect the target adversely; (b) there were persistent overtures or "horseplay" (e.g., as in sexual advances) when the target clearly and repeatedly indicated that the behavior was unwelcome; and (c) the response to aggression clearly exceeds self defense (Graham et al., 2006).

Developmental psychologists generally have used the term *aggression* to refer to behavior intended to harm or injure another individual (Huesmann & Moise, 1999; Parke & Slaby, 1983). Determining that behavior, such as shown in the case of the two adolescents noted earlier, is both motivated by, and harmful to another may be difficult at times, and has led some to suggest omitting intention because it unnecessarily encumbers the definition (e.g., Loeber & Hay, 1997). However, there is practical importance to determining intention. In the case of everyday aggression by adolescents, teachers, parents, and other observers, do in fact make inferences about intentions based on some of the following earmarks: (a) co-occurrence of behaviors (e.g., hitting, pushing); (b) reciprocal non-verbal behaviors (e.g., both combatants with parallel shoulders, intense gaze, raised fists, etc.); (c) some awareness of the context (e.g., intensifying argument, rivalry over a soccer ball); (d) and explanations of the motivations (i.e., intentions) of both of the participants following the altercation. Indeed, observers attempt to identify a perpetrator and victim because possible consequences might be quite different following intentional acts versus accidental behaviors.

Researchers have tended to reserve the term violence, rather than aggression, for an instance in which there is actual injury or the risk of injury to a victim (Archer & Browne, 1989; Loeber & Stouthamer-Loeber, 1998). Violence has been described as "the exercise of physical force so as to injure persons . . . that causes bodily injury . . . and/or forcibly interferes with personal freedom" (Archer & Browne, 1989, pp. 10–11). Consistent with that definition of violence, but adding the connotation of illegality, is the FBI Uniform Crime Report definition of four violent index offenses, namely, homicide, aggravated assault (with a weapon or yielding harm), forcible rape, and robbery (UCR, 2002). For purposes of consistency, current use of the terms aggression and violence will be used to describe behavior intended to harm another, with violence also connoting actual injury or increased like-lihood of injury (as in robbery), greater intensity or severity, and greater likelihood the acts would be considered illegal.

Developmental psychologists also have studied the origins of aggression from infancy and early childhood years through the adult years (see review by Coie & Dodge, 1998), and have made important distinctions between motivational processes fueling angry and impulsive aggression, that is, reac-tive aggression, and aggression intended to achieve the goals of obtaining something (e.g., money, deference) from the opponent, that is, proactive aggression. Such motivational distinctions between the two forms of aggres-sion have been reliably distinguished by teachers in ratings of third grade boys (Dodge & Coe, 1987), and in parent ratings of young children (Marcus & Kramer, 2001). Yet reactive and proactive aggression are highly related to one another, and distinctions are not always easy to make. A middle school child who is insulted one day, stews about the affront for a few days, and then overreacts to a mild slight by the same peer, might be said to be reactively aggressive. But there also may be an element of planning designed to gain some outcome such as revenge or regaining respect the perpetrator perceived he had lost. Finally, developmental psychologists have noted that by age 8 children have developed a characteristic level of aggression across many situ-ations. They have also found that aggression is stable over time and predicts to adolescent aggression (Huesmann & Moise, 1999; Loeber & Dishion, 1983), and childhood aggression predicts well to violence in adolescence (USDHHS, 2001; Farrington, 1991). Aggression is often a developmental precursor of later violence, a point to be discussed more fully in Chapter 2.

Distinguishing Aggression and Violence from Other Antisocial Behavior

The study of both aggression and violence are important to this current exploration because they have similar motivational processes, and lie on a continuum of intensity, injury, and illegality. Aggression and violence also are distinct from other antisocial behaviors such as drug abuse, stealing, smoking, and vandalism. Typically, measures of aggression and violence have been shown to be correlated to a low or moderate degree with measures of other antisocial behaviors, but also are quite distinct, at least based on stud-ies using self-reported problems noted by adolescents. Regarding aggression, factor analytic studies of problem checklists, such as the Youth Self-report (Achenbach & Edlebrock, 1987), a 118 item self-report measure of adolescents' problems, has shown that adolescent problems can be empirically sorted into eight scales (plus an "other problems" scale). The scales are those such as anxious-depressed (items include "lonely," or "cries"), physical aggression (items include "fights," "attacks"), delinquent behavior (items include "sets fires," "steals"), and attention problems (items include "trouble concentrating"). The scales measuring physical aggression, including items such as argues, fights, attacks others, have been related only positively and moderately ($r = .45$) with delinquent misbehavior, including items such as lie/cheats, alcohol or drug use, or steals, suggesting some overlap or communality with other antisocial behaviors, but also uniqueness of problems with physical aggression (O'Keefe, Mennen, & Lane, 2006). Factor analysis of a twenty three item self-report measure of the antisocial behaviors of 6th through 8th grade students also has shown aggressive antisocial behaviors were relatively distinct from non-aggressive antisocial problem behaviors (Marcus & Betzer, 1996). Non-aggressive antisocial behaviors, such as "sneaking into a movie," and stealing items worth more than $25, were moderately related (i.e., $r = .65$) with aggressive antisocial behaviors such as throwing rocks and bottles to scare people, or beating someone.

Another study of high school students measured 10 problem behaviors among a large sample of high school students from 25 Canadian high schools ($n = 7,430$) (Willoughby, Chalmers, & Busseri, 2004). Problem behaviors such as smoking, sexual activity, minor delinquency (e.g., stealing, vandalism), major delinquency (e.g., carrying a weapon, joining a gang), and direct aggression (e.g., pushing, kicking, and hitting someone), were assessed as to the adolescent's frequency of participation. Factor analysis of the ten items initially revealed three positively but modestly related dimensions: (a) a "syndrome" factor (comprised of alcohol, smoking, and marijuana use, hard drug use, sexual activity, and minor delinquency); (b) an "aggression" factor (comprised of direct aggression; e.g., pushed, hit someone, and indirect aggression; e.g., spreading rumors, daring another student to hurt another); (c) and a "delinquency" factor (e.g., major delinquency such as carrying a gun as a weapon, joining a gang, as well as minor delinquency such as shoplifting, and wrecking others' property). Thus, the three forms of problem behaviors were relatively unique. A stronger case for specificity rather than generality of problem behaviors appeared when the frequency of participation in each of the three domains was examined. Engagement at a high level of involvement was reported for two problem behaviors for only 15% of respondents. In addition, high-risk involvement was found to co-occur among alcohol use, minor delinquency, and direct aggressive behaviors, but co-occurrence among other behaviors was rare. The authors' findings tended to support the contention that involvement in one type of problem behavior, such as aggression, does not necessarily mean involvement in another problem behavior, such as stealing or drug use.

Finally, research using survey methods has shown that nine school-related survey items from the Youth Risk Behavior Survey, such as smoking, marijuana use, selling drugs, and theft, and being threatened or injured with a weapon, related positively but modestly with weapon possession on school property (correlations ranging from $r = .13$ to $r = .26$) (Furlong & Bates, 2001). Moreover, some of those who reported having carried weapons six or more times had responded negatively to all of the other survey items (Furlong & Bates, 2001). Risky behaviors that are common among high school students may not easily be summed to equal a more general behavioral risk-taking propensity.

Longitudinal studies also have shown us that aggression and violence by mid-adolescence, at least prior to participation in the most serious violent crimes, are relatively distinct from other antisocial behaviors. A meta-analysis of 58 prospective longitudinal studies concluded that there was a moderate positive correlation between a more general measure of antisocial and substance abuse behaviors, assessed prior to adolescence, and those who displayed later violent crimes toward persons (average correlation, $r = .33$). This composite measure of antisocial and substance abuse problems also failed to identify 66% of those who later were violent (Derzon, 2001). An important longitudinal study of the early development of over one thousand boys from the Pittsburgh Study (Loeber & Stouthamer-Loeber, 1998), showed that those committing violent acts, and escalating their level of aggression along an "overt pathway" toward violence (i.e., annoying, aggressive behavior followed by bullying, fighting, strong armed robbery), were different from those escalating over time on a "covert pathway" (i.e., stealing, breaking and entering). Those on the "overt" pathway were different from those on the "covert" pathway in important ways, according to findings from the Pittsburgh Study and additional research literature reviewed. Specifically, those on the overt, as contrasted with covert pathway had the following characteristics: (a) more likely to confront victims; (b) evidenced angrier emotion; (c) possessed thinking processes that were deficient (in terms of generation of solutions to interpersonal conflicts) and/or emphasized perceptions of hostile intent by others when none existed; and (d) had a lower resting heart rate. As overt pathway boys progressed through school, they were a clearly distinct group. Later in adolescence, and at the most severe levels for adolescents on both pathways, there was crossover between types. In fact, the specialization versus generalization controversy in the criminology literature regarding offenders may be partly resolved by noting that these two paths taken by adolescents are distinct prior to evidencing the most serious offending behavior. Covert offenders escalating along their path, for example, may eventually come into violent face-to-face confrontation with victims, after which they may become a serious violent offender with both covert and overt behavioral features. Cross-sectional surveys and official records of violent crimes, both over the course of adolescence, can begin to tell us about the developmental course of aggressive and violent behavior.

Reliability and Validity of Surveyed Aggression and Violence

The U.S. Department of Health and Human Services (USDHHS), Centers for Disease Control and Prevention (CDC) in Atlanta, Georgia, monitors the population of the United States for the presence of important threats to health and safety, including risky behavior by adolescents. The current review will present findings from the Youth Risk Behavior Surveillance System, developed in 1989 by CDC to monitor the causes of injury, death, and other social problems among youth in the United States. CDC's Youth Risk Behavior Survey (YRBS) questionnaire included seven aggressive, violent or violence-related items that had been administered to a nationally representative sample of 9th to 12th graders in the United States every two years since 1991. The seven items were the following: (1) carrying a weapon, such as a gun, knife, or club in the last 30 days; (2) being in a physical fight in the past 12 months; (3) being in a physical fight in the past 12 months, after which they were treated by a doctor or nurse; (4) carrying a weapon, such as a gun, knife, or club *on school property* during the past 30 days; (5) being in a physical fight *on school property* during the past 12 months; (6) being threatened or injured with a weapon, such as a gun, knife, or club *on school property* during the past 12 months; and (7) not going to school one or more times, in the past 30 days, because they felt unsafe at school, or unsafe on their way to or from school.

As in the case of any measurement instruments in the behavioral and social sciences, it is important to ask to what extent we may place our trust in the results of survey findings. More specifically, it is important to know whether the measures of violence and violence-related behaviors are reliable and valid. Reliability is the extent to which questionnaire responses yield results that are consistent (e.g., over brief periods of time, within the measure). Validity refers to the extent to which the survey items are a good representation of what they purport to measure. Research on the original development of the YRBS has been described elsewhere (see Kolbe, Kann, & Collins, 1993).

Recently the reliability of the YRBS questionnaire was examined in a racially diverse sample of 4,619 youths ages 13 through 18 (Brener et al., 2002). All of the seven, aggressive and violence-related behavior items showed "moderate" to "substantial" agreement when re-administered two weeks later to the same individuals. In addition, prevalence rates for five of the seven items on second administration did not statistically differ from the first administration prevalence rates. One item, "in a physical fight" during the past 12 months, went down in prevalence (from 34.6% to 30.3% prevalence rate). Responses to another item (i.e., "injured in a physical fight during the past twelve months") went up (i.e., from 2.9% to 4.4%) from the first to second administration. The authors suggested keeping all seven items because they maintained either moderate correlation, or maintained stability in prevalence from time one to time two.

A second reliability indicator is the extent to which similar prevalence rates are obtained by those using similar questions who also have sampled nationally representative adolescents at similar points in time. This issue of inter-test reliability (sometimes referred to as reliability of the behavior) will be revisited once YRBS survey items have been presented. Recently, Brener, Grunbaum, Kann and colleagues (2004) explored whether directions containing stronger appeals for respondent accuracy, called "strong honesty" appeals, might yield different results from three different national surveys, and whether offering respondents complete anonymity produced different similar results than did offering confidentiality without anonymity. Brener et al. found that whereas differences in wording occasionally produced significantly different prevalence estimates, none of the three questionnaires examined produced consistently higher or lower prevalence estimates. Neither did stronger appeals for accuracy lead to lower or higher prevalence rates. Surveys of nationally representative samples with similar wording produced similar prevalence estimates. Our confidence in prevalence data would be enhanced by cross-survey consistency with alternate modes of question presentation.

Validity can be addressed by examining the ability of self-report measures to predict to other behaviors such as future arrests for violent behavior (i.e., predictive validity), the consistency of the internal structure of a self-report measure (i.e., construct validity), and the extent to which respondents truthfully report their behavior when asked (i.e., face validity). Construct validity was noted earlier in factor analytic studies of self-reported behavior problems (see Marcus & Betzer, 1996; Willoughby et al., 2004). Self-reported violent behaviors factored into dimensions that were moderately related to other antisocial behaviors among high school and middle school students, and with responses clustering into distinct dimensions, at least one of which is identifiable as aggression or violence.

The development over the past thirty years of large scale, self-report survey instruments, such as the YRBS (Kann et al., 1995), the Monitoring the Future study (MTF) (Johnston, Bachman, & O'Malley, 2000), and the National Crime Victimization Survey (NCVS) (Bureau of Justice Statistics, 2000), has been used to monitor yearly changes and individual differences among adolescents in the United States. Nationally representative sampling of adolescents throughout the United States are key to each of the studies, although there are differences in methods of gathering data. Most important for each of the measures is that adolescents report what they have actually done. Unlike widely used objective self-report measures of personality problems, such as the Minnesota Multiphasic Personality Inventory – Adolescent version (MMPI-A) (Butcher, Graham, Williams, & Kanner, 1992), which has built in ways to detect lying, distortion (e.g., faking good or faking bad), and other ways to detect bias in responding, surveys have no such safeguards. Also, unlike the MMPI-A, which asks respondents specifically about getting into fights when drinking, or breaking and destroying things, and items representing the signs and symptoms of emotional disorders, the YRBS asks specifically whether the individual has carried a weapon on school property, or been forced to have sexual intercourse. Such questions are sensitive not only because they are personal, but because they are asked of respondents in a school setting where such behaviors are illegal, and the individual can be subjected to serious repercussions if discovered by authorities.

Variations in prevalence rates have been studied in relation to the wording of survey questions, and also whether the students' responses are collected with no identification that might permit association with their responses (anonymity), or in a way that permits some linkages between responses so as to facilitate later follow-up (confidentiality). Research has found that the YRBS, which provides anonymity, yields estimates of prevalence (for those of similar grade, and year of data collection) that are slightly higher than the MTF estimates for "carrying a weapon" (Coggeshall & Kingery, 2001). In addition, the Coggeshall and Kingery study found that surveys with similar wording yield prevalence estimates that are generally similar for aggression and violence questions, and that questions asking adolescents to rate behavior over a longer period of time (e.g., last 6 months vs. last month) yielded higher prevalence estimates. As noted earlier, another study of a large sample of high school students (n = 4,140) found that variations in wording alone did not produce differences in prevalence estimates, when conditions of anonymity were provided for YRBS and MTF questions; prevalence estimates were robust for wording differences (Brener et al., 2004). In sum, estimates based on the YRBS should produce estimates that are an accurate reflection of student behavior, with minimal differences from other survey questions about behavior within a similar time frame. Once YRBS data are presented, comparisons with other surveys will be undertaken.

Predictive validity has been established both by examining self-report survey items, and confidential interview responses in relation to logically related criterion variables. For example, one study investigated the relation between self-reported violent offending (i.e., those inflicting cuts, bleeding, unconsciousness, or hospitalization) and later official arrest records in a five-year longitudinal study called the Denver Youth Survey (Huizinga, Esbensen, & Weihner, 1996). Seventy four percent of self-reported violent offenders were later arrested, although typically for more non-violent than for violent offenses, the latter having a higher frequency of occurrence (and therefore were easier to predict).

Recently, self-reported violent behaviors were successfully used to predict any serious violence (i.e., court conviction for any violent offense, self-report index offenses, or homicide conviction), and more specifically to court conviction for homicide (Loeber, Paridini, & Homish et al., 2005). The sample in Loeber and colleagues, consisted of 1,488 boys from Pittsburgh, Pennsylvania, who were followed longitudinally for 4 years from 1st, 4th, and 7th grades. Contrasting those boys who showed any serious violence with boys who were non-violent, the following self-reported behaviors were more likely to be acknowledged by violent boys: gun carrying, weapon use and carrying, gang fighting, gang membership, drug use, peer substance use, and peer delinquent behavior. Moreover, those committing homicide (n = 33), versus those committing "any violence" (as above) were more likely to self-report gang fighting, carrying (any) weapon, peer delinquency, positive attitude toward substance use, and selling hard drugs. Despite the sensitivity of such self-reported behaviors, boys had acknowledged important behaviors that predicted later onset of the most serious of violent behaviors.

It is important to note that developmental trends and gender differences using different measurement instrumentation are also seen in survey responses from self-report instruments such as the YRBS. Loeber (1982) reviewed research relating to developmental trends in aggression, using parent ratings, and concluded that pre-pubescent and early adolescent years represented a peak in aggression levels, and that aggression levels declined during the remainder of adolescence. Loeber and Hay (1997) showed that, according to parent ratings in the Pittsburgh Study (using the Child Behavior Checklist) aggressive behaviors such as physical fighting showed decreases from ages 12 to 15, after which the percentage of those *initiating* physical fighting declined to age 16. Yet, the same study noted that violence (i.e., strong arming, attacking someone) increased steeply between ages 11 and 15 before tapering off. These data would predict age-related trends toward greater aggressive behavior in the middle school through early high school years (9th grade), and declines in prevalence rates thereafter. The developmental course of serious violent behaviors may, however, continue to escalate during mid-adolescence. Elliott's (1994) research findings, based on longitudinally gathered interview data, showed that ages 15 to 17 were a time for the greatest escalation and prevalence for serious, self-reported violent offending. Serious violent offenders were those who had committed three or more of the following: aggravated assault, strong armed robbery against students, strong armed robbery against others, gang fighting, and sexual assault. Elliott reported that boys were more likely to evidence a pattern of serious violent offending (i.e., three or more serious violent behaviors); there were three times as many serious offending boys than girls. Serious violent offenders were most prevalent at age 17 (3.7%), for those who had never before been so classified, after which the prevalence of first time serious violent offending declines to age 21 (Elliott, Huizinga, & Morse, 1986).

In summary, the data from the YRBS, in order to be consistent with previous research, would need to show aggression at a peak in middle school and early high school years. More serious violent behaviors may not decline until late high school. Official reports of criminal violence, however, are likely to reveal increases throughout the 12 to 17 year age range.

Findings from the Youth Risk Behavior Survey

The exact questions from the YRBS may be found in Table 1.1. The seven questions were administered within a 90 item, anonymous, biennial survey to a nationally representative sample of students in grades 9 through 12. Sample sizes ranged from 10,904 to 16,296 per year.

Table 1.2 presents the data for aggressive, violent, and violence-related behaviors among high school students for the years 1993 through 2005. The data show a decline throughout the 1990s in five of the seven violent behaviors, with increases in five of seven noted for the year 2005. No declines over time were evidenced in being injured in a physical fight. Contrary to the general trend toward decline in violent behaviors since 1993, data show increases in being threatened or injured with a weapon in school and in feeling unsafe

TABLE 1.1. *Violence and violence-related questions from the Youth Risk Behavior Survey*

Violence Questions:
1. "During the past 30 days, on how many days did you carry a weapon such as a gun, knife, or club?"
2. "During the past 12 months, how many times were you in a physical fight?"
3. "During the past 12 months, how many times were you in a physical fight in which you were treated by a doctor or nurse?"

School Violence Questions:
1. "During the past 30 days, on how many days did you carry a weapon such as a gun, knife, or club on school property?"
2. "During the past 12 months, how many times were you in a physical fight on school property?"
3. "During the past 12 months, how many times has someone threatened or injured you with a weapon such as a gun, knife, or club on school property?"
4. "During the past 30 days, on how many days did you not go to school because you felt you would be unsafe at school or on your way to or from school?"

Source: Brener et al. (1999).

in school and on the way to and from school. Despite reductions over time in some forms of aggression and violence, there has been a steady prevalence rate for threats or injuries with a weapon in school, suggesting that more serious fighters have remained a student concern. Possibly in reaction, students have become more fearful of being harmed in or around schools. Clearly self-reported aggressive and violent behavior fluctuates over the 13-year period, with a trend downward to the early 21st century for most behaviors, and an upturn in five of the seven behaviors in 2005.

TABLE 1.2. *Violence-related behavior among high school students – United States, 1993–2005: Prevalence rates (percentages) by year*

	1993	1995	1997	1999	2001	2003	2005
Violence							
Carried weapon	22	20	18	17	17	17	19
In physical fight	42	39	37	36	33	33	36
Injured in physical fight	4	4	4	4	4	4	4
School violence							
Carried weapon	12	10	9	7	6	6	7
In physical fight	16	16	15	14	13	13	14
Threatened or injured with a weapon	7	8	7	8	9	9	8
Unsafe to go to school	4	5	4	5	7	5	6

Source: Youth Risk Behavior Survey: 1993–2005 (USDHHS, 2006b) (percentages rounded).

Table 1.2 also shows that prevalence estimates are time bound. To compare different surveys of nationally representative high school students, for purposes of reliably knowing what is happening in the real world, it is important to select specific years in which multiple surveys have been instituted. Comparison of survey results for particular years also may bolster our confidence in the validity of prevalence measures as well because they accurately reflect true behavioral trends. Therefore, in order to contrast the survey results on similar violent behaviors, the years 1994–1995 were selected in order to examine the convergence of three data sets: the YRBS (USDHHS, 2006b); The National Longitudinal Study of Adolescent Health (Add Health) (Add Health, 2006); and Monitoring the Future (MTF) (Johnston, Bachman, & O'Malley, 2000). Specifically, in the YRBS survey for 1995, the 39% of high school students had been in a physical fight in the previous 12 months. The Add Health data for 1994–1995 indicated that 31% of high school youth had engaged in a physical fight in the previous years (USDHHS, 2006b). The YRBS yielded somewhat higher prevalence rates for physical fighting among high school students, possibly due to the fact that anonymity was provided on the YRBS but confidentiality provided on the Add Health survey because the latter required a longitudinal follow up.

Shifting to work or school settings, surveys were likely to yield lower prevalence rates because of adult monitoring in those settings. The MTF reported prevalence rates for "serious" physical fighting at "work or school," for 10th and 12th graders: 19% of 10th graders and 15% of 12th graders answered in the affirmative (Johnston et al., 2000). The YRBS data for 1995, noted in Table 1.2, also show that 16% of high school students fought in school. The prevalence rates for the YRBS and MTF surveys for the same years appear roughly comparable, despite slight variations in question wording and context. In addition, MTF had asked students about "serious" fighting and placed the context at school and work rather than school alone, thus lowering the possible prevalence rate.

Grade Trends in Aggressive and Violent Behaviors

Table 1.3 presents violence and violence-related behaviors by grade level in violence and violence related behavior for the YRBS. To show these grade level differences, prevalence levels for each behavior were averaged across the 13-year period, and are presented for each grade level. Six of the seven aggressive and violent behaviors were more prevalent among 9th graders than among students in the other three grades. Being injured in a physical fight was prevalent at a constant level throughout the high school years.

TABLE 1.3. *Violence-related behavior among high school students – United States,*
1993–2005: Average prevalence rates (percentages) by grade

	Grade 12	Grade 11	Grade 10	Grade 9
Violence				
Carried weapon	16	18	19	21
In physical fight	30	34	38	44
Injured in a physical fight	4	4	4	5
School violence				
Carried weapon	7	8	8	8
In physical fight	9	12	16	20
Threatened or injured with a weapon	6	7	9	11
Unsafe to go to school	4	5	5	7

Source: Author re-analysis YRBS data (USDHHS, 2006) (percentages rounded).

Comparison of YRBS grade trends in Table 1.3 can be made with MTF data
for the years 1992 through 2004, for the purposes of cross-survey validation.
The average prevalence rates for the thirteen years, by 12th, 10th, and 8th
grades for MTF data also shows the prevalence of serious fighting was greater
in lower grades (i.e., 12th grade: 17%; 10th grade: 19%; and 8th grade: 23%)
(ICPS, 2005). In addition, MTF data show that hurting someone badly enough
to require a bandage or doctor was also greater in lower grades (12th grade:
13%; 10th grade: 14%; 8th grade: 17%) (Johnston et al., 2000). MTF grade
trends for violent behaviors mirror the same direction as YRBS grade trends;
the lower the grade the more prevalent the involvement in violence.

One further source of cross-validation of grade trends in violence, as
well as an opportunity to understand distinctions between the prevalence of
serious predatory violence among adolescents, and more common forms of
physical fighting, is provided in a 1994–1995 Add Health data set for aggression,
violent, and violence-related behaviors among middle school and high school
students (Add Health, 2006). The data presented in Table 1.4 report Add
Health prevalence rates in 1995 for 7th through 12th grade students who
were interviewed at home. Descriptive information for the representative
sample yielded the following: racial composition was 62% White; gender 51%
male; mothers' education was 43% high school graduate or less; mean age
15 years. The Add Health results presented in Table 1.4 support the YRBS
findings in a number of ways. First, the YRBS report of greatest prevalence of
high school violence in 9th grade is supported by Add Health data for eight
of the ten behaviors. One slight exception is "someone pulled knife...,"
which peaks in 10th grade before declining by 12th grade. The other item
showing no grade variation was "someone shot you," which remains relatively
steady at 1% during high school. In addition, it is interesting to note that

TABLE 1.4. *Prevalence of aggressive and violent behavior (percentages) by grade (Add Health, n = 20,745): 1994–1995*

Violent Behaviors	12th Grade	11th Grade	10th Grade	9th Grade	8th Grade	7th Grade
Interpersonal violence						
Serious physical fight	25	28	32	35	39	38
Seriously injured someone	13	17	21	22	22	21
Take part in group fight	14	18	20	22	23	23
Perpetrated violence						
Used weapon in fight	6	6	6	7	7	6
Pulled knife or gun on someone	4	5	5	5	6	3
Used weapon to get something	3	5	5	5	5	4
Carried weapon at school	9	9	10	11	11	6
Victim of violence						
Someone pulled knife/gun on you	14	14	15	14	12	8
Someone stabbed you	4	5	6	6	6	5
Someone shot you	1	1	2	1	1	1

Source: Author analysis based on Add Health (2006) Full Wave I Data Set (percentages rounded).

eight of the ten behaviors evidenced increases from 7th to 9th grades before declining by 12th grade. In sum, there is a rise in prevalence rates by the middle school to early high school years, with declines in most behaviors thereafter.

The Add Health data also yields important information about the relative prevalence of different kinds of aggressive and violent behavior that are not assessed in other surveys. Add Health data are also classified by perpetrator and victim roles. Ninth grade is a peak year for aggressive and violent behavior, and can serve as a useful example. First, those forms of aggression in which parties are likely to share roughly equivalent contributions are referred to in the table as "interpersonal." They are most common, involving from 22% to 35% of 9th graders. The reader will recall this high prevalence for physical fighting, as compared with other forms, was also noted in YRBS findings. Such conflicts are likely to result from interpersonal disputes or arguments and were common relative to perpetrated violent behaviors. Second, perpetrated violent acts ranged from 11% carrying a weapon to school to 5% robbing someone with a weapon. The importance of the roughly 8% of adolescents perpetrating serious violent behaviors will be revisited in Chapter 2 with a discussion of a qualitatively distinct groups of seriously violent adolescents.

Violent victimization ranged from 14% having a knife or gun pulled on them to 1% actually being shot. More serious violent behaviors, and both perpetration and victimization, are clearly not rare events in the lives of 9th grade students. Third, violence-related injury also is not a rare occurrence among 9th graders, involving from 22% harmed by physical fighting, 6% stabbed, and 1% shot in a year's time. Fourth, use of weapons among 9th graders was also not a rare occurrence, and ranged from 11% carrying a weapon at school, 5% using a weapon in a robbery, 7% using a weapon in a fight, to 6% being stabbed, and 1% being shot. The grade trend toward lower prevalence rates for perpetrated acts such as use of weapons in a fight in higher grades, may reflect the disappearance from the school of the most violent perpetrators, despite attempts by Add Health to interview those who had recently been in school. In the future, aggressive and violent behaviors in late middle school and early high school will require further monitoring because both are common occurrences in the lives of young adolescents and a threat to their safety.

Gender and Race Differences in Surveyed Aggressive and Violent Behavior

The YRBS data allow for inspection of aggressive, violent, and violence-related behaviors by gender and by race. Table 1.5 presents these data for the years with prevalence rates averaged for 1993–2003. Males were approximately two times more likely than females to engage in physical fighting, being injured in a physical fight (i.e., both in school and generally), and being threatened or injured with a weapon on school property. Males were approximately four times more likely than females to carry a weapon. Males and females were equally likely to feel it is unsafe to be in school, to go to school or return from school, and therefore stayed out of school as a result. The greater prevalence of aggression, violence, and violence related behaviors among males, as compared with females, is a well known finding in developmental psychology (see review by Coie & Dodge, 1998), as well as research on self-reported violent behaviors (USDHHS, 2001). The survey results in Table 1.5 are also consistent with a recent meta-analysis of research studies using various naturalistic methods of data collection (i.e., self-report, observational, peer reports, and teacher reports), involving 264 separate studies (of over 150,000 males and females) in ten countries around the world (Archer, 2004). Archer (2004) found differences in favor of males over females across all age groups (i.e., from childhood through old age), in all countries, and for physical and verbal aggression. Archer's review found no gender differences in anger; in the case of indirect aggression, differences were found in favor of females over

TABLE 1.5. *Average prevalence rates (percentages) for violence-related behavior among high school students – United States, 1993–2003 by gender and race*

	Gender		Race		
	Male	Female	White	Black	Hispanic
Violence					
Carried weapon	31	8	18	20	21
In physical fight	46	28	35	43	41
Injured in physical fight	5	3	3	6	5
School violence					
Carried weapon	13	4	8	9	10
In physical fight	20	9	13	19	17
Threatened or injured with a weapon	11	6	7	10	10
Unsafe to go to school	5	5	3	8	9

Source: Author analysis of USDHHS (2006b) (percentages rounded).

males in late childhood and early adolescence. Most recently, a meta-analysis of studies show that physical and verbal victimization is greater among males in elementary, middle, and high school years (Rose & Rudolph, 2006).

Blacks and Hispanics, noted in Table 1.5, both show a relatively equal level of involvement in violence and violence-related behaviors in the YRBS data. Both Blacks and Hispanics reported a greater involvement in all aggressive and violent behaviors than Whites. Blacks showed from 13% to 78% greater involvement than Whites for all forms of aggressive and violent behavior, whereas for feeling unsafe at, or to or from, school showed 123% more Blacks felt unsafe than Whites. Racial-ethnic differences of this magnitude have been reported in other national surveys that were roughly similar. Consistent with YRBS findings, MTF reports indicated that a self-reported, composite Violent Index Rate (i.e., a combination of hitting an instructor, serious fighting, gang fighting, injured other, and armed robbery) also showed a 10% greater rate for Blacks as compared with Whites (Johnston, 2000 cited in USDHHS, 2001). Also, Blacks have self-reported 20% greater rates of assault with injury and 60% greater armed robbery than have Whites (Maguire & Pastore, 1999, cited in HHS, 2001, p. 29).

Cross-National Comparisons of Surveyed Aggression and Violence

Recently, some of the YRBS questions, plus one measuring bullying have been administered in five different countries (Smith-Khuri et al., 2004). This cross-national study of the prevalence of violence and violence related behaviors has the added advantage of extending downward to middle school students.

TABLE 1.6. *Prevalence rates (percentages) for violence-related behaviors among 6th, 8th, and 10th grade students in five countries*

Violence	Country					Total
	Israel	Ireland	United States	Sweden	Portugal	
Carried a weapon	16	10	10	–	6	11
In physical fight	45	45	40	39	31	40
Injured in physical fight	18	18	16	–	12	16
Bullied others	43	25	39	15	36	34

Note: re-calculated to reflect prevalence rates as in previous tables.
Source: Smith-Khuri et al. (2004).

The average ages (with rounding) were 12 years (6th grade), 14 years (8th grade), and 16 years (10th grade). The sample sizes per country ranged from 3,721 to 5,168. The data show that prevalence rates are relatively consistent across countries for all age groups combined. In addition, males were more involved in fighting than females (e.g., fighting involved from 50% to 66% of boys and from 15% to 30% of girls). Consistent with earlier findings on grade differences in MTF, Add Health, and YRBS data, prevalence rates in all countries showed that rates for physical fighting were equivalent for 6th and 8th graders, and both were significantly higher than for 10th graders. Table 1.6 presents these data. Cross national prevalence rates show middle school students more aggressive than high school students for all measures.

Official Crime Statistics

The survey data contained in the YRBS surveys do not represent more serious violence among adolescents. Serious violent behaviors for adolescents, namely, homicide, and arrests for four violent crime index offenses (i.e., murder, forcible rape, robbery, aggravated assault), simple assault, and weapons carrying, can be seen in data gathered by the FBI's Uniform Crime Reports, based on reports from police headquarters across the United States. Crime reported to police has typically been seen as a small fraction of what adolescents self-report. This gap exists because much violent behavior goes unreported, and may occur prior to arrest by the police. Also, adolescents themselves may be the best reporters of what they have done. Crime report data can help us to understand changes with age and over time for more serious crime, but they vary with trends and biases among law enforcement agencies over time and around the country, and are usually not viewed as useful for estimating prevalence rates. Table 1.7 presents data on homicide victims, ages 12 through 17, for the years 1990 through 2002, as well as the

TABLE 1.7. *Homicide victims, for ages 12 through 17, for the years 1990 through 2002: Uniform Crime Reports – United States: Supplemental Homicide reports*

Age of Victim	1990	1991	1992	1993	1994	1995	1996	1997	1998	1999	2000	2001	2002	Row Total
12	51	35	58	49	51	55	35	39	39	20	30	28	33	523
13	76	75	88	111	106	94	63	51	57	46	31	25	39	862
14	120	161	187	212	179	179	119	90	91	78	80	58	61	1,615
15	226	227	312	318	336	293	247	177	144	127	116	125	134	2,782
16	339	441	455	515	450	481	379	338	245	220	179	197	200	4,439
17	542	599	629	682	682	644	534	460	392	365	318	299	307	6,453
Column total	1,354	1,538	1,729	1,887	1,803	1,746	1,377	1,155	968	856	754	732	774	16,672

Source: Author analysis based on FBI (2006) data.

totals per year (i.e., columns) and totals by age (i.e., rows). The data show an increase in homicide victims to 1993 and then a tapering off until 2001, after which the trend started upward again for all age groups. In 1993, the greatest number of homicides involving adolescents were recorded than in any year since 1976, the year when recording began. The average number of homicides per year was 1,282, or four per day for those ages 12 through 17. Interestingly, homicide data are consistent with YRBS data presented in Table 1.2, where the YRBS data showed the highest prevalence rates in 1991 and 1993, tapering off to 2001.

The trend for homicides for the age groups considered in Table 1.7 was the opposite of survey data results presented earlier. For homicide data for those age 12 and older, there was a 60% to 87% increase in homicide deaths with each year increase in age. Surveys of crime victims also have shown adolescents to be at greater risk than other age groups. Data from the National Crime Victimization Survey (NCVS), a survey of 42,000 households two times per year, also show that those ages 12 to 15 years, and those 16 to 19, experience the highest rate of violent victimization of any age group across the lifespan (Snyder & Sickmund, 1999).

Gender and Race Differences in Homicide

Consistent with the focus here on broad differences among sub-populations of adolescents, Table 1.8 presents the data on homicide victims, for the years 1990 through 2002, for males versus females, and for Whites versus Blacks. Between 1990 and 2002 there were 13,504 males and 3,168 females who died as a result of homicide. This indicated that males, ages 12 through 17, were four times more likely than females to be murdered. Between 1990 and 2002, 7,501 Whites and 8,931 Blacks were murdered, making Blacks 19% more likely to be murdered than Whites, despite the fact that Blacks are only about 14% of the population.

Arrest Data for Violent Crimes by Adolescents

Arrests of adolescents for violent crimes are also reported by police headquarters around the United States to be included in the Uniform Crime Reports. Violent crimes, for which adolescents have been arrested, are defined in Table 1.9

Table 1.10 present the arrest rates per 100,000 persons ages 10–17 for the four Violent Index Crimes (i.e., the first four in Table 1.9) plus the rates for simple assault and weapons arrests for the years 1990 through 2003. As was

TABLE 1.8. *Homicide victims, for ages 12 through 17, by gender and race, for the years 1990 through 2002 – United States*

	1990	1991	1992	1993	1994	1995	1996	1997	1998	1999	2000	2001	2002	Total
Male	1,078	1,278	1,407	1,541	1,510	1,402	1,134	943	767	676	596	582	590	13,504
Female	276	260	322	346	293	344	243	212	201	180	158	149	184	3,168
Whites	596	654	734	772	723	768	610	681	494	401	356	340	372	7,501
Blacks	723	844	943	1,060	1,010	907	714	765	447	413	370	361	374	8,931

Source: Author analysis based on FBI (2006) data.

TABLE 1.9. *Definitions of four violent index crimes and other assault (simple)*

Criminal Homicide-Murder and Non-Negligent Manslaughter: The willful (non-negligent) killing of one human being by another.

Robbery: The taking or attempting to take anything of value from the care, custody, or control of a person or persons by force or threat of force or violence and /or putting the victim in fear.

Aggravated Assault: An unlawful attack by one person upon another wherein the offender uses a weapon or displays it in a threatening manner, or the victim suffers obvious severe or aggravated bodily injury involving apparent broken bones, loss of teeth, possible internal injury, severe laceration, or loss of consciousness.

Forcible Rape: The carnal knowledge of a person, forcibly and/or against that person's will, or not forcibly or against the person's will where the victim is incapable of giving consent because of his/her temporary or permanent mental or physical incapacity (or because of his/her youth). (USDHHS, 2001, p. 17)

Other Assault (Simple): Assaults and attempted assaults where no weapons are used and which do not result in serious or aggravated injury to the victim. (USDJ, 2002)

the case for homicides, the arrests for violent index crimes reached a peak in 1993 to 1994, and then tapered off to the lowest rates for violent crimes seen since 1980. However, the rate for aggravated assault in 2003 remained 26% higher than in 1980. Also, the arrests for simple assault remained 138% higher and weapons arrests 25% higher than in 1980. Thus, arrests for some criminally violent behaviors did not recede back to the levels of the 1980s.

The yearly trends in arrests for the four violent index crimes noted in Table 1.10 are also consistent with NCVS prevalence rates for 12 to 17 years olds from 1993 to 1998 (Lynch, 2002). NCVS results showed increased rates of offending, i.e., for total incidents of three serious violent offenses (namely, aggravated assault, robbery, and forcible rape) from 1987 to 1993, followed by steady declines from 1993 to 1998. NCVS data also showed declines in prevalence of robbery and aggravated assault from 1993 to 1998. The year 1993 represented the highest rate of offending, according to NCVS data, for any of the years from 1980 through 1998.

Table 1.11 compares the arrest rates for violent crime index offenses separately for the years 1994 and 2001 by ages 12 through 20. Also, for these two years, intended to be representative of arrest rates for the 8 year span, the rates of arrest show dramatic increases from ages 12 and under to 13 to 14 years of age. Also, for these two years, the jump in arrest rates was from 19 to 14 times as great for the older of the two age groups. From age 15 onward, with increases in age, the increases in arrest rates ranged from 22% to 74%, until

TABLE 1.10. *Juvenile arrest rates (per 100,000 persons ages 10–17 years), for violent crimes by offense, 1990–2003*

Violent Crimes	1990	1991	1992	1993	1994	1995	1996	1997	1998	1999	2000	2001	2002	2003
Violent crime index	428	461	482	504	525	516	459	441	368	337	308	296	277	273
Murder and non-negligent manslaughter	12	13	13	14	13	12	10	8	7	5	4	4	4	3
Forcible Rape	22	23	22	22	20	19	19	18	17	16	14	14	14	13
Robbery	155	175	175	185	199	199	176	161	109	94	86	81	75	76
Aggravated assault	239	295	273	282	293	286	255	253	235	223	204	197	184	181
Simple assault	538	608	623	663	714	738	765	768	768	747	719	717	700	712
Weapons carrying, possessing, etc.	304	311	342	421	219	194	176	173	148	137	116	114	105	115

Source: National Center for Juvenile Justice (2005) (rounded).

TABLE 1.11. *Juvenile arrest rates for violent crime index offenses (per 100,000 persons) by age for 1994 and 2001.*

Age	1994	2001
12 and under	24	20
13–14	491	293
15	853	477
16	1,052	582
17	1,122	662
18	1,153	759
19	992	753
20	909	699

Source: FBI (2003) (rounded).

age 18, after which the rates decline. Arrest rates of adolescents for violent crimes are the highest of any age group across the lifespan.

Table 1.12 contrasts male and female and contrasts White and Black arrestees for the years 1990 through 2003. When arrest rates for violent crimes were averaged for the 14-year period of time, arrest rates were approximately six times greater for males than females, and five times greater for Blacks than Whites. Data from the NCVS also has shown that rates (per 1,000) for perpetrated robbery and aggravated assault, for the years 1993 through 1998, were six times greater for boys as compared with girls for acts committed without additional associates present (Lynch, 2002). NCVS data for the same time period also showed that four times as many incidents were reported perpetrated by Blacks than by Whites. Thus, NCVS survey data are consistent with gender and race differences in arrest rates. Snyder (2004) also noted that there were gender differences in violent crime over that time that are not reflected in the above. Snyder noted that from 1993 to 2002, aggravated assault rates for men went down 29%, but women went up 4%. In addition, and for the same time period, the increase in simple assault for males was 4% and for females was 41%. Changes in female arrest rates for violent crime will need to be carefully watched for changes in relation to male rates for violent crime arrests.

Summary

The definitions of aggression and violence, both behaviors intended to harm others, lend themselves to comparisons along a dimension of motivation to harm and actual harm, and from behaviors that are of questionable legality

TABLE 1.12. *Juvenile arrest rates (per 100,000 persons ages 10–17) for violent crime index offenses by year, gender, and race, 1990–2003*

	1990	1991	1992	1993	1994	1995	1996	1997	1998	1999	2000	2001	2002	2003	Average Rate
Male	736	792	818	849	879	856	757	723	594	542	490	471	440	434	670
Female	105	112	127	139	153	158	144	143	130	122	117	111	105	103	118
White	254	283	292	299	315	308	292	271	255	242	220	212	196	186	259
Black	1,434	1,504	1,579	1,664	1,697	1,668	1,399	1,138	984	856	820	789	736	752	1,215

Source: National Center for Juvenile Justice (2005) (rounded).

to those that are considered illegal by law enforcement entities. Aggressive behaviors, as self-reported, tend to remain highly prevalent among middle school and young high school students, are more prevalent among males than females, and more prevalent among minority groups. Surveys of nationally representative samples of adolescents show that prevalence of most aggressive and some violent behaviors decreases from early to later high school years. Grade and gender differences are consistent among different survey results for the same years. Grade- and gender-related trends in aggressive behaviors surveyed also appeared to be relatively consistent across nations surveyed.

A different trend was noted for violent crimes among older adolescents. Data based on Uniform Crime Report data showed that violent crimes increased dramatically in early adolescence and then more modestly but steadily from early to late adolescence. Both self-reported aggressive and violent behavior, and rates of arrest for violent crimes, plus the number of adolescent homicide victims, increased during the early 1990s and have generally decreased since that point in time. The FBI's use of terms such as "epidemic" and "unprecedented" to describe violent crimes in the early 1990s appears to have been reflected in both self-reported and official arrest rates of aggressive and violent behavior.

2

Developmental Pathways to Violence

The cross-sectional surveys and official crime statistics presented in Chapter 1 indicated that there were two main developmental trends in adolescent aggression and violence. The first, as surveys of nationally representative samples of middle and high school students showed, was that the middle school through early high school years, roughly ages 11 through 14, represented a peak time in which conflicts erupted into physical aggression, as well as for slight increases in the prevalence of more serious violence perpetration and victimization. Following early adolescence, and with some noteworthy exceptions (e.g., the stable prevalence rate for being shot), the prevalence of aggression and some forms of violence decline during the remainder of the high school years. This rise and fall of relatively common forms of aggression and violence was contrasted with a second trend. Homicide and arrests for seriously violent crimes show an escalation toward a peak at ages 18 and 19, before declining, or a relatively steady prevalence rate for the most serious self-reported violence. Explaining this bifurcated trend within the context of pre-adolescent and adolescent development is the main focus of the current exposition.

Understanding these two important trends in aggression and violence requires an appreciation of individual adolescent development and the social context of adolescence that triggers interpersonal violence. Moreover, it requires an understanding of both child and adolescent development, with special attention to subgroups of children and adolescents at greatest risk for the most serious violence; those who have veered off the mainstream developmental path. Examination of key predictors of common forms of aggression and serious violence has been aided considerably by longitudinal studies of both mainstream and at-risk children and adolescents instituted over the past 40 years, and by the ability to combine those studies meta-analytically in order to fully understand the developmental trajectories taken by seriously violent youth. For this reason, the main focus of the current analysis shifts to longitudinal studies, those in which the same individuals are observed over time.

Adolescence as a Period of Multiple Transitions

Adolescence is clearly a time of transitions in contexts, and in personality, physical, academic, and social domains, transitions that are managed by most, albeit with considerable difficulty by some. The first, and most obvious, transition is that of school setting changes. Adolescents are likely to transition from elementary school to middle school, and then from middle school to high school. School setting transitions have not specifically been linked to increased aggression or violence, but research has documented poorer academic work and increased dislike for school experiences (Wigfield & Eccles, 1994), and lowered self-esteem (Simmons & Blyth, 1987), which appear more pronounced with an increased number of transitions. Transitions from school to school often disrupt friendships and teacher–child relationships that have sustained children through grade 5, and undermine emotional bonds with peers, teachers, and schools. That resulting social disconnectedness for some students has been linked to dropping out of school shortly after middle school (Marcus & Sanders-Reio, 2001).

The study of adolescence as a stage in human development, marked by pubertal changes at the beginning, and assumption of adult legal status/completion of basic education at the end, has sparked enormous controversy, debate, and research investigation surrounding one important issue: the extent to which adolescence is seen as a period of great destabilization of individual development, or "storm and stress," as Hall suggested more than 100 years ago. Of the two main divergent opinions, one is best represented by developmental psychologists who see the disruptions of puberty as affecting a small portion of adolescents. The other, represented by mental health researchers and professionals, sees most adolescents as suffering major personality disruption as a result of pubertal upheavals. The two perspectives are best summarized by two chapters in a stage-segmented review of research in developmental psychology using roughly the same body of literature to address the evidence for or against the concept of storm and stress of puberty (Wolman, 1982). The first chapter, representing developmental perspectives, concluded that adolescence was "not universally a stressful period ... (and does) not involve major upheavals, maladaptive developments or angry, antagonistic ... relations with parents ... yet some adolescents experience some of these negative events and others experience all of them" (Lerner & Shea, 1982, p. 507). The second, or mental health perspective, concluded that adolescence is "certainly a period of impressive transitions; the changes are vast and occur rapidly . . . (and) ample evidence at all levels . . . support that turmoil in early adolescence is a fact" (Siegel, 1982, p. 541). For current purposes, it is important to describe the precise ways in which pubertal changes, and trends later in adolescence, may heighten the risk for aggression and violence.

Adolescence and Multiple Personality Transitions

Adolescence clearly is a time when there are multiple social and personality transitions taking place, requiring personal resources and navigation that some may achieve with relative ease, some achieve with great difficulty, and some achieve not at all. The two contrasting points of view on adolescence noted earlier have taken divergent perspectives on pre- versus post-pubertal changes concerning adolescent boys. For example, there is the classic research by Offer (1969). Whereas Offer's longitudinal research has been cited as support for difficult transitions for only a minority of boys, the research suggests stormier transitions for most boys. Despite Offer screening out boys who had behavior disorders, and the group consisting of 84% who went on to college, the research concluded that early adolescence was a difficult time for boys. Specifically, 23% evidenced "continuous growth" (i.e., smooth, non-abrupt changes in behavior), 35% showed "surgent growth" (i.e., developmental spurts with periods of conflict and turmoil), and 21% evidence "tumultuous growth" (i.e., with intense periods of crisis, stress, and problem behavior). Fully 56% of those boys experienced some disruptions in development and relationships, which potentially may have heightened interpersonal conflict and vulnerability to aggression. (Note: another 21% appeared to be a mixture of surgent and continuous growth processes.) More recently, a longitudinal study of both boys and girls, from the beginning of 7th grade to the end of 8th grade, assessing angry and depressed emotions, found that 45% of the group consistently showed elevations in emotional distress across the two-year period (Roeser, Eccles, & Sameroff, 1998).

Some research reviews concerning potential disruptions of adolescence have pointed vividly to a time of heightened distress and disruptions in development. Some of those disruptions appear during early adolescence, some in middle, and some in later adolescence. For example, one important review of research identified three forms of disruptions in adolescence for which there was ample research support: "1. *conflict with parents*. Adolescents have a tendency to be rebellious and to resist adult authority. In particular, adolescence is a time when conflict with parents is especially high; 2. *mood disruptions*.

Adolescents tend to be more volatile emotionally than either children or adults. They experience more extremes of mood and more swings of mood from one extreme to the other. They also experience more frequent episodes of depressed mood; 3. *risk behavior.* Adolescents are more likely to cause disruptions of the social order and to engage in behaviors that carries the potential for harm to themselves and/or the people around them" (Arnett, 1999, p. 319). In addition, the three forms of disruption occurred at different periods in adolescence. Arnett found that conflict with parents appeared in early adolescence, mood disruptions in middle adolescence, and risk behaviors in late adolescence. Moreover, normative changes such as increased conflict with parents were more likely to occur in non-traditional societies, such as in the United States, where expectations for acceptable behavior for adolescents were less well defined.

It is important to re-examine the research bases for these three disruptions in development specifically with regard to aggression and violence, so that trends in aggression and violence can be better understood in a developmental context. The first of these disruptions was increased parent–adolescent conflict, which continues to be an important area of longitudinal research. Early research had clearly shown that adolescents' conflict with their parents and siblings increased in early adolescence. For example, conflicts between adolescents and their parents and siblings were found to average twenty incidents per month (Montemayor & Hanson, 1985), and daily conflicts in early adolescence increased when compared with those of pre-adolescents (Larson & Richards, 1994). Two recent longitudinal studies also have shown that negative affect expressed toward parents increased markedly from ages 12 through 15, but that it decreased thereafter (Kim, Conger, & Lorenz, 2001). Another 3-year longitudinal study of adolescents from ages 11 through 14 showed that one fourth of boys and one third of girls reported deterioration in the relationship with their parents over this period of time: 20% to 30% of adolescents perceived marked deterioration, 10% marked improvement, and 55% to 70% perceived relative stability (McGue, Elkins, Walden, & Iacono, 2005). Increased conflict with parents may have beneficial effects on development by serving to increase autonomy as development proceeds toward adulthood. Yet, increased adolescent conflict with parents is clearly experienced by many.

This trend toward deterioration in parent–adolescent relationships, for at least a sizeable minority of adolescents, occurs at a time when adolescents are shifting from life primarily within the family context to one with much greater peer involvement. Research has shown that from pre-adolescence to adolescence the time spent with parents diminishes while time spent and conformity with peers increases (see review in Rubin, Bukowski, & Parker, 1998). Furthermore, the middle school and early high school years mark the time in which associations with deviant peers becomes a good predictor of aggression and later arrest (see Coie & Dodge, 1998, pp. 831–834 for a review of research). Recently, and for example, a study of students in 24 middle schools in southern California has found that violence perpetration was highly correlated with violence perpetration by one's friends, and with membership and identification with high-risk groups of peers (Mouttapa, 2005). Thus, combining both developmental trends toward greater autonomy from their families and toward greater involvement with the peer culture, early adolescence is a time when relationships with parents shift gradually toward more adult-like relationships with parents, and toward greater vulnerability to peer influences. Conflicts between age peers, and between groups of young adolescents can potentially increase the likelihood of aggression or violence.

The second trend likely to elevate conflict and interpersonal aggression noted by Arnett concerned the pubertal onset of mood swings and depressed mood. The weight of the evidence in one important review of research clearly linked hormones, mood, and behavior as a challenge for early adolescent development (Buchanan, Eccles, & Becker, 1992). In particular, Buchanan and colleagues supported the following associations with hormonal surges identified by longitudinal investigations: (1) heightened activity, excitability, and rapid behavioral responses to stimulation; (2) increased anger and irritability, primarily in boys; (3) increased anxiety in boys; and (4) increased aggression among adolescent boys (Buchanan, Eccles, & Becker, 1992). Pubertal disruptions were closely linked to mood and behavior in early adolescence, and possibly served to increase the prevalence of more common forms of boys' aggression. Moreover, boys at puberty evidenced the greatest increases in testosterone levels between the ages of 12 and 14 (Lee et al., 1974), and a twenty-fold increase from ages 10 to 17 (Fairman & Winter, 1973), thus possibly contributing to both aggression and emotions consistent with aggression (e.g., irritability) that appears in the middle school years. Recent evidence for the impact of puberty on depressive mood, however, suggested that middle and high school girls were most vulnerable. For example, recent research concerning the appearance of depressive symptoms from childhood through adolescence showed that mood declines were present for both girls and boys, but that the increases in depressive symptoms between grades 5 and 8 were mainly experienced by girls (Cole et al., 2002). That finding also was consistent with earlier research regarding increased depression among girls in adolescence (Petersen et al., 1993). In sum, whereas girls were at greater risk for increased internal distress, boys were at greater risk for anger, irritability, interpersonal conflict, and aggression as related to pubertal changes.

There are additional ways in which pubertal changes may influence aggression and violence beyond the influence of puberty on emotional stability. Pubertal changes also result in a growth spurt second only to that of infancy. For girls, this growth spurt is regulated by estrogen, beginning around age 10 and ending at about age 14, leading to alterations in fat deposits, skeletal growth, and so on; this growth spurt occurs about two years earlier for girls than for boys (Fairman & Winter, 1973; Tanner, 1970). The growth spurt for both boys and girls results in an average yearly growth in height that is three times greater at age 15 than at age 11 (Tanner, 1970). However, boys gain primarily in muscle mass with accompanying increases in coordination, speed, and strength (Ramos, Frontera, Llorpart, & Feliciano, 1998; Tanner, 1970). For those reasons, early physical maturation for boys is likely to have multiple effects on aggression and violence. That proposition also has ample research support. First, research has shown that boys who mature earlier, and are thus likely to be bigger and stronger, were more likely to be among those who bully younger and smaller peers (Olweus, 1993). Bullying was shown in Chapter 1 to peak during pubertal transition in middle school years and then decline during the high school years in all six countries in which it was assessed (Smith-Khoury et al., 2004). Perhaps the most convincing evidence regarding the relation between maturity in boys (measured as appearance of underarm hair, facial hair, and voice change), and violent behavior (measured as self-reported fighting, weapons use, injury relating to fighting) was found for a diverse, nationally representative sample of 11 through 17 year olds (Cota-Robles, Neiss, & Rowe, 2002). In that study, pubertal maturity predicted to violent behavior, beyond the influence of age and ethnicity. Second, the gender difference in adolescent growth between boys and girls has been associated with a rapid divergence between male and female aggression and violence prevalence rates, making male gender one of the most potent predictors of violent or serious delinquency by early adolescence (Lipsey & Derzon, 1999). Third, although testosterone concentrations has been linked with aggression in boys in some studies, even prior to puberty, recent research evidence has suggested that testosterone increases alone may not be responsible for increased aggression among boys (Archer, 2006). It appeared that the physical maturation produced by hormonal changes, rather than the hormonal changes alone, was likely to be responsible for elevated aggression. Fourth, the appearance of sexual maturation in males may likely increase rivalry for the attention of females. Research has found that the most common motivation for violence between dating partners was given as jealousy (Sugarman & Hotaling, 1989), and for aggression between friends was jealousy (Parker, Low, Walker, & Gramm, 2005).

The third change in adolescence noted by Arnett (1999), and one of the most frequently studied forms of adolescent personality and behavior concerns the prevalence of many forms of risk taking behavior. Nationally representative surveys of adolescents in grades 9 through 12, since the early 1990s, have shown increased risk taking with greater age. Increases in risk taking behavior have been shown for many different forms of risk taking behaviors in 2003, according to the Youth Risk Behavior Survey (YRBS) (USDHHS, 2006b). Whereas 28% of high school students acknowledged having taken their first alcoholic drinks (i.e., more than a few sips) before entry to high school, from 9th through 12th grades, respectively, from 36% to 56% drank at least one alcoholic beverage in the last 30 days, and from 20% to 37% binge drank (defined as 5 or more drinks in a row) in the past 30 days. Drug use also increased from 9th to 12th grades, according to the 2003 data. Prevalence rates for marijuana smoking increased from 19% to 26%, cocaine use from 4% to 5%, methamphetamine use from 6% to 13%, and smoking more than two packs of cigarettes a day from 10% to 18%. Other elevations in high-risk behaviors revealed in that same YRBS yearly data were that from 9th grade to 12th grade, from 21% to 49% engaged in sexual intercourse with one or more partners in the past 3 months, and from 3% to 6% acknowledged having gotten their girlfriends pregnant. From 9th to 12th grades prevalence rates for insufficient exercise rose from 28% to 40%. Finally, one meta-analysis of risk taking research revealed that boys are more likely than girls to engage in risk taking behaviors (Byrnes, Miller, & Schafer, 1999). Therefore, although risk-taking behaviors are not rare in 9th grade, engagement in various risk-taking activities typically doubles by 12th grade. Aggression and violence may, in part, be a consequence of increased risk taking in adolescence. Greater risk taking in later adolescence may motivate serious violent behaviors.

Cognitive development in adolescence that is average or above may facilitate school adjustment whereas limited cognitive ability may increase frustration and aggression. Adequate cognitive development is a major requirement for negotiating the shift from childhood through adolescence as relates to aggression and violence because it is important to coping with the demands of increasingly complex school learning. Increasing cognitive sophistication for some, but not others, widens the achievement gap between those advancing and those lagging behind intellectually. In a broader sense, poor academic advancement represents a failure to acquire the cognitive skills needed to benefit from advanced schooling, and achieve a place in a highly complex society.

Adolescence has typically been seen as a stage during which abstract reasoning, ability to reason scientifically, and other cognitive skills approaches adult levels for most (Sigelman & Rider, 2003). But there also are individual differences in level of cognitive sophistication achieved. Intelligent quotient (IQ) can be taken as one global measure of intellectual functioning. The Wechsler Intelligence Scale for Children-IV (WISC-IV) (Wechsler, 2003) has been widely used and researched as a measure of intelligence quotient. The WISC-IV assesses cognitive progress, and how much adolescents have gained in school related (i.e., crystallized) and non-school related (i.e., fluid) intellectual domains. Although too often the major focus is on the individual's global IQ score (which has an average of 100, and standard deviation of 15) the IQ test score is comprised of a number of subtests that increase in difficulty, and each is age graded. Each year, in order to remain at the same IQ score, individuals would need to demonstrate increased attainment on most subtests. As individuals progress in age, so does the expectation of greater advancement intellectually in such cognitive domains as abstract verbal reasoning, memory for facts and information, spatial reasoning, and so on. Individuals with intelligence quotients that are below average, and who may have lowered academic achievement, may not keep pace with the intellectual advancements of their peers. Adolescents with limited school achievement during both childhood and adolescence may also find that the demands of advanced mathematics, understanding forms of government, or learning foreign languages is increasingly difficult, and they may find themselves falling further behind. Failing to keep pace intellectually and academically is likely to make adaptive transitions to middle school and high school academic subjects difficult, disliked, and frustrating for some, thereby promoting disengagement from mainstream peers and from the schooling process. Frustration and anger also resulting from rising school expectations will be revisited in Chapter 4.

Early Development of Violent Behavior

Starting the developmental story with a stage approach to adolescence does not consider the individual differences adolescents bring with them into puberty. The remainder of this discussion of the developmental context of adolescent aggression and violence begins with the early history of a smaller group (i.e., less than 10%) of individuals who are less equipped to cope with the transitions required of most adolescents. A case presentation of a child referred in middle school for seriously violent behavior, suggests some early precursors of later violent behavior.

I first met Tony when he was 13 years of age. His parents were interested in counseling because of his mounting difficulties in middle school. His behavioral and academic problems began long before this meeting. A child born to a drug-addicted mother, Tony was adopted by a couple who tried their best to contain him from his earliest years. In kindergarten, Tony jumped across the tops of the desks, and required stimulant medication to help him focus minimally on schoolwork. His parents tried many forms of punishment in order to reduce his impulsive and aggressive behavior, but his father acknowledged nothing worked, either then or now. Tony remained highly impulsive and aggressive, and gradually fell behind during the elementary school years. In middle school Tony now erased assignments from a book teachers had given him as a reminder of due dates, and he now was years behind his peers academically.

Tony told me when we first met that he had attacked a boy in school because two days earlier the boy had said something he didn't like. The case was pending in juvenile court after he had been arrested. Opening a girl's blouse in school, bragging about his penis size, running up a multi-thousand-dollar bill for 1-900 "sex calls," breaking and entering houses to gather "loot" that he stashed in the woods, and frequent fighting in school were among the most recent difficulties that overwhelmed the coping resources of both home and school. These acts were only the tip of the iceberg. Tony was now the leader of a small gang of like-minded, tough peers and said to me that they ran the school. He bragged that the students and teachers were afraid of them. Toward the end of my contacts with Tony, he showed me something he had written: "for some reason, I love violence; guns, knives, anything to do with violence; I don't know why." Tony stopped coming to counseling after he had been arrested for bringing a gun clip and live ammunition to his school, and for breaking into and entering a house in his neighborhood.

The Centrality of Aggression in the Development of Violence

There are a number of paths or trajectories toward seriously violent behavior proposed by developmental psychologists in order to describe the life course children such as Tony have followed. The paths are from disruptive behavior in early elementary school to middle or high school violence. All models of early development have in common either preschool or early elementary school aggressive behavior as an important precursor of later escalation to violence. However, models differ in the centrality, and even the importance of aggression, versus other non-aggressive conduct problems, as a key risk factor along the developmental path toward violence.

The simplest model proposes that aggression, practiced and intensified by individual children over the years, plays a central role in the development of violence by middle school. There are a large number of longitudinal studies, dating at least from those done at the Fels Research Institute in Ohio in the 1930s to 1950s (e.g., the *Birth to Maturity* study of Kagan & Moss, 1962), and many others not to be reviewed here, concluding that aggression is remarkably stable from childhood through adolescence. A review of these studies may be found in a reference work concerning aggression and violence in childhood and adolescence (Coie & Dodge , 1998, pp. 801–802).

There is little question, based on these studies, that aggressive behavior is among the more stable of human characteristics from childhood through adolescence. Moreover, correlations between aggression at age 8 and later violence, alcohol, and theft offenses in adolescence (Pulkkinen, 1982), and between aggression at age 8 and conviction for both violent and non-violent criminal behavior in early adulthood (Farrington, 1991; Huesmann, Eron, Lefkowitz, & Walder, 1984) also have confirmed the aggression–violence association.

More controversial are the reasons for the stability of aggression. The continuity of aggression is thought to be a consequence of "cumulative negative effects of this behavior, individual dispositions, or some combination of both" (Elliott & Tolan, 1999, p. 33). The answer to this crucial question of whether it is the aggression that is stable, or the consequences of aggression that make it so, has importance for the timing of prevention efforts, such as the importance of intervention before the age of 8, and whether the most intensive prevention efforts should be directed at the individual child, the family–school–child nexus, or both. Some have contended, on the basis of longitudinal data, that it is all over by age 8, and the cascade and accumulation of effects will have already begun by age 8, will continue through childhood, and will become increasingly resistant to change. Some, to the contrary, have contended that continuities in the environment, serious individual psychopathology, and extremely high scores of some children, do not account for the stability of aggression across situations and over time (Huesmann & Moise, 1999). More specifically, they hold that aggressive children "have acquired more scripts and beliefs that lead them to respond more aggressively in more situations . . . (and) situational factors play a major role in determining which scripts and beliefs (are) acquired by any individual" (Huesmann &

Moise, 1999, p 75–76). For example, individuals may learn to show high levels of aggression in situations in which they are insulted or disrespected. Citing research by Eron and colleagues (Eron et al., 1974; Huesmann et al., 1984; Lefkowitz et al., 1977), and using both peer ratings and self-report measures on 285 individuals at ages 8, 18, and 30, Huesmann and Moise concluded the following: (a) a 22-year continuity correlation coefficient for aggression of .40 to .50 was not unreasonable; (b) continuity was strong for both males and females; and (c) aggression was stable at *both* high and low levels, and not solely for those with extreme high scores.

Most recently, a study in six sites and three countries combined longitudinal data sets in order to define the early course of children's aggressive behavior in relation to adolescent delinquency (Broidy et al., 2003). The six research studies defined childhood physical aggression as physical fighting, bullying, and initiating fights. Self-reported violent delinquency in adolescence was defined as gang fighting, attacks with weapons, and attacks on people. Non-violent delinquency, defined as stealing or breaking and entering, also was assessed in early to mid adolescence. Physical aggression for both boys and girls was found to be highly stable for children in all six sites. Only in the two U.S. sites was there evidence of increasing aggression during middle school among boys and girls. Of greater significance for later violent behavior, a small but identifiable group of boys (i.e., 4% to 11%) and girls (i.e., 0% to 14%) were chronically aggressive throughout childhood. The results for boys showed that physical aggression was the most consistent predictor of violent offending in adolescence, after statistically teasing out the effects of early hyperactivity, non-aggressive conduct problems (e.g., stealing, lying), and oppositional behavior (e.g., disobedience). For girls, partly because of the lower average levels of delinquency in adolescence, data from four of the sites did not link girls' childhood aggression to delinquency in adolescence, despite the presence of a discernible, chronically aggressive group of girls in the childhood years.

Aggression in childhood has been shown not only to be a good predictor of later violent behavior but research studies have found that it shaped the character of later violent behavior as well. Aggression was more strongly associated with interpersonal forms of violence rather than crimes that did not entail face-to-face confrontations. Highly aggressive behavior at age 13 (Statin & Magnusson, 1989), and at age 8 (Pulkkinen, 1982), was found more strongly associated with violence than with property offending in late adolescence for both males and females. In addition, aggressiveness rated by teachers at age 13, for both males and females, related positively with both more serious and more frequent crimes (Statin & Magnusson, 1989).

An important caveat should be provided to the reader about linkages between early aggression and later violence. Researchers using longitudinal data have also become aware that many, if not most, boys who are aggressive in the elementary school years will desist from aggressiveness, thus effectively exiting the path toward violence (Loeber & Stouthamer-Loeber, 1998). Perhaps the presence of fewer risk factors, or more protective factors may have aided that desistance. Consistent with that caveat, correlations between childhood aggression and later violence have generally been modest. Lipsey and Derzon's (1999) meta-analysis of 155 longitudinal studies, for example, found an average correlation of .21, and this association held for both males and females, and between aggression and both self-reported and official arrest measures of later violence by mid-adolescence.

Childhood Aggression and a Resulting Cascade of Effects

Tony's experiences in early elementary school were likely to have perpetuated his conflicts with peers and teachers, setting him on a sequential path of events toward violent behavior by early adolescence. What this cascading of effects might look like has been an important research area for developmental psychologists. One research study focused only on kindergarten children, and can illustrate that sequential unfolding fairly well – within a single school year. Children who were deemed highly aggressive have been found to have consistently aggressive behavior from the beginning to the end of the kindergarten year, with correlations for teacher-rated aggressiveness (e.g., fighting, bullying, taunting peers) ranging from .69 to .71 for two cohorts of kindergarten children (Ladd & Profilet, 1996). Moreover, that study of kindergarten children showed that aggression was highly and negatively associated with prosocial behavior toward peers (e.g., helps, recognizes feelings, kind toward peers; $r = -.60$ and $r = -.65$), and strongly positively related to a measure of peer rejection and exclusion by peers (e.g., measuring not much liked by peers, peers avoid, and peers refuse to let child play: $r = .59$ and $r = .50$). Thus within one year alone, aggressive children showed consistent levels of aggression, failed to develop pro-social behavior skills, and were increasingly rejected by peers.

If kindergarten difficulties had represented the end of Tony's problems with peers in school the outcome might not have been so disastrous. However, research also showed that highly aggressive behavior, subsequent peer rejection, and failure to develop socially competent relationships with peers, were likely to continue for highly aggressive children throughout elementary school and into middle school. First, highly aggressive boys, ages 9 to 11, tend to select other highly aggressive boys as friends (Poulin & Boivin, 2000), thus compounding the social rejection from mainstream peers, resulting in isolation and reduced play with those who possess greater social skill. Longitudinal studies of elementary school children have also shown that, among boys, peer rejection in kindergarten predicted increased aggression by third grade, that is, beyond the levels shown in kindergarten (Dodge et al., 1990). The combination of aggression and peer rejection has been shown to increase both children's negative expectations of peers and their own aggressiveness from 1st to 6th grades (Bierman & Wargo, 1995). Finally, a longitudinal study of a predominantly African-American group of 3rd grade boys and girls (n = 327) followed the boys through grades 6, 8, and 10. They found that 3rd graders who were both highly aggressive *and* rejected by peers were more likely in 10th grade than those with other 3rd grade classifications (e.g., non-rejected aggressive, rejected non-aggressive) to acknowledge having committed a serious illegal offense (e.g., felony theft, felony assault, robbery) (Miller-Johnson et al., 1999). For boys, the combination of peer rejection and aggression predicted only to felony assault; for girls, rejection alone predicted minor assault.

Tony was representative of a small group of boys and girls whose aggressive and violent behavior had likely developed over a long period of time, and whose cumulative behavior difficulties had spilled over into the broader community. With behavior problems beginning often before the start of school, and descriptive labels applied to them as "life-course-persistent" offenders (Moffitt, 1993), and "early starters" (Patterson, DeBaryshe, & Ramsey, 1989), they constitute about 7% to 8% of boys and 2% to 3% of girls (Elliott, Huizinga, & Morse, 1986) who became "serious violent offenders" in adolescence. This "early starter" sequence, for example, outlined the sequential development of early aggressive behaviors. Early coercive interaction patterns between parent and child had led to the development in the child of a conduct disorder, and to school failure and rejection by mainstream peers in early elementary school. By middle school "early starters" had identified with pre-delinquent and delinquent peers, thereby arriving at an endpoint on a path taken by the most seriously impaired and antisocial children (Patterson, DeBaryshe, & Ramsey, 1989).

Early vs. Late Onset Violence

Early onset violence (i.e., that which occurs before age 12) has been an important organizing concept for those who propose a single childhood pathway from aggression toward serious violence. A study of two birth cohorts, has shown that the probability of committing a future violent offense increases from .26 after the first offense to .50 after the sixth offense (Tracy, Wolfgang, & Figlio, 1990); the frequency of violent offenses increases with the accumulation of prior arrests for violent crime. Moreover, longitudinal data from the National Youth Survey (NYS) revealed that those with onset before age 12 were more likely than those initiating after age 12 to have evidenced serious and chronic offending careers (Tolan & Thomas, 1995). Yet Tolan and Thomas cautioned that early onset timing of violence contributed only 6% additional influence (i.e., variance) as compared with 31% attributed by prior levels of psychosocial predictors, and early onset contributed minimally once delinquency had already started. Using the same NYS data, others had found that "serious violent offenders" (evidencing three or more serious violent behaviors in a year) had, on average, violent careers lasting only about 1 1/2 years, making it difficult to predict future serious violence beyond that point, based on the presence of violent behaviors alone (Elliott, Huizinga, & Morse, 1986). Thus serious violent careers may be relatively short and may not have predictive significance for future behavior. Moreover, a longitudinal study of aggression from ages 6 through 15, in samples from Canada, United States, and New Zealand had found no evidence of a late onset form of aggression for boys or for girls (Broidy et al., 2003). Late onset violence may require further study in order to determine whether it too has a special course of development, as in the case of early onset violence.

Longitudinal research has addressed important distinctions between the early development of those who later become seriously violent, and those who show few signs of violence until early adolescence. A taxonomy of two paths taken by those who persist in aggressive behavior by either (a) escalating to violent behavior in late childhood and early adolescence, that is, "life-course-persistent" (LCP) offenders, or (b) those greater in number who begin aggressive and violent behaviors during adolescence, that is, "adolescence-limited" (AL) offenders, has been proposed with explanations of etiology and predictions regarding the forms of later offenses (Moffitt, 1993). The early starters, or LCP offenders, are described as more permanently rather than temporarily engaged in antisocial behaviors, are documented as more extreme and frequent offenders, and later more likely to become violent. This group is likely to become violent specifically because of neuropsychological damage resulting from maternal drug abuse, or poor nutrition during the mother's pregnancy. This yields early and lasting effects in areas of poor cognitive control, "difficult" infant temperament, and poor impulse control, leading to persistent cycles of negative maternal–child interaction during infancy and childhood (Moffitt, 1993). It is important to note that the LCP offender suffers from individual psychopathology, which differs from AL offending, which typically mirrors adult-like problem behaviors (e.g., smoking, driving while intoxicated). AL offenders lack the cumulative and disabling elementary school history of LCP offenders (e.g., school failure, rejection by peers). More importantly, the AL offenders are able to shift from this path once adolescence is completed. AL offenders appear to be more like those who earlier were described as engaging in post-pubertal, normative aggression, whereas LCP offenders were more like the less than 10% who engaged in more serious violence.

Recent research evidence has continued to accumulate in support of the distinction between LCP offenders and AL offenders. Contrasts between those committing violent versus non-violent crimes in adolescence, according to longitudinal research, have shown that a key difference is that the LCP offenders evidence deficiencies in impulse control at the ages of 3 and 5 (i.e., defined as inability to modulate impulse expression, lack of persistence in problem solving, and emotionally negative reactions to stress) (Henry, Caspi, Moffitt, & Silva, 1996). Moreover, LCP offenders show cognitive deficits in spatial and memory functions at age 17 (Raine et al., 2005), and atypical family structure and functioning (e.g., five or more changes in residence) (Henry et al., 1996).

Multiple Developmental Pathways from Childhood through Adolescence

Some have proposed that children travel along multiple pathways toward violence in adolescence, and may reach a similar violent apex from different directions. One model of multiple pathways from early elementary school years through adolescence, proposes one pathway for violent and two pathways for non-violent offenders, both leading to violence during adolescence. Children during the elementary through high school years are described as following an "overt," "covert," or "authority conflict" pathway (Loeber & Hay, 1994; Loeber & Stouthamer-Loeber, 1998). All three pathways involve gradually escalating behaviors. In addition, all pathways escalate to serious forms of offending that are mixtures of violent and non-violent forms. Based on a longitudinal study of nearly 1,500 boys from Pittsburgh, Pennsylvania, this team of researchers described escalation along the "overt" pathway in which children progressed from "minor" forms (e.g., bullying, annoying others), to moderate forms of aggression (e.g., physical fighting, gang fighting), and finally to severe forms of violence (e.g., rape, attack). With each year on the pathway, there are progressively fewer boys who remain on the pathway, and fewer who initiate the more severe forms of violence. The "covert" boys progressed from "minor" covert behaviors such as shoplifting and frequent lying, escalating to property damage (e.g., vandalism, firesetting), and finally to serious delinquency (e.g., fraud, burglary, serious theft). The third pathway, called "authority conflict," progressed from stubborn behavior, to defiance/disobedience, to authority avoidance (e.g., truancy, running away). At the beginning of the pathways, the boys appear to be distinct groups, although sharing some of the behavioral characteristics of those on the other pathway. Despite the presence of some cross-over behaviors, "overt" offenders differ from others. Overt offenders were more confrontational, angrier, and possessed more cognitive distortions and deficiencies than those on the other pathways. At the pinnacle, or apex of the pyramid, however, it was difficult to tell the three groups apart. For example, at the apex of escalation, if a "covert" offender broke into enough homes, it was likely that they eventually would come face to face with their victims, and behave violently. At the pinnacle, as an "overt" offender once told me, "if I'm stronger than him, and he can't hold onto his stuff, then its mine." Overt offenders may eventually find that they can use their aggression to get what they want from others. A contrary line of evidence suggests, however, that specialization actually increases with continued referral to juvenile court (Farrington et al., 1988). This alternative observation leaves open the issue of whether specialization is descriptive of early or later offending careers.

Independent verification of the three developmental pathway models has come from analysis of two longitudinal data sets, the NYS and the Chicago Youth Development Study (CYDS) (Tolan & Gorman-Smith, 1999). The NYS is a study begun in 1976 and uses a probabilistic sampling of U.S. households. In the NYS study, youth were 12 to 17 years of age when the study started (n = 1, 453), and interviews on five occasions served as data for this re-analysis. The first four waves of the CYDS (Tolan et al., 1997 involved boys (n = 238) with complete interview data who were 5th and 7th graders at the time the study began. The CYDS boys were, in contrast to the NYS children, a predominantly minority, high-risk group.

To test the pathway model, those who became violent offenders, along with those who became serious violent offenders (but were non-violent) were contrasted as to the sequencing of escalating behaviors, and whether either group started earlier in their behaviors than other youth (Tolan & Gorman-Smith, 1999). Results of this re-analysis, for the NYS and CYDS youth, showed that from 82% to 89% of participants fit within the escalatory sequencing prescribed by the three pathways model. For example, from among the violent offender groups, violence came after fighting for 91% of the NYS and 93% of the CYDS youth. Finally, for the NYS group only, the violent offender group evidenced an earlier onset of problem behaviors than authority conflict, moderately serious delinquency, and the serious delinquency groups. Tolan and Gorman-Smith caution that findings are not applicable to females, and that escalatory processes in aggression levels suggest risk factors but not precursors or pathognomonic markers for later violence.

Longitudinal Risk Factors for Later Violence or Serious Offending

At this point in time, there are many longitudinal studies that have examined early risk factors among those 6 to 11 years of age, and those that have identified risk factors for violence among 12 to 14 year olds. A recent meta-analysis of 155 longitudinal studies has examined 68 studies for risk factors among 6 to 11 year olds, and 87 studies involving those 12 to 14 years of age with regard to the prediction of either violent or serious delinquency or criminal behavior at ages 15 to 25 years of age (Lipsey & Derzon, 1999). The specific criterion at ages 15 to 25 was physical aggression or threats of physical aggression against persons (i.e., called violent behavior), and "index offenses or offenses of comparable seriousness." The inclusion of index offenses or offenses of comparable seriousness may appear somewhat off message from the current focus on violence. However, it is important to note that Loeber's pathway model proposed that at the apex of the pyramid, where the most serious behavior may be found, the covert and overt offenders may be indistinguishable. The meta-analysis used studies coming mostly from the United States, with a significant portion from the United Kingdom and Scandinavian countries. The results were adjusted for differences (e.g., in timing, proportion of minorities, ages) between studies. Table 2.1 presents the results of meta-analysis in the form of correlations (i.e., r) and odds ratios (OR). Odds ratios refer to the increased odds of being in one category when the value of the predictor increased by one unit. Predictors are grouped into three categories by odds ratio, from the strongest (OR = 8 or better), to moderate (OR = 4 to 8), and small (OR = 2 to 4). Terms used in the table are provided in examples beneath the table.

Perhaps the most noticeable trend among the moderate to strongest predictors is that characteristics of individuals (e.g., gender, general offenses – law violating behaviors, aggression) accounted for seven of the ten moderate

TABLE 2.1. *Risk factors for violence or serious offenses based on longitudinal studies*

Ages 6 to 11	Ages 12 to 14
Strongest predictors: Odds Ratio 8 or Better:	
General offenses (r =.38, OR = 16.68)	Social ties (r =.39. OR = 18.54)
Substance use (r =.30, OR = 8.31)	Antisocial peers (r =.37, OR = 15.09)
Gender (r =.26, OR = 18.5)	
Moderate Predictors: Odds Ratio 4 or Better:	
Aggression (r =.21, OR = 4.40)	General offenses (r =.26, OR = 6.20)
Ethnicity (r =.20, OR = 4.12)	Gender (r =.19, OR = 5.17)
Antisocial parents (r =.23, OR = 5.04)	
Small Predictors: Odds Ratio 2 or Better:	
Problem behavior (r =.13, OR = 2.59)	Physical violence (r =.18, OR = 3.61)
IQ (r =.12, OR = 2.42)	Aggression (r =.19, OR = 3.85)
Medical/physical (r =.13, OR = 2.59)	Person crimes (r =.14, OR = 2.77)
Psychological condition (r =.15, OR = 2.96)	Problem behavior (r =.12, OR = 2.42)
	IQ (r =.11, OR = 2.26)
School attitudes/performance (r =.13, OR = 2.59)	Psychol. condition (r =.19, OR = 3.85)
	School attit./perform. (r =.19, OR = 3.85)
Parent–child relations (r =.15, OR = 2.96)	Antisocial parents (r =.16, OR = 3.16)
Other family characteristics (r =.12, OR = 2.42)	Broken home (r =.10, OR = 2.12)
Social ties (r =.15, OR = 2.96)	Family SES (r =.10, OR = 2.12)

Key to terms: **general offenses** = property crimes, status offenses; **substance use** = alcohol, tobacco, illicit drug use; **ethnicity** = minority status; **social ties** = few social activities, low popularity; **antisocial peers** = peer criminality, peer normlessness; **antisocial parents** = criminal parent, parent psychopathology, violent; **problem behavior** = aggressively inclined, antisocial, poor behavior ratings, temper tantrums; **medical/physical** = problems in developmental history, medical condition, physical development; **psychological condition** = behavior characteristics, high daring, impulsive, psychopathology; **parent–child relations** = punitive discipline, low parent involvement, low warmth, poor parent–child relationship; **person crimes** = violence, sexual offenses; **school attitudes/performance** = dropped out of school, low achievement, low interest, poor quality school; **other family characteristics** = high family stress, marital discord, large family size; **broken home** = separated from parents.
Source: Modified and reduced from Lipsey & Derzon (1999).

to strongest predictors for both age groups taken together. This suggests that measurement of individual differences such as these, as might be part of a screening measure, could serves as a basis for predicting which children might be most at risk by age 15. Second, risk factors differ in strength depending on the age of the child. For example, among the social factors that are moderate to strong predictors, when social factors, that is, those such as "antisocial parents," "antisocial peers," and poor "social ties," appear they are strongest when the child is embedded in or dependent on that system. For younger children 6–11 years of age, parent–child relationships are small predictors, but parent–child relationships were not found to be as important during adolescence. Yet poor social ties and antisocial peers were poor predictors in childhood, but were strong predictors when peer relationships most strongly affected them – in adolescence. The practical significance of these findings is that prevention efforts directed at the system most central to the children's lives at that age span is likely to be most effective. For example, parent training for the parents of younger children, and group focused work with older adolescents, are likely to be most efficacious. Finally, the huge contribution of unalterable factors such as gender, ethnicity, and physical handicaps, may make prevention efforts somewhat more difficult, but may potentially be counter-balanced by prevention focused on a greater number of changes in early drug use or abuse, behavior change, and so on, so as to reduce their impact.

Summary

The age-related trends toward increased aggressive behavior in middle and early high school years, but often dramatic increases in more violent behaviors in the high school years, were here examined within a developmental context. Longitudinal studies, and cross-sectional studies of developmental changes, and increased risk for aggressive behaviors in early adolescence co-occur with and appear related to many disruptions accompanying puberty. Disruptions of school and social relationships, puberty-related increases in mood regulation difficulty, increases in size and strength, and increases in conflict with parents appear to heighten personal distress for a significant minority of young adolescents. Such personal distress appears related to increases in aggressive behaviors. Once past early adolescence, many of the risk factors appear to ameliorate, along with the prevalence of the most common aggressive behaviors.

The developmental paths taken by those who later will engage in seriously violent behavior in adolescence appear to have their beginnings at least at the start of elementary school. Aggressive behavior, along with a cascade of effects of that behavior, such as peer rejection and poor social skill development, suggest a longer developmental sequence beginning with early neuro-cognitive deficits, and for less than 8% of boys and less than 3% of girls, a path of increasing escalation of aggressive behavior toward greater likelihood of injury, and criminal arrest for the most serious of violent behaviors. Whereas most of those on this path toward seriously violent behavior will exit before reaching the apex, their early development is marked with, for example, serious legal offenses, substance abuse, adverse family influences, and school learning difficulties, all of which appear before adolescence is reached. Individuals in this small, but not rare, subgroup appear more seriously handicapped by additive and numerous risk factors, which likely make exit from the path increasingly less likely the longer they remain on it.

3

Personality Risk Factors for Aggression and Violence

Over the last 60 years, advances in test construction, and greater sophistication in the creation and analysis of test items by which individuals might rate themselves, have been dramatic. Such advances have yielded a variety of basic personality traits. Particular personality traits, in turn, have been linked with aggression and violent behaviors in adolescence. However, efforts to reduce personality to a fundamental set of traits also has depended on which particular test items were provided for self-description purposes (Zuckerman et al., 1993). The resulting associations between trait measures of personality and aggression and violence also have depended on which basic personality traits have been measured.

One important attempt to define the structure of personality was dubbed the "Alternative Five." The measure consisted of five dimensions that take into account the psychobiological components of personality, and was designed so that traits would be replicable for both gender and various age groups (Zuckerman et al., 1993). The results of this empirical work were the following five personality traits: (1) *impulsive sensation-seeking.* " ... lack of planning and the tendency to act impulsively ... experience seeking, or the willingness to take risks for the sake of excitement or novel experience"; (2) *neuroticism-anxiety.* "items describe emotional upset, tension, worry, fearfulness, obsessive indecision, lack of self-confidence, and sensitivity to criticism"; (3) *aggression-hostility.* " ... a readiness to express verbal aggression ... rude, thoughtless, or antisocial behavior, vengefulness, and spitefulness"; (4) *activity.* " ... need for activity and an inability to relax and do nothing ... preference for hard or challenging work, an active busy life, and high energy level"; (5) *sociability.* " ... number of friends one has and the amount of time spent with them, outgoingness at parties, and a preference for being with others as opposed to being alone and pursuing solitary activities" (Zuckerman et al., 1993, pp. 759–760). Work on describing the major dimensions will continue to spark much debate, disagreement, and further research. But this model gives us a starting point from which we can organize our approach to adolescent personality and its relationship to aggression and violence.

There are also models by which we can conceptualize the ways in which personality traits might influence aggression and violence. The models typically take a personality trait by situation/context perspective. For example, the General Aggression Model (GAM) (Anderson & Bushman, 2002; Joireman, Anderson, & Strathman, 2001) proposes that the individual brings into any given situation personality traits that predispose them to respond aggressively or non-aggressively to given contextual factors (e.g., threat, constraints). The resultant behavior is an interaction of the two sources of influence. A particular adolescent who is angry and has a history of aggressive or violent behavior may respond aggressively at a party, given alcohol consumption, and an argument over a female interest. Another individual, without an aggressive personality trait, might simply respond by turning his attention elsewhere. Personality motivates the individual, or reduces the motivation of the individual to behave aggressively in that setting.

The section that follows will focus on different kinds of facilitators and inhibitors within the personality that influence the likelihood of aggressive behavior. The selection of personality constructs is not exhaustive, but identifies those most frequently studied among adolescents, and most reliably associated with aggression or violence. As important as which factors have been enumerated by prior research to explain the interaction of personality and context, is an explanation of *how* each operates. To address this issue of how each has influence, we draw on trait mechanisms of motivation, moderation, and mediation.

Motivators, Moderators, and Mediators of Aggression and Violence

Personality traits and situational influences may hold sway over behavioral outcomes by motivating behavior toward aggression-motivating. Or the personality trait may influence where and when the behavior is more or less likely to occur-moderating. Or the personality trait might work within the individual by altering the processes by which the individual interprets the situation-mediating. Personality traits may operate as motivational constructs. Motivation has been described as "a driving force . . . responsible for the initiation, persistence, direction, and vigour of goal-directed behavior" (Colman, 2001, p. 464). Motivation includes biologically based drives as well as social motivations such as domination or harm toward others, and is goal directed.

Personality traits, viewed as relatively enduring patterns of thoughts, feelings, and behavior, and encompassing a motivational readiness to respond in certain ways, have been found to increase during adolescence in some ways (e.g., social dominance), or remain relatively stable during adolescence in other ways (e.g., conscientiousness) (Roberts, Walton, & Viechtbauer, 2006). Examples of motivators might be the pursuit of sensation seeking in varied and risky ways, or simply a readiness to respond in a hostile fashion (i.e., a hostile attitude). Traits typically vary from low, or possessing little of that characteristic, to high and possessing more of that characteristic. For current purposes, we are interested in which personality traits continue to have motivational influence over aggression and violence throughout adolescence.

A second and third mode of influence, perhaps best thought of as indirect influences, suggested in a classic article by Baron and Kenny (1986), are *moderators* and *mediators*. A moderator is a variable that "effects the direction and/or strength of the relation between an independent or predictor variable and a dependent or criterion variable" (Baron & Kenny, 1986, p. 1174). The criterion variables we are most interested in are aggression and violence, and the moderators may be, qualitative (e.g., gender, race, class) or quantitative (e.g., level of reward), and may be both situational or person variables. Gender, as noted in earlier chapters, is a well known qualitative factor related to both aggression and violence. With regard to situational moderators, an adolescent with aggressive or impulsive personality traits might be more likely to be aggressive under conditions of threat or provocation, such as when insulted or challenged to fight, but shows relatively little aggression in non-provocative situations. One such moderating situational context in the broadest sense of the word is neighborhood. Operating both currently and over time, research has shown that impulsive adolescents were more likely to become violent if raised in more impoverished neighborhoods, where there may have been broader expectations of behavior, than if raised in a more affluent neighborhood with more guidance and narrower expectations for behavior (Lynam et al., 2000). Impulsivity may "flower" into violence in one moderating setting, but not another. As suggested in previous discussion of the early development of aggression and violence, being male or belonging to a gang, may provide many opportunities for aggression to manifest.

The workings of mediation, operating as a filtering mechanism within the individual, have become clearer with more sophisticated research and statistical methods. Mediators are "various transformational processes internal to the organism ... (that) ... intervene between output and input ... (and) explain how external physical events take on internal psychological significance"

(Baron & Kenny, 1986, p. 1176). In the case of mediators, we ask what internal cognitive or emotional processes of the individual might be most closely linked with behavioral aggression or violence. Examples of mediators would be a cognitive readiness to interpret ambiguous gestures or looks by another adolescent as aggressive (i.e., a hostile attribution bias). Other mediators would be recalling that aggression must be responded to aggressively in order to save face, or compassion for an opponent's injuries that curtails or de-escalates a physical fight (i.e., empathy). Where possible, distinctions here between trait motivators, moderators, and mediators will be made.

Personality Motivators for Aggression and Violence: Sensation Seeking

One of the better researched domains for description of personality *motivators* of aggression and violence, and a component of the Alternative Five model is "impulsive sensation seeking" (Zuckerman et al., 1993). Zuckerman (1994) describes four forms of sensation seeking as follows: (1) *boredom susceptibility:* an aversion to repetitive and/or boring tasks and people; (2) *disinhibition:* or seeking release or disinhibited social behavior via alcohol, partying, and so on; (3) *experience seeking:* or pursuit of an unconventional lifestyle via unplanned activities and/or hallucinatory drugs; and (4) *thrill and adventure seeking:* or seeking unusual sensation via exciting and/or risky sporting activities. Noteworthy is the adolescent who travels long distances to find excitement, initiates hostile teasing of classmates, or jumps into the middle of a fray in the lunchroom in order to break the boredom, all in pursuit of novel forms of excitement. Zuckerman's (1994) review of research provides considerable research support for associations between sensation seeking motivational processes and a number of measures of aggression, with stronger associations noted for thrill and adventure seeking. Currently it is important to show that sensation seeking motivation may serve to result in aggression or violence for adolescents.

Research has attempted to define a small, qualitatively distinct group for whom sensation seeking might be an important motivation toward serious violence, the less than 10% of individuals who are life-course-persistent (LCP) offenders identified by Moffitt (1993). In a recent longitudinal study of males ages 12 through 31, researchers found those who were identified in early adolescence as LCP offenders evidenced more criminally violent behavior (e.g., armed robbery, assault), and higher sensation-seeking traits than those whose offenses ended in adolescence (White, Bates, & Buyske, 2001). Those higher in sensation seeking personality traits were not only higher in aggressive behavior, but were more seriously and persistently violent as well.

Conscientiousness refers to "individual differences in the propensity to follow socially prescribed norms for impulse control, to be task- and goal-directed, to plan ahead, to delay gratification, and to follow norms and rules," (Bogg & Roberts, 2004, p. 887). This polar opposite of sensation seeking has been studied across age groups as a personality variable linked to various health-related behaviors. Conscientiousness is the opposite of disinhibition and experience seeking. A recent meta-analysis of studies with varying age groups showed that conscientiousness related moderately and negatively (generally below $r = -.30$ or less) with aggressive delinquency (e.g., conduct disorders, vandalism, physical threats). Moreover traits related to conscientiousness correlated better with measures of interpersonal aggression, such as, fighting, or using a weapon in an attack than with convictions for non-violent crime, incarceration, and sexual violence (Bogg & Roberts, 2004).

Another study of adolescents ages 12 through 18, had assessed trait impulsivity in a short-term longitudinal study of Spanish adolescents (Luengo, Carillo-de-la-Penca, Otero, & Romero, 1994). Measures of impulsivity, defined as disregard for the consequences of behavior, and a lifestyle focused on the present, predicted to self-reported aggression one year later, suggesting that impulsivity may be a relatively stable trait. A study of impulsivity in 16 year olds had shown stronger correlations with emotional aggression rather than instrumental aggression (Raine et al., 2006). Interpersonal aggression and violence in adolescence appears motivated by personality processes such as impulsivity and sensation seeking, and aggression and violence also related negatively with personality traits such as delay of gratification and following social rules.

There are two studies involving college students, rather than adolescents, which have helped us to further understand the ways in which sensation seeking as a motivator might have its effects, as well as the ways in which sensation seeking might be subject to important moderators and mediators. Identifying qualitatively distinct groups for whom sensation seeking was a particularly important motivation, was the goal of a recent study of college students (Swett, Marcus, & Reio, 2005). A measure of "fight-seeking" was constructed using items measuring thrill and adventure seeking, items reflecting a need to have an intensity of stimulation in one's life, a wish to do dangerous things, a craving for excitement, and taking risks for fun. In addition, items were added to tap whether individuals intentionally sought out physical fights or verbal arguments with others, after which they felt calmer, more relaxed. Interestingly, the items measuring thrill and adventure seeking and seeking arguments and physical conflict were highly inter-correlated, suggesting that intentionally seeking physical and verbal conflicts with others, and seeking thrills and adventure had a similar motivational basis. The results of this investigation also indicated that those males and females who were fight seekers, and scored in the top 8% on the fight seeking measure (n = 35; 17% female) were more likely to report the following: (1) they engaged in a greater number of physical fights with strangers, with opponents in private settings, and fights in which alcohol consumption was involved; (2) they engaged in a greater number of verbal arguments that later became violent conflicts, and were more likely to blame their opponents for starting the fights; and (3) were less likely to use fight prevention strategies such as avoiding or disengagement from verbal arguments, and finding alternative forms of excitement. Fight seekers were thus sensation seekers, motivated to seek out arguments and physical confrontations with others in a variety of ways, and they possessed few skills by which they could avoid fighting to begin with, or de-escalate fighting once initiated.

A second study of college students, and an important recent study of sensation seeking and aggression, explored the mediation of sensation seeking motivation by other emotional processes (Joireman, Anderson, & Strathman, 2003). The results of this study were that those rated high in sensation seeking, versus those with lower scores, were more motivated to participate in aggressive activities in future studies of aggression and violence. Thus, high sensation seekers were motivated to seek out situations likely to elicit aggression and violence. Second, high sensation seekers, versus low sensation seekers, and specifically those high on boredom susceptibility, disinhibition, and thrill and adventure seeking, were more likely to be more physically and verbally aggressive (correlations ranged from .20 to .46), and less likely to consider the future consequences of their behavior. The third and most complex finding concerned the ways in which sensation seeking motivation was mediated by internal cognitive and emotional processes, for both women and men. For men specifically, sensation seeking had direct effects on physical aggression, but indirect effects as well. The indirect effects were on lowered concern for future consequences, more hostile attitudes, and greater angry emotion. In other words, the effects of sensation seeking motivation were intensified when males were less mindful of future consequences, had more hostile attitudes, and were angrier. For women, sensation seeking had no direct effects on physical aggression, but had indirect effects through lowered concern about future consequences of their behavior, more hostile attitudes, and greater angry emotion. Thus, sensation seeking may function to increase aggression differently in men versus women because it is mediated differently by internal psychological processes such as general attitudes of hostility, and anger, thus resulting in greater or lesser aggression. Although these mediation effects have not yet been demonstrated for adolescents, we might speculate that for those adolescents who are high sensation seekers, but also take account of the future consequences of their behavior, possess less hostile attitudes, and are less angry, the outcome would less likely be aggression or violence.

As research studies of early development of adolescent aggressive and violent behavior have increased in complexity they have incorporated multiple, potential correlates of violence within a single study. The conclusions of those studies have aided our understanding of how strongly sensation seeking motivates violence, when contrasted with other predictors. For example, one recent study provided interviews yielding personality traits and violent crimes committed by a diverse group of adolescents when they were between 13 and 19 years of age. Participants were then re-interviewed 4 1/2 years later (Cooper, Wood, Orcutt, & Albino, 2003). The interview items measured the following: (1) "thrill and adventure seeking" (i.e., preference for dangerous, reckless, or risky behaviors); (2) "impulsivity" (i.e., tendency to act hastily and without thought, and inability to resist urges and cravings); (3) "negative affect" (i.e., a combination of items measuring depression, anxiety, and hostility); and (4) "maladaptive forms of emotion coping" (i.e., problems coping with anger, problems coping with negative emotions, failure to cope with problems). The results showed moderate and positive correlations between the personality measures and the number of self-reported violent crimes. Correlations with personality measures ranged from high with number of truant acts, alcohol use, and gender (B > G), and correlations leveled off at lower levels with thrill and adventure seeking and the other personality variables. However, more complex analysis, allowing entry of all variables in a single model predicting to high risk behaviors showed that it was "thrill and adventure seeking" that predicted equally and uniquely to both violent crimes and alcohol abuse (but not to poor school achievement or sexual behavior) at the beginning of the study. Avoidance coping, likewise, contributed to a degree slightly less than thrill and adventure seeking to violent acts. Interestingly, impulsivity did not specifically predict to violence in this model, given the presence of thrill and adventure seeking and avoidance coping. A component of sensation seeking predicted to violent crimes 4 1/2 years later to a greater degree than did impulsivity, and sensation seeking contributed to about the same extent as did avoidant coping styles.

Individual differences in personality traits conceptually related to sensation seeking assessed at the end of adolescence also have been helpful in predicting four health-risk behaviors at age 21, including convictions for violent crimes (Caspi et al., 1997). This longitudinal study, known as the Denedin Study, completed in New Zealand, utilized ten scales from the Multi-dimensional

Personality Questionnaire. Those who were violent offenders at age 21 ($n = 38$), when contrasted with those who did not engage in any health risk behaviors ($n = 728$), were similar to those engaging in other health risk behaviors, but violent offenders were more extreme in their personality trait scores. Specifically, and with regard to impact (or effect sizes represented, by convention, as small $= .20$, medium $= .50$, large $= .80$), those who were violent at age 21 were likely at age 18 to have the following personality traits (note: sensation seeking related variables italicized): (1) higher on aggression ($d = 1.44$); (2) higher on alienation ($d = 1.01$); (3) *lower on traditionalism* ($d = .77$); 4) *lower on control* ($d = .73$); lower on social closeness ($d = .69$); and (5) *lower on harm avoidance* ($d = .39$). Specifically, with reference to Zuckerman's sensation seeking subcomponents, these results show that those convicted at age 21 of violent offenses were, at age 18, less likely to desire a conservative social environment (low traditionalism), less likely to be reflective, cautious, careful, rational, and planful (low control), and less likely to avoid excitement and danger and to prefer safe activities (low harm avoidance).

Three additional studies from outside the United States have provided support for sensation seeking and its relation with aggression and violence by younger adolescents. A recent study of Swedish 8th graders evaluated self-reported violent behaviors (including robbery, fighting, injuring another, and assault with a weapon) (Eklund & Klinteberg, 2005). Alcohol abuse was defined as self-reported intoxication or consuming large amounts of alcohol. Personality was assessed using the fifteen traits of the Karolinska Scales of Personality. Nineteen percent of the boys and 7% of the girls had engaged in five or more violent behaviors. When boys and girls who were violent were contrasted with those who were non-violent, the violent adolescents were more impulsive (i.e., acted on the spur of the moment, talked before thinking, and engaged in quick decision making), and were more likely to avoid monotony (i.e., needed change and action; thrill seeking; avoiding routines). Second, a Belgian study of male students ages 12 through 18 ($n = 794$), revealed that those classified either as suicidal-violent ($n = 21$), or violent only ($n = 142$), and had higher sensation-seeking scores than those either in the suicidal ($n = 40$) or control group ($n = 591$). The measure of sensation seeking in the Belgian study was the Reynolds and Kamphaus (1992) instrument. However, use of the same measure translated for a sample of 7th grade boys in Singapore, showed positive correlations between sensation seeking with a teacher rated measure of conduct problems and hyperactivity, but not aggression (Ang & Wood, 2003). The Singapore study's use of a sample of younger students, teacher ratings as versus self-reports of behavior, less seriously violent students, and possible cultural differences in terms of the meaning of sensation seeking items make comparisons across cultures difficult. However, the results also suggest that further validation of sensation seeking measures with those of varied cultural backgrounds, and middle school ages, is needed to differentiate developmental processes from more deviant processes in the middle school years.

Personality Motivators and Mediators: Negative Affect

Common to all trait models of personality is the relatively enduring trait dimension of negative affect. Known as "neuroticism," negative affect includes the presence of emotional upset, lack of self-confidence, sensitivity to criticism, tension, worry, and fearfulness. Conceptualized as a mediator between environmental influences and behavioral output, there have been many studies linking aggressive and violent behavior to angry and depressive affect. For example, and as noted earlier, difficulty in coping with negative affect (i.e., anger and other negative emotions), were second in potency to thrill and adventure seeking in the prediction of violent crimes at two points in time (Cooper et al., 2003).

Emotion has reliably been classified as varying on two dimensions: (1) valence, or positive to negative affect; and (2) degree of intensity or arousal, from low to high (Feldman, 1995; Green, Goldman, & Salovey, 1993). Moreover, research on emotional valence has shown that some people typically show predominantly positive affect and calm, relaxed, and happy emotional experiences, whereas others show mainly negative affect such as angry, fearful, anxious, and depressed emotions (Green, Goldman, & Salovey, 1993). Positive and negative emotional experiences appear not to co-exist intrapersonally, and the tendency to experience one suppresses the other. Research on emotionality in adolescence has helped us to better understand the triggering role of negative affect as well as the protective role of positive emotions.

Emotions also have been described as incorporating specific action tendencies, with the meaning of "emote" itself meaning to move toward. For example, anger has been linked with an urge to attack someone, and fear with an urge to escape (Frijda, 1986; Frijda, Knipers, & Schure, 1989). Conversely, positive emotions also have been described as possessing action tendencies, those such as an urge to approach and continue activities, and generate prosocial behaviors such as to create, play, and cooperate (Frederickson, 2002).

Emotions can be thought of as social constructions in that they are what most people think of when they describe anger, fear, or sadness. More specifically with regard to anger, angry emotions have been described by people in terms of prototypical components, with "fuzzy boundaries," containing the following: (1) an instigation (e.g., frustration); (2) a cognitive component (e.g., obsessing about being wronged); (3) a physiological component (e.g., emotional arousal with tightened muscles); and (4) a behavioral component (e.g., aggressive actions toward the perceived agent of frustration) (Russell & Fehr, 1994). Anger, as a state of physiological arousal in preparation for aggression, has been described as providing a bridge between instrumental or motor components of behavior and the cognitive component of hostility (i.e., the feelings of ill will and injustice), which thereby increases the likelihood of physical or verbal aggression (Buss & Perry, 1992). However, anger, according to a major theory of angry aggression known as the Cognitive Neo-Associationist Theory, does not cause aggression itself, but is an important by-product of the initial cause of aggression, and accompanies, *motivates*, and directs aggression toward the perceived agent of frustration (Berkowitz & Harmon-Jones, 2004).

Based largely on a program of laboratory research studies, angry or emotional aggression has been described as having the following antecedents: (1) one is kept from reaching a goal (i.e., the interference has motivational relevance); (2) we perceive that the agent is responsible for the negative event; (3) the agent is blameworthy; (4) there is a perceived injustice or unfairness; and (5) we feel that attacking the source gives us a measure of control over the event (Berkowitz & Harmon-Jones, 2004). Moreover, according to this model, both angry emotion and aggressive behavior are the culmination of a multi-stage process in which there is negative affect generated in an "anger-aggression" syndrome (i.e., of thoughts, feelings, memories, and motor impulses). A fear syndrome is evoked at the same time (occasionally even suppressing anger), and the eventual expression of this syndrome is finally influenced by higher order cognitive processes (e.g., interpretations, social rules, anticipated costs and benefits), all of which alter the eventual behavioral expression. Not surprisingly, there is a large body of research concerning the association between anger and aggression in adolescence.

Personality Motivators and Mediators: Anger

The extent to which anger is a relatively stable trait during adolescence, and the extent to which it has reliably been associated with aggression, has been the subject of a number of longitudinal and psychometric research studies. "Trait anger," or the extent to which individuals of varying ages evidence a propensity to become angry, has been studied using a measure called the State-Trait Anger Expression Inventory, or STAXI (Spielberger, 1988), and the more recent STAXI-2 (Spielberger, 1999) measures. The original, 44-item scale had been factor analyzed and shown to have a single dimension ranging from low levels of irritation or annoyance, to high levels of fury and rage. However, the STAXI-2 measure of anger has been used to further distinguish between a predisposition toward anger called "trait anger;" as measured by self-report items such as "I am quick tempered," and "state anger;" a more transient anger measured by items such as "I feel irritated." Furthermore, the STAXI-2 measure has allowed for distinctions between "anger-out," a predisposition to openly express motoric components of anger (e.g., "I argue with others"), "anger-in," a tendency to hold in anger (e.g., "I boil inside, but I don't show it"), and "anger-control," or efforts to control the expression of anger (e.g., "I control my angry feelings").

Cross-sectional data show that males and female adolescents, as compared with samples of early adult and older adult males and females, evidence more trait anger and have greater difficulty controlling angry feelings (Spielberger, 1999). One caveat on interpreting these developmental trends as genuine developmental differences is that the groups are not entirely comparable with regard to educational status. Yet important to current focus on adolescents is a contrast of adolescent and post-adolescent individuals. A contrast of middle and high school students, as compared with college students, showed that both males and females declined in trait anger and anger-out, and improved in anger control with increasing age (Spielberger, 1999). Theoretically, anger-out would more strongly and positively relate to aggression and violence. Also efforts to control the outward expression of anger (e.g., "I take a breath and relax") would be expected to relate negatively with aggression and violence.

There have been no published longitudinal studies of the stability of the STAXI or STAXI-2 measure during adolescence. However, some studies have used items similar to those contained within the different trait anger scales. For example, one study utilized a composite measure of emotional distress, comprised of both self-rated symptoms of anger and of depression in the previous two weeks, and found emotional distress to be moderately stable from the beginning of 7th grade to the end of 8th grade; 45% of all middle schoolers consistently showed elevations in emotional distress for the two-year period (Roeser, Eccles, & Sameroff, 1998). Another longitudinal research study of Latino and White Non-Latino 9th through 12th graders, using a measure of trait anger (items such as "I am quick tempered"), showed anger to have low to moderate stability through high school (Swaim, Deffenbacher, & Wayman, 2004). In addition, Swaim et al. demonstrated that angry aggression, as measured by items such as "when I get angry, I hit others," also was relatively stable from 9th through 12th grades. Moreover, for trait anger and angry aggression, there was a strongly and positively related; those who rated themselves as high on trait anger were highly likely to be angrily aggressive. Finally, another short-term longitudinal study tracking a highly diverse group of New York City adolescents from 6th grade through 7th grade, showed no mean changes in anger for boys, but an increase in anger for girls (Nichols, Graber, Brooks-Gunn, & Botvin, 2006). In sum, there is some support for low to moderate stability of trait anger during adolescence; some evidence of mean elevation of trait anger during middle and high school, with declines thereafter; and moderate positive correlations between trait anger and angry aggression during adolescence.

The functional role of trait anger, as a motivator and mediator, in relation to aggressive behavior, has received some attention from studies of college students, but not by studies of adolescents per se. As reviewed earlier, one study of college students found that the influence of sensation seeking was mediated by anger for both males and females (Joireman et al., 2003). Specifically, the presence or absence of angry emotional traits significantly increased or decreased the relationship between sensation seeking and aggression for both men and women. However, other research also suggests that angry emotion influences decision making. Specifically, that study found that angry emotion influences individuals to both make riskier choices, and also to make more optimistic assessment of estimates to outcomes of risk choices (Lerner & Keltner, 2001). The interpretation of anger and its relation to high-risk behaviors, based on the Lerner and Keltner study, would suggest more of a motivational role, and thus an influence over both behavior and cognition, rather than a mediational mechanism between personality and aggression. Finally, and reminiscent of the Cognitive Neo-Associationist theory, both anger and aggression toward the perceived agent of frustration, and specifically the cognitive components of anger alone (i.e., obsessive thoughts of hostility or revenge) have been found to be moderate predictors of self-reported aggression and externalizing problem behaviors (as rated by mothers) for children and adolescents ages 7 through 16 (Schneiring & Rapee, 2004). The means by which anger influences aggression and violence, that is, by virtue of its mediation or motivational properties, or primarily due to its physiological or cognitive mechanisms, remains an important area of investigation in adolescence.

The relation between anger control mechanisms and aggression during the middle school years has been demonstrated in a short-term longitudinal study of 6th graders followed to 7th grade (Nichols et al., 2006). Anger control difficulty (e.g., "I have trouble controlling my temper") was found to be positively associated with self-reported aggression among 6th grade students. Also, anger related negatively with self-control (e.g., "when I have to wait in line, I do it patiently"). Most importantly, anger control predicted uniquely to aggression, beyond the effects of five other control variables (namely, gender, baseline aggression, ethnic group, self-control, and family structure) in 6th grade and predicted uniquely to higher levels of aggression the next year in 7th grade. Anger control efforts may take different forms, some of which predict better to aggression. Tangney and colleagues (1996) classified the anger coping mechanisms of 7th through 11th graders as destructive (e.g., physically aggressive), symbolic (e.g. shaking fists), displacement to an object, and constructive mechanisms (e.g., considering long-term consequences to the other person). Teacher-rated aggression related positively with destructive, symbolic, and displacement coping methods, and negatively with constructive coping. More mature means of coping can promote better anger regulation.

A study of the relation between anger and serious violent behavior during grades 9 through 12, was particularly noteworthy because the sample involved over 3000 students, and enabled matching of the dangerously violent adolescents (n = 484) with a group matched on age, gender, ethnicity, urban versus rural residence, and family structure (Flannery, Singer, & Wester, 2001). A dangerously violent (DV) subgroup was defined as those who had self-reported either shooting at or shooting someone or as attacking or stabbing someone with a knife (in the past year). This group comprised 15% of the total sample and was 28% female. Comparing the DV group versus the rest of the sample, a measure of anger significantly increased the likelihood of membership in the DV group by 4.15 fold for females, and 3.81 fold for males (which was also the largest of any predictor).

Research evidence for the relation between anger and aggression in adolescence also has been supported by studies of trait anger and "anger-out" associated with laboratory simulations of real life frustrations for adolescents. Two studies investigated anger and aggression in relation to simulations of everyday frustrations experienced by adolescents: (1) peer interference causing a failed video-game attempt; and (2) being bumped by a peer in the hallway on the way to class. The first study asked 7- to 13-year-old boys, most of whom had been clinic referred, to use their imaginations while they listened to a vignette in which an interfering peer appeared to cause a video-game failure (de Castro et al., 2005). The participants were asked to describe their own and the other's emotions and behavior. The results showed that the respondent's level of trait anger was positively and moderately related to their verbalization of physically aggressive responses. In addition, boys who had been classified as either reactively *or* proactively aggressive by their teachers, as compared with peers who were neither, had greater difficulty regulating negative emotions such as anger. Aggressive boys, as compared with their peers, had difficulty finding ways to distract themselves or think differently about the situations in order to make themselves feel better. Moreover, those classified as reactively aggressive, versus proactively aggressive, were angrier, perceived more hostile intent by the interfering boy, and saw the interfering boy as happier at the respondent's misfortune. The second simulation study, asked high school students (mean age = 16) to listen to an audio simulation of a situation in which a student bumps into them in a school hallway (Di Liberto, Katz, Beauchamp, & Howells, 2002). When respondents were asked about their thought processes in response to the bumping incident, adolescents classified as high anger (on the "anger-out" portion of the STAXI-2), said they had less control over their angry emotions. In addition, high anger-out students were more likely to have had histories, in the previous year, of either being suspended from school or arrested by the police for aggressive behavior.

Another important study of the relation between STAXI subscales of trait anger, "anger-out" and anger control subscales and aggression involved incarcerated adolescent boys (Cornell, Peterson, & Richards, 1999). Despite being a homogeneous group of adolescents, and therefore likely to reduce the overall size of correlations, the staff-rated physical aggression toward staff and toward peers during their period of incarceration related positively with anger-out and trait anger, and negatively with anger control. The anger out average for this incarcerated group was at the 75th percentile when compared with the original adolescent norms for the STAXI. Finally, a combination of the three anger scales, plus a history of the number of prior violent offenses jointly predicted to the number of physical aggressive acts during the period of incarceration.

The moderate stability of anger during adolescence, at least for adjacent years, and low to moderate associations between both aggression and violence with trait anger, anger-out, and anger control difficulties for adolescents, suggest that anger and angry aggression are positively related during adolescence, but both have an unsubstantiated relation with "cold" aggression. Attempts to understand angry aggression, however, does little to advance understanding of emotions involved with instrumental or proactive aggression. The precise nature of the relation between anger and angry aggression, that is, mediation or motivational, and cognitive versus emotional components of anger, is an important thrust of current research and remains somewhat murky at present.

Personality Motivators and Mediators: Depressed Mood/Clinical Depression

The second form of negative affect that has been studied in relation to aggression and violence in adolescence is depressed mood and clinical depression.

Depression is clearly one form of negative affect within the major models of normal personality functioning, but one that also has been defined as a unique clinical disorder. Depressed mood, as studied in adolescence, will here refer to the presence of depressed mood in the previous 2 weeks, or to the number of symptoms of a depressive disorder present at the time of evaluation. The number of symptoms of a clinical disorder, as present in the last 2 weeks, may be any of those that are indicative of a clinical depression, but not necessarily those sufficient to comprise a clinical depression. Clinical depression, however, will refer to the presence of a Major Depressive Episode, that is, a set of symptoms noted in DSM IV-TR (American Psychiatric Association, 2000), for the previous 2-week period. That constellation of symptoms, denoting a clinical depression according to DSM IV-TR, must represent a deviation from previous functioning, and significantly impaired social or occupational functioning. Clinical depression, known as a major depressive disorder, is both a more severe and more complicated version of depressed mood. Moreover, the symptoms must include at least five of the following: (1) depressed or irritable mood; (2) diminished interest or pleasure in activities; (3) weight loss or gain; (4) sleep problems; (5) psychomotor agitation or retardation; (6) fatigue or loss of energy; (7) feelings of worthlessness or inappropriate guilt; (8) diminished ability to think or concentrate; and (9) recurrent thoughts of death (note: symptoms 1 and 2 must be present; American Psychiatric Association, 2000). Noteworthy in DSM IV-TR is that with children and adolescents, there may be no depressed mood, but instead an irritable mood for the previous two weeks, thus representing a linkage with angry negative affect.

There have been recent attempts to conceptually link normal and abnormal personality around common underlying temperament dimensions of negative affectivity, positive affectivity, and disinhibition (vs. constraint) (Clark, 2005). This theory links the temperament underpinnings of normal and abnormal development by virtue of their stability over the course of lifespan development, with abnormality simply comprising more extremes on those three temperament dimensions. The extent to which depressed mood and, to a lesser extent, clinical depression has been relatively stable or recurrent during adolescence, and associated with aggressive and violent behavior in adolescence, has been supported in a number of studies over the past 20 years.

Depressed mood has been found to be relatively stable during adolescence. As stated earlier, a composite measure of both depressed mood and anger over the previous 2-week period was found to be relatively stable from the beginning of 7th grade to the end of 8th grade (Roeser et al., 1998); 45% of middle schoolers were stably distressed from 7th through 8th grades. A second source of support for stability of depressed mood comes from a longitudinal study of adolescent boys from ages 13 to 17 years of age (Beyers & Loeber,

2003). The measure of depressed mood was the thirteen-item Short Mood and Feelings Questionnaire (Angold et al., 1995). The items on the measure asked respondents whether they were, for example, unhappy or lonely during the previous 2-week period. Results of that study showed that there was a moderate average correlation between depressed mood as evidenced by adolescent boys for the 4-year period, and for pairs of adjacent years. A third longitudinal study used the Children's Depression Inventory, as completed by adolescents from grades 7 through 9 (Cole & Martin, 2005). Results of this study also showed that both self-rated depression and parent ratings of depression were moderately stable for adjacent years and across the 3-year span of time.

Studies in which depressed mood and measures of aggression or violence have been employed have provided modest support for a positive association between the two. A longitudinal study of 13- to 17-year-old students showed a low positive association with the average depressed mood and parent ratings of aggression over the 4-year period (Buyers & Loeber, 2003). Perhaps a more important finding by Byers and Loeber was that when participants were 13 years of age, depression contributed uniquely to parent rated aggression, after controlling for the effects of many other factors (namely, poor parent–child communication, family socioeconomic status, peer delinquency, and school achievement). The authors interpreted the effects of depression on aggression as due to its effects on increased shame and lowered empathy, which they believed co-occurred with subclinical depression. Since there is evidence that depressed mood also relates consistently with a number of different forms of antisocial behavior (such as alcohol use, sexual activities, rule-violating behavior) (Rohde, Lewinsohn, & Seeley, 1991), it is important for future research to help clarify what it is that explains the association between depressed mood and interpersonal violence. It may be the lowered empathy or increased shame, or it could be the increased irritability that clinicians often see in depressed adolescents, suggesting that the impact of depression is due to the irritability-anger component of depression.

The study of clinical depression and the symptoms of a depressive disorder has focused both on adolescents as perpetrators of aggression or violence and as victims of aggression or violence by others. The evidence seems more consistently to support the association between violent victimization and clinical depression for both adolescent males and females. First, the National Survey of Adolescents (U.S.) involved a national, household probability sampling of adolescents ages 12 through 17 (n = 4,023) (Kilpatrick et al., 2003). This study provided prevalence, co-morbidity (co-occurring diagnoses), and risk factor correlates for Major Depressive Episode (as well as Post-Traumatic Stress

Disorder and Substance abuse/dependence). The 6-month prevalence rate for Major Depressive Episode was 7.4% for boys and 13.9% for girls. Adolescents also were asked whether they had been violent victims of a physical assault, with or without a weapon. The study findings revealed that having experienced a physical assault contributed significantly and uniquely to the presence of a Major Depressive Episode beyond the effects of many demographic factors, namely, age, gender, ethnicity, family members having drug/alcohol problems, and either witnessing violence or personal sexual assault.

Two additional studies assessed the presence of clinical symptoms of depression, but not a major depressive disorder, in both perpetrators and victims of violence, and allowed for separate analyses of both male and female adolescents. First, one study of perpetrators contrasted two matched groups of adolescents grades 9 through 12: a dangerously violent group of males and females (15% of sample; 28% females) who had self-reported, in the past year, either attacking or stabbing someone with a knife or shooting at or shooting someone; versus a non-violent group (Flannery, Singer, & Wester, 2001). The dangerously violent and control groups were carefully matched on gender, age, ethnicity, areas of residence, and family structure. Odds ratios were given to show the relative increase in risk for violence for each of the personality measures. Males in the dangerously violent perpetrator group, versus non-violent group, evidenced greater anger (odds ratio = 3.81 to 1) but did not differ from controls in the presence of depressive symptoms. Females, however, evidenced both greater anger (odds ratio = 4.15 to 1) and greater depression (odds ratio = 6.37 to 1). Similar gender differences in depression for those who were victims and perpetrators, were found in another study of adolescents in grades 9 through 12 (Prinstein, Boergers, & Vernberg, 2001). Results from the Prinstein and colleagues study revealed that both males and females who were victimized by aggression reported more depressive symptoms. However, among violent perpetrating males there was no elevated level of depressive symptoms, whereas violent perpetrating females showed greater depressive symptoms. Finally, a recent longitudinal study in which depressive symptoms and delinquency were measured during adolescence showed that for females depressive symptoms both preceded and followed violent victimization, but delinquency preceded depression for males (Wiesner, 2003). There is a consistent body of research showing that violent victimization is related to serious depression in both males and females, but violent perpetration appears more reliably linked with depressive symptoms in females.

Research in which perpetrated violence or aggression is studied among adolescents individually and clinically diagnosed with a major depressive disorder is rare. One such study involved adolescents ages 13 through 17 (n = 74) who were not contrasted with a similar control group of undiagnosed adolescents (Knox et al., 2000). The results of this study showed that 24% showed frequent physical aggression in the home, 30% received detention at school for aggression, 14% reported being arrested for aggressive behavior, and 80% reported significant aggression either in the home or community setting. The authors interpreted elevations in aggression among depressed adolescents as possibly due to depression-related deficiencies in the regulation of emotion, to cognitive distortions (e.g., selective attention on negative stimuli), or possibly to prior victimization having led to the major depression.

Personality Motivators and Mediators: Empathy

There has been considerable lack of clarity as to whether empathy should be considered a personality trait, a situation-specific emotional state, or a multi-phased experiential process, and this confusion has impeded research and limited our understanding of empathy (see Duann & Hill, 1996). However, methodological problems have not reduced the enthusiasm of researchers who, for example, describe empathy as a key component of emotional intelligence (Goleman, 1995; Mayer, Salovey, Caruso, & Sitarenios, 2001), and a critical component of moral emotions and behavior beginning in early childhood (Eisenberg, Spinrod, & Sadofsky, 2006; Eisenberg, 2006).

Empathy has been generally described as the ability to understand another's perspective, feel compassionately for the other (although this empathy-based trait has sometimes been called sympathy), and respond in tailored fashion to others' needs. The study of empathy has provided a central theme for the study of morality and aggression/antisocial behavior in childhood and adolescence for over thirty years. Theoretically, those individuals with higher levels of empathy have been viewed as more likely to develop important prosocial behavioral skills and competencies, as well as qualitatively better emotional bonds with others, in part as a response to warm empathic parenting (see review by Eisenberg, 2006). Conversely, those with lower levels of empathy would be more likely to evidence aggressive and violent behaviors because they are insensitive to the pain they cause others. In addition, those low in empathy are unable to understand the reasons others behave the way they do, and, consequently, do not develop more effective, non-violent ways of coping with interpersonal disputes. Whether empathy sets the individual on a lifelong course of connectedness, or social and emotional responsiveness to others, or repeated aggression toward others leads to rejection and isolation from others, and desensitization to the effects of aggression on others, the evidence for the importance of empathy to aggression and violence continues to grow now as it has over the past 50 years.

Researchers have been divided as to the nature of what empathy is. Some place relative emphasis on the cognitive components of empathy, such as accurate perception of the others' feelings, or abilities to understand others' points of view (see Hogan, 1969). Others place greatest emphasis on the extent to which the individual experiences or shares the emotions of others, as in compassion or matching emotions (e.g., Miller & Eisenberg, 1988; Mehrabian & Epstein, 1972). Most have incorporated both cognitive and emotional components (e.g., Davis, 1983). A relatively complete definition of empathy, should include the ability to correctly perceive the emotions of others (i.e., label and discriminate among emotions), correctly understand the perspective and role of the other (i.e., role-taking, perspective-taking), and respond emotionally to the others' plight both emotionally and behaviorally (Feshbach & Feshbach, 1982). Sympathy and compassion represent behavioral outcomes in response to others' needs that some see as a derivative but not a necessary component of empathy (Eisenberg, 2006). Others have felt that the presence of a behavioral outcome was central enough to empathy to require expanding its meaning to the wish or motivation to behaviorally respond to them, as one might to someone being bullied (Olweus & Endresen, 1998).

Empathy has been frequently examined in relation to major dimensions of personality, and with regard to its stability during adolescence. There is evidence for the association between the "Index of empathy for children and adolescents" (Bryant, 1982), a measure of emotional empathy derived from a Mehrabian and Epstein measure, and major dimension of personality (the Big Five) (Del Barrio, Aluja, & Garcia, 2004). In that study of Spanish adolescents ages 12 to 17 years, emotional empathy was moderately related to a sociability or "friendliness" personality trait. Another study attempted to describe empathy, particularly the empathic concern and perspective taking dimensions of the Interpersonal Reactivity Index (IRI) (Davis, 1980), in relation to a number of interpersonal measures of personality (Gurtman, 1992). In that study, empathic concern and perspective taking were positioned within a circumplex model of traits and at the nurturance or love axis of the model.

The stability of empathy as a personality trait has also been the subject of study during the years of adolescence. Empathy, as measured by the IRI has been found to be highly correlated from the 9th to 12th grades for perspective taking, empathic concern, and personal distress. This research also found there were significant increases in perspective taking and empathic concern during the high school years, but declines in personal distress, the latter thought to be a less mature form of emotional responsiveness to others emotions (Davis & Franzoi, 1991). A longitudinal study of 13- to 16-year-old Norwegian adolescents further explored systematic developmental changes in empathy for both boys and girls (Olweus & Endresen, 1998). Consistent with Davis and Franzoi, Olweus and Endresen found that both boys and girls increased in empathy when the distressed other (e.g., one who was bullied or isolated) was a girl, but boys' empathy for other boys actually declined during this 4-year period. This finding suggested that the potential inhibitory influence of empathy for boys might also decline during this period of time. In addition, this study found for those in grades 8 and 9, and among the top 5% of empathic adolescents, that 97% were girls; and among the lowest 5% of empathic adolescents, 95% were boys. Moreover, from grades 6 and 7 to grades 8 and 9, boys had gone, respectively, from 24% in the top regarding empathic concern, to 5% in the top group on empathic concern. The authors suggested that gender differences and gender changes in empathy represented role adoption by both; boys were adopting competitive values of toughness and reputation and girls were adopting roles relating to emotional support and nurturance. Finally, an interesting difference appeared in correlations between empathy scores and two measures of negative affect (i.e., depression and anxiety). For boys, but not girls, their own negative emotionality related positively with total empathy; empathy for boys required the presence of some personal emotional distress. For girls, emotional distress was unrelated to total empathy.

Beginning with an early meta-analysis of research on empathy and aggression, in which various forms of empathy measurement (e.g., questionnaire, picture story, and non-verbal responses to emotion stimuli) were considered, measures of emotional empathy, such as the Mehrabian and Epstein (1972) Questionnaire Measure of Empathy (later renamed the "Emotional Empathic Tendency Scale" in 1997) showed consistent but modest negative associations with measures of aggression. More recently, a meta-analysis of 35 studies of both cognitive and emotional measures of empathy, as related to offending in adolescent samples, found that violent offenders showed the lowest empathy of all, particularly those who were adolescent offenders, and specifically on cognitive measures of empathy (Jolliffe & Farrington, 2004). The Jolliffe and Farrington study was a meta-analysis that was particularly significant since official records of violent crimes were the validity criterion used, but use of this criterion also may have minimized the variability, frequency, and severity of violent behavior.

Other research studies have been more supportive of the relation between emotional empathy and prosocial and aggressive behaviors in adolescence.

An often cited review of empathy measures found that the Questionnaire Measure of Empathy (emotional empathy), as well as the Hogan Empathy Test (a cognitive measure) related positively with measures of sociability, helping behaviors, for studies using samples of adolescents (Chlopan, McCain, Carbonell, & Hagen, 1985). A contrast between conduct disordered (and aggressive) and non-disordered boys and girls, ages 14 to 17, found conduct disordered adolescents to have lower scores on the empathic concern scale of the IRI, the empathy index from Bryant's measure, a measure of emotional arousal (responses to videotaped stimuli), as well as on measures of cognitive empathy (Cohen & Strayer, 1996).

Recent studies have focused on the mediational role of empathy in relation to aggression among young adolescents. The role of empathy as a mediator of aggressive behavior was supported by two studies. The first research study found that the positive correlation between social intelligence and aggression actually increased, when the effects of empathy were statistically partialled out (Bjorkqvist, 2000). Yet another study of Finnish children, ages 10, 12, and 14, utilized sociometric methods by which students rated their same-sex classmates on social intelligence, empathy, and aggression in physical, verbal, and physical forms (Kaukianen et al., 1999). The measure of empathy used here required students to rate those who, for example, correctly perceived the emotions of others, assumed the roles and perspectives of their classmates, and who were emotionally responsive to others. Items on the empathy scale included, for instance, "when I feel bad, I think that s(he) understands," and s(he) "notices quickly if others get hurt by a situation"; items were highly interrelated. Social intelligence was assessed by ten items measuring person perception, social flexibility, and accomplishment of personal goals, using items such as "able to get along with people" and "able to persuade others to do almost anything." Consistent with their hypothesis and theory, empathy and social intelligence were strongly and positively related. However, instead of empathy being redundant with social intelligence, in relation to aggression, it was a unique contributor to aggression. Specifically, empathy and physical aggression related moderately and negatively for 10, 12, and 14 year olds, when the effects of social intelligence were statistically partialled out: greater empathy appeared related to diminished aggression regardless of social ability and skill possessed by middle school students.

Empathy also has been studied in relation to serious violent offending, and using a variety of research methods. Empathy has been found to be a protective factor for both adolescent males and females with regard to serious offending behaviors in a group of incarcerated individuals, 56% of whom had committed serious violent crimes (e.g., murder, robbery)

(Broidy et al., 2003). Furthermore, research has focused on very low levels of empathy among those whose psychopathology suggests serious deficiencies in interpersonal relationships. Among psychopathic adolescents, there appear to be two main clusters of symptoms defining psychopathy among 12 to 16 year olds: (1) a cluster consisting of interpersonal arrogance, manipulativeness, and affective unresponsiveness, including callous-lack of empathy, and (2) impulsive and irresponsible antisocial behavior (Kosson et al., 2002). Using a rating system devised for a structured interview with incarcerated boys, those scoring higher on the psychopathy checklist were more likely than those with lower scores, to have had a history of violent charges in the criminal justice system, to have used weapons and a greater variety of weapons, had higher aggression ratings by parents, and had poorer quality emotional attachments to parents (Kosson et al., 2002). Other research has focused specifically on the empathy–psychopathy association, using the psychopathy checklist with a homogeneous sample of incarcerated males in the United Kingdom in order to more fully assess both empathy and psychopathy (Dolan & Rennie, 2006). The findings from that study showed that a measure of emotional empathy (derived from the Eysenck & Eysenck "Impulsivity, Venturesomeness & Empathy" measure), related negatively with both the interpersonal dimension, as well as the behavioral or lifestyle dimension of psychopathy.

One set of research studies explored a particularly low level of empathy in relation to serious violence. The trait of emotional coldness or unresponsiveness in a small group of adolescents, identified personality traits described as "callous, unemotional," as assessed by teachers and parents, in relation to the seriousness of violent behavior. Callous unemotionality was defined as both low empathy (i.e., "not concerned about the feelings of others") and low emotionality (i.e., "does not show emotions") (Frick et al., 2003). Late elementary school to early middle school adolescents with a combination of more symptoms of conduct disorder and higher ratings of callous-emotionality were more likely to evidence more severe and proactive aggressive patterns of conduct (Frick et al., 2003). Other research findings linked psychopathic symptoms with violence in a sample of male prison inmates ages 16 to 21 (Kruh, Frick, & Clements, 2005). That study found those inmates with both greater callous/unemotional and impulsive/conduct traits (i.e., psychopathic) were more likely to have a greater frequency and variety of violent acts, incrementally beyond that which was predicted by violence history and demographic factors. Their findings showed patterns of violence that were cross situational, and their violence was proactive rather than provoked (Kruh, Rick, & Clements, 2005). Extremely low empathy, particularly within an emotionally shallow personality apparently plays an important role in serious personality problems. Impaired attachment relationships and very low empathy, when coupled with impulsivity and conduct problems, serves as an important precursor of unemotional, and serious violent behavior.

A final study of low emotional empathy and serious violent behavior was undertaken with the development of a Risk of Eruptive Violence Scale (REV) (Mehrabian, 1997). The study revealed a complex interrelation of negative emotionality, empathy, and anger as well. Thirty five juvenile inmates were rated as to the severity of their violent acts, that is, from non-violent offenses (such as drug offenses), to high frequency use of weapons, serious injuries, and murder. They were administered the REV scale, a thirty-five-item measure of the extent to which individuals did not display anger to others, but seethed beneath the surface. Items included those such as "I sometimes experience smoldering pent-up anger that I am unable to express," and "my violent daydreams and thoughts give me energy and make me feel better." For the incarcerated sample, the REV correlated highly and positively with their history of violent behavior. In Mehrabian's second, related study of college students, the REV scale related positively with other measures of angry aggression, negatively with Mehrabian's measure of emotional empathy, and positively with personality temperament measures of negative affect (e.g., "nasty" feelings), and feelings of dominance and control (e.g., "I control situations . . . "). Although not yet validated on adolescent populations, this second study suggests that greater angry aggression is related to lowered empathy and increased negative affect, linking three personality risk factors reviewed earlier in this chapter.

The manner in which empathy functions to mediate both emotions and aggressive behavior in younger children, in relation to anger and depression, suggest a promising avenue for further research with adolescents. Recent research with 6 and 7 years olds addressed whether healthier emotional adjustment in general may serve to promote role-taking and thus reduce angry emotion as children develop, thus disentangling the associations between happy emotions, empathy, and anger (Schultz, Izard, & Baer, 2004). In this study, as with studies in adolescence, emotional empathy related negatively with children's aggression. In addition, this study showed that children higher in empathy (vs. lower) were also happier, were less angry, and were less likely to see other children as angry when in fact they were not. Although, unfortunately, empathy was omitted from the final model, this research supported the progression from happier emotions, to more accurate perceptions of others' angry emotions, to lowered aggressive behaviors. Similar models with middle and high school students might promote further understanding of the emotion, empathy, and aggression associations.

Summary

This chapter reviewed the research evidence on the relation between personality traits and aggression and violence in adolescence. Personality traits related to aggression and violence as motivators, mediators, or moderators. Among the personality traits most frequently studied in relation to aggression and violence are sensation seeking, negative affects such as anger and depressed mood, and empathy. Sensation seeking, and especially the subcomponents of thrill and adventure seeking and impulsivity appeared to be reliable motivators of aggressive and violent behavior, but were mediated by the presence of anger, which served to intensify the associations. Some research evidence suggested that sensation seeking also motivates individuals to seek out situations in which they are more likely to behave aggressively, thus suggesting that sensation seeking also may motivate toward moderating influences of situations. There is, however, little research on developmental changes in sensation seeking, or stability of sensation seeking during adolescence.

Personality traits relating anger and depression have shown good stability during adolescence, from the middle through high school years, with some suggestions of increases in negative affect with puberty. Trait anger, as well as anger-out, and poor anger controls also appear to increase in early adolescence, with anger controls increasing over the years of adolescence. Thus trait anger and anger control difficulties appear greater at times when aggression also appears greater. Trait anger consistently predicted to both aggression and violence in samples of adolescents. Depressed mood also showed good stability over the years of adolescence, albeit showed more modest correlations (than with anger) to measures of aggression and violence. Research combining both measures of sensation seeking and negative affect show that both contribute uniquely to the prediction of aggression and violence.

Perhaps the clearest research examples of personality traits serving as mediators of aggression and violence are those involving empathy. Whether considered mainly as a cognitive trait, or as an emotionally responsive trait, both empathy components negatively correlated with a variety of measures of aggression and violence. It is more difficulty to physically hurt another when you can either understand why they have behaved in a certain manner or hurting them simultaneously causes empathic pain in oneself. Perhaps the clearest examples of empathy deficits appear in psychopathic individuals, and particularly those with callous-unemotional traits. It is in that case that violent behavior becomes more likely. Unfortunately, studies have just begun to show some associations among motivators such as sensation seeking, negative affect, empathy, and their joint relations with aggression and violence.

4

Situational Risk Factors for Aggression and Violence

The belief among personality researchers and mental health practitioners that behavior is a function of both personality and situation is generally accepted as an obvious truth. Yet, because aggression and violence are relatively rare in human interaction, the prediction of dangerousness has not been possible using clinical methods or personality measurement alone. As suggested recently by Mulvey and Cauffman (2001), school violence is difficult to predict because it typically occurs in a social context rather than in isolation, and changes rather dynamically with daily occurrences in the lives of adolescents, thus suggesting the importance of careful attention to situational variation. Predicting violence might be comparable to that of charting the path of a leaf (i.e., personality) in the wind (situation), where under some circumstances one or the other may give you the most useful information, sometimes one or the other may be best, and more often than not both will be most helpful.

Consider the following example of a 17-year-old frequent alcohol drinker and fighter who was recently arrested for allegedly attacking and robbing a fast food deliveryman. Due to his recent arrest and 5 weeks of sobriety, a threatening encounter with a rather large acquaintance led to a different encounter than usual. Cornered outside a restaurant, despite accusations that he had snitched on the antagonist, direct invitations to fight, and threats to "bitch slap" his girl friends in front of male companions, the 17-year-old did not fight. Instead, he summoned up creative resources, including putting on a mask of "no fear," joking, ridiculing the physical posturing of his opponent, and reasoning to rebut the accusations, all leading to a non-violent ending. One can easily imagine that if the same encounter had taken place in a private rather than public situation, if he been drinking hard liquor, if there had been an unpleasant interaction earlier with friends, and if the threat of court appearance and possible jail time had not been present, any or a combination of any of these provocations might have led to violent conflict.

At the time individuals launch into aggression with antagonists there are a number of proximal or situational risk factors operating within the setting that may serve to increase the risk or decrease the risk of physical conflict. There are important reasons to examine situational influences on aggression and violence. First, previous discussion of personality traits that individuals take with them across situations and over time, such as anger or empathy, indicated that personality traits are limited in their ability to predict to aggressive response in particular situations, usually they do not account for more than 25% of the variance or difference in aggression (i.e., a correlation of $r = .50$ squared), and they rarely contribute much more when considered among multiple factors. Second, emotions such as anger and empathy, found in earlier reviews to be relatively stable personality traits, also appear in relatively transient forms, rising and falling with many factors such as heat, hunger, and frustrating circumstances. Personality factors may in fact recede in importance as more temporal factors become more prominent; it is likely that almost anyone would be more aggressive under certain circumstances such as threat to one's life or loved ones. In the mid 20th century, research had fairly well established that moral behaviors such as those investigated in the Hartshorne and May studies on dishonesty were both situationally specific and cross-situationally general. Predicting what someone would do required both knowledge of what they usually do and what kind of situational influences might be operating at the time. Following a description of situational dynamics related to aggression, and a review of some of the most important and best researched situational influences on aggression, an examination of violent episodes among middle and high school students will help piece together some of the multiple situational influences over violent episodes among middle and high school students. This chapter will end with a summary model of developmental, personality, and situational influences (Chapters 2 through 4) on aggression and violence.

Situational Influences and the "General Aggression Model"

There have been relatively few attempts to propose a general model for situational triggers for aggression and violence. This may be because there had been considerable confusion as to how situations should be conceptualized (Funder, 2006). Funder suggests that it is important to classify situations in terms of both "psychologically important" aspects of a situation, such as the personal perception of a situation, and objective features of a situation, such as the identity of individuals present, or the nature of the task the individuals are engaged in. In this way, we can describe the person-situation combination in which the expression of aggression becomes most likely.

The General Aggression Model (GAM) (Anderson & Bushman, 2002) proposes a taxonomy of psychologically salient situational factors, with both subjective and objective features, that research has found to trigger aggressive behavior. In this model, individual factors (as reviewed in Chapters 2 and 3) that are relatively enduring or relatively enduring such as male gender, trait anger, values, beliefs, goals, and cognitive scripts, are supplemented by factors operating within a given situation, so as to cue, provoke, frustrate, irritate, or provide relative cost/benefit information and thereby trigger or sustain aggression between people. The GAM was designed to replace an earlier model of emotional aggression with one that places greater emphasis on cognitive factors such as perceptions of objects, beliefs about people, and understandings about how people behave in given circumstances. However, it is important to note that the GAM also includes knowledge about when affects should be experienced, when affect should influence judgment and behavior, and provides a rule as to the circumstances under which aggressive retaliation should take place (e.g., a time when anger is high and fear of consequences is low). It is also important to note that anger has a special role within this model, as it did in their earlier affective aggression model, and one that is more important than suggested in Berkowitz's CNA theory of aggression. Specifically, the GAM proposes that anger may play a causal and situational role in aggression in the following ways: (1) anger may reduce inhibitions against aggressive retaliation; (2) anger may sustain attention to provocation over time (recall the Chapter 3 discussion of Mehrabian's eruptive violence); (3) by focusing attention on who is responsible for frustration and ways of responding; (4) by priming aggressive scripts; and (5) by energizing behavior and increasing arousal levels (Anderson & Bushman, 2002).

A specific research example of the interplay between a number of situational and personality influences on aggression is presented in a recent meta-analysis of situation, cognition, anger, and sympathy in relation to aggression (Rudolph, Roesch, Greitmeyer, & Weiner, 2004). Twenty-five of the studies assessed whether participants perceived personal harm to be controllable by the other individual, and thus responsible for the harm (or not), and had assessed anger, sympathy, and aggression. They found, consistent with CNA and GAM theories, that when an individual perceived that the agent was indeed in control and responsible for the harm (an attribution of control and responsibility), anger increased and sympathy for the perpetrator lessened, resulting in greater aggression. The authors interpreted the results to mean that when the individual experiences great physical discomfort, as in the case of hot temperatures, individuals might actually overestimate the negative intents of others and experience increased anger, thus increasing the likelihood of aggression.

The GAM proposed a provisional taxonomy of situational influences over aggression that here may serve as a model for situational effects regarding adolescent aggression and violence. The first of the six situational domains is *provocation*. Provocation refers to triggers such as insults, physical aggression, or interference in one's goals. A previous review of research on individuals of all ages concerning provocation in "real world settings," studies investigating a diverse set of provocations, such as verbal insult, stealing one's property, attacking one's self-esteem, and actual physical attack, showed provocation to be strongly related to both self-reported aggression and violent crime (e.g., as noted in police reports), and related to aggression in laboratory experiments (Anderson & Bushman, 1997). The second situational influence was *frustration*, defined as the blocking of goal attainment and one's determination that the antagonist was responsible for the failure to attain the goal. The third form of situational influence was *pain and discomfort*, which includes anything (e.g., sight, sound, temperature extreme) that would be experienced as aversive, painful, or discomforting. Their previous review of research concerning pain/discomfort and aggression or violence showed that violent crime and aggression in natural settings increased with higher temperatures, but research in laboratory settings had not consistently demonstrated that association (Anderson & Bushman, 1997). Their fourth situational influence was *drugs and alcohol*. Drugs and alcohol were believed to enhance the effects of frustration and provocation. Their previous review showed that alcohol consumption related well to violent crime in "real world" settings, but yielded a small to moderate effect size impact in laboratory studies (Anderson & Bushman, 1997). The fifth area of situational influence was *incentive*, which meant anything that would increase the relative benefit to cost ratio of aggression (e.g., obtaining money or material goods, lowered likelihood of getting caught). Their previous review concerning anonymity as a cost-lowering risk factor for aggression (as in larger crowds, more bystanders, hidden identity at night or with cover) showed moderate effects in real world settings and large effects in laboratory research (Anderson & Bushman, 1997). The sixth area was *aggressive cues*, which included the presence of weapons, or exposure to violent video games or movies. Earlier review of the effects of media violence on aggression showed moderate to large effect sizes in field studies and large effect sizes in laboratory studies (Anderson & Bushman, 1997). Both personality and situational influences, according to the GAM, may contribute to the internal state of cognition, affect or arousal level, leading to an appraisal and decision-making process and, eventually, to either thoughtful or impulsive action. The review that follows relates specifically to situational factors for adolescent aggression and violence.

Provocation

Provocation to aggression includes both real and imagined triggers to adolescent aggression and violence. The first to be discussed, and the subject of enormous research investigation over the past 25 years is that of a perceptual and cognitive bias present in aggressive and violent individuals that distorts incoming information to provide the perpetrator with a justification for aggressive acts and astound others who may be observing. I recall making a rather mild comment that I hoped would be useful to a highly aggressive 15 year old in order to help resolve a conflict with a competitor for his girlfriend's attention (his original plan was to put him in the hospital), only to have him move forward in a threatening and intimidating manner as if I had just insulted him. This cognitive distortion is referred to as a hostile attribution bias. The second is a form of provocation in which aggressive individuals attack others verbally, and sustain arguments leading to conflict escalation and eventual aggression. The third form of provocation involves a tendency for some adolescents to exploit a size and power differential with peers who are perceived as weaker, and for some who are both bullies and victims of bullying to be among the most vulnerable to provocation and yet frequent perpetrators as well.

A recent analysis of interviews of seventeen seriously violent male offenders, ages 16 to 20, who had committed a total of forty-one violent crimes leading to their incarceration, suggested the kind of provocation that triggers violence in their personal definitions, interpretations, and justifications for their violent acts (Lopez & Emmer, 2002). Their explanations were divided into two sets of belief-based motives for violence in response to situational influences: vigilante crimes and honor crimes. The offenders intentionally ignored the possibility of negative consequences of their violence (such as arrest, prison time, retaliation) once provocation was perceived. *Vigilante crimes* (constituting 25% of all incidents) had as its main goal the protection of others. Their violence was perceived as entirely justified and was accompanied by no regret or remorse afterward. Gustavo, age 18, attacked with a baseball bat a neighbor whom he had suspected of pedophilia. Another was Stone, age 17, who saw another boy helping his own brother to fight Stone's brother, leading Stone to ride by on bicycle while stabbing his brother's foe in the leg. *Honor crimes* were those in which there was a defense of self in response to either a real or perceived threat (i.e., self-preserving), and those in which the honor of one's gang was perceived to have been threatened. Self-preservation motives (constituting 39% of all incidents) were exemplified by Woody, age 16, who stabbed an opponent (also armed with a knife) who had wrapped himself around Woody in order that Woody would both save himself and not be perceived as a "punk"; both physical and psychological self-preservation were paramount. An example of a gang crime (37% of all crimes), committed in defense of the gang, was a drive by shooting described by Frederick, age 17, who collaborated with his gang to publicly humiliate (to the point of dropping fliers at the scene!) because rivals had disrespected their "hood" and their "set." Common to both vigilante and honor crimes was the endorsement of violence as an acceptable and preferred method of dealing with perceived provocation and were guided by hyper-masculine values and norms. Characteristic of honor crimes (75% of all incidents) was a readiness to take offense at others as trying to show them up as weak, unmanly, or unworthy of respect, a hostile attribution bias well known to those familiar with aggressive and violent adolescents.

The tendency for aggressive and violent adolescents to perceive and think differently from their peers, specifically in a biased manner, has been the subject of a number of research investigations. As an exemplar of this line of research, boys in fourth and seventh grades were classified as non-aggressive, moderately aggressive, and severely violent (Lochman & Dodge, 1994). Classification as non-aggressive and aggressive were based on teacher ratings and behavioral observations in the classroom; boys classified as severely violent were those in a special program in which a panel of raters had rated them as assaultive toward self, others, or property, and emotionally handicapped. The boys were presented with video-recorded vignettes with child actors portraying conflicts with peers and authority figures, and the boys were asked to imagine being the protagonist. The antagonist was portrayed as either benign, clearly hostile, or ambiguous with regard to intentions. Afterward, children were asked to recall and interpret the intentions of the antagonist, and complete a measure of interpersonal problem-solving strategies. The results of this study showed that the adolescent group generated significantly more physically and verbally aggressive solutions and labeled more anger and sadness in the antagonist than did the younger children. In addition, the violent adolescent group, as compared with the other two adolescent groups, generated fewer solutions by which protagonists could solve the problem, recalled fewer relevant interpersonal cues, and interpreted ambiguous antagonist behaviors as aggressive. The presence of a hostile attribution bias was also evident in research with a sample of delinquent male adolescents in a maximum-security prison; here a hostile attribution bias was positively correlated with reactively aggressive behavior and violent crimes (Dodge, Price, Bachorowski, & Newman, 1990). Were we able to collect in situ data on cognitive processes right after episodes, we would probably see more clearly the appearance of a hostile attribution bias in their responses to actual conflicts.

A recent meta-analysis of forty-one studies of hostile attribution bias and aggression, in children and adolescents, showed a low correlation between cognitive bias and aggression ($r = .17$), and a smaller but significant effect size for those age 12 and over ($r = .12$). The largest effect sizes were for those studies in which actual interaction was simulated as a way to gather "real life" information ($r = 55$) and those involving boys ($r = .22$) (Orobio de Castro et al., 2002).

The second form of provocation concerned a more obvious tendency for physically aggressive adolescents to also be verbally argumentative. An exploration of both individual anger and a school's angry climate (i.e., schools containing more angry students), as associated with verbal/physical conflict, was carried out in a 2-year longitudinal study of male 10th graders attending eighty-seven randomly selected high schools (Brezina, Piquero, & Mazerolle, 2001). The results of that study provided evidence for both school and individual differences in fighting and arguing with peers, and an association between individual anger and peer conflict. Results also showed that fighting and arguing with peers was affected by school climate of anger (i.e., aggregated anger), controlling for individual anger and other variables; "a student was more likely to engage in fights and arguments with schoolmates if he (attended) a school that harbors a relatively angry student population, controlling for (the student's own level of anger)" (p. 375). Both individual and context-related anger related positively with both physical and verbal peer conflict.

The original norming and development of the Aggression Questionnaire (Buss & Perry, 1992; see also Collani & Werner, 2005, with German adolescents and adults) provided evidence that those who were more argumentative and disagreeable tended also to be more physically aggressive ($r = .45$), angrier ($r = .48$), and more hostile ($r = .25$) (Buss & Perry, 1992). Other research using the Aggression Questionnaire with two samples of incarcerated male and female juvenile offenders, ages 15 to 17, and young offenders, ages 18 to 21, found that verbal aggression related moderately with psychological/verbal bullying (i.e., name calling and intimidation), and physical bullying behaviors (e.g., hitting and kicking; psychological aggression) and verbal aggression related moderately with physical aggression ($r = .47$) (Ireland & Archer,

2002). More revealing were the differences between those classified as "pure bullies," "bully/victims," "pure victims," and those uninvolved in bullying. Surprisingly, it was bully/victims, among the 15 to 17 years olds, who consistently had the highest levels of physical aggression, verbal aggression, hostility, and anger among all the groups. The authors interpreted the bully/victims' motivations as striving to communicate that they are not weak, and attempting to ward off future victimizations. This "fighting back" is reminiscent of adolescents in the United States who have been bullied, who also bully others, and who ultimately fight back by snapping and killing fellow students in a shooting spree.

Since the early research by Olweus in Norway in the 1970s (1993), the study of bullying and victimization by bullies has garnered considerable research interest around the world. Although bullying may vary widely from embarrassing sounds intended to disrupt a student giving a speech in English class, to slapping someone in the head while passing the school stairwell on the way to classes, or to taking someone's lunch out of their desk while they are away, such repeated victimization is often recalled many years later. Recent research, in fact, finds that adults most often recall bullying experiences occurring between the ages of 11 and 13 (Eslea & Rees, 2001). Indeed, bullying is most common during middle school years (Nansell et al., 2001; Haynie et al., 2001; Shafer et al., 2005; Pellegrini & Long, 2002), and varies in definition from single incidents within a 2-week time period (Ireland & Archer, 2002) to three or more instances in the past year (Haynie et al., 2001). Research has examined forms as subtle as teasing and excluding another (Espelage, Holt, & Henke, 2003) to a focus on hitting or shoving (Unnever, 2005). Bullying is typically regarded as a subset of aggressive behaviors in which there is repeated aggression by a bully toward a victim and there is a power differential in which the bully is bigger, stronger, and of higher status. The acts are very likely recalled later because of the embarrassment, shame, fear, or other emotions making the incidents highly salient. There is fairly good consensus on the four middle school roles of bully, victims, bully/victims, and non-involved individual (e.g., Haynie et al., 2001; Unnever, 2005), as well as the special vulnerabilities of those in the bully/victim roles.

Bully/victims are those who are both likely to be repeatedly victimized and to repeatedly victimize others. Bully/victims, as compared with bullies, have been found to have less control over anger, poorer social competence, and more depressive symptoms (Haynie et al., 2001), greater anger and hostility (Ireland & Archer, 2002), and evidence greater reactive but lower proactive aggression (Unnever, 2005). At the individual level then, bully/victims appear more easily provoked. Bully/victims also have been found to have more unstable relationships with peers. They have been found, as compared with bullies, to be more likely to be verbally bullied by others and to have fewer friends (Unnever, 2005), as well as to have more deviant friends (Haynie et al., 2001). A recent short-term longitudinal study has shown that those who bully or physically fight tend to associate in cliques with others who also bully and physically fight, and (for boys and girls) peer group influences overshadowed grade and individual aggression levels in predicting to later aggression levels (Espelage et al., 2003). In all, the bully/victim appears at greater risk for increased aggression, has greater response to provocation from others' aggression, due both to their individual vulnerabilities as well as their social networks.

Provocation may be clearly observable, as in verbal insults nested within verbal arguments that escalate to physical aggression. Provocation also may be seen in a hypersensitive, psychological readiness to interpret others' intentions as malevolent and threatening, requiring a prompt overreaction as a deterrence and warning to others that they will fight if provoked. Seriously violent adolescents appear poised to react to perceived disrespect to self and compatriots, but also to violations of their sense of justice without need to establish guilt or innocence in an impartial manner.

Frustration

Common to adolescents responsible for twelve school-based shooting episodes in the United States during the 1990s was that they were white males, averaging 15 years of age, of normal intellectual and physical functioning, with both peer and family relationships that were highly conflicted, and they had experienced a triggering event shortly before their rampage (McGee & DeBernardo, 1999). More specifically, the precipitating event involved experiences of frustration or humiliation, rejection, and censure or discipline. Frustration may be experienced in academic work, peer relationships, or any domain in which goals are thwarted. Central to a reformulation of the frustration-aggression principle are the following factors likely to increase frustration, from which aggression is but one, albeit least likely outcome: (1) a repeated inability to attain one's goals or obtain rewards that are expected; (2) perceiving the agent of frustration as unfair or arbitrary; (3) personalizing the agent's actions; and (4) having few resources (i.e., personal, cognitive, social) with which to cope with stressors – all likely to increase both anger/fear and aggression (Berkowitz, 1993).

The middle and high school years are likely to present many frustrating experiences, with academic hurdles being among the leading candidates.

Different scenarios describing a poor student–school "fit," have suggested possible variations on the nature of mounting frustration for various students leading to different forms of violent behavior, all of which center around a disengagement, or "dis-identification" with the academic mission of the school (Osborne, 2002). The first of these scenarios is a devaluing or dis-identification with academics due to a history of poor learning outcomes, which then leads to identification with peers having similar experiences. This scenario is similar to Patterson et al.'s (1989) early starter model in which early antisocial behavior leads to poor school performance and to later association with pre-delinquent peers in late elementary school or early middle school. The second is the frustration due to the student's dis-identification with academics yet being forced to attend school for legal reasons. The student is compelled to engage in 6 hours or more of frustration each day. The third scenario is the acquisition by the student of unrealistically high expectations that the student is unable to meet, a difficult situation in which students are required to perform at high levels. They feel pressured to perform by parents and teachers, but are unable to succeed, get help, or in any other way resolve the situation. The fourth scenario is a poor person–school environment fit in which peer rejection plus an inability to devalue or cope with various social relationships leads to considerable frustration.

Evidence for the first and second of Osborne's scenarios, in which there is dis-identification with academics prior to 9th grade leading to poor achievement or violence by the end of 10th grade, can be found in two separate research studies (Osborne, 2004). In the first study, they found that substantially reduced academic motivation prior to entry to 9th grade led to lowered grade point averages and increased referrals and absenteeism by the end of 10th grade. A second study employed data from a large, nationally representative sample of high school students in the United States. Osborne found that poor academic motivation was associated with cutting classes, missing school, dropping out of school, as well as physical fighting, transfers for disciplinary reasons, and being arrested by the police (Osborne, 2002). Support for scenario four can be found in longitudinal studies presented earlier in this volume (see Chapter 2), in which a combination of both peer rejection and aggression related most strongly to violent outcomes in adolescence.

The difficulty students have with both academics and physical fighting, however, likely starts earlier during middle school years, if not before, and both frustration with poor achievement and fighting may exert independent influence on later academic work during the high school years. A sample of high school students was classified as either "off track" for a regular high school diploma, or "on track" for a regular diploma, and this was followed by a review of school records for these boys and girls for 6th through 8th grades (Tobin & Sugai, 1999). The authors were interested in grade point averages and violent physical fighting during the middle school years as predictors of later high school academic tracking. In 6th grade, and consistent with Osborne's scenarios one and two, girls and boys whose school records indicated that they had non-violently misbehaved in a manner suggesting academic frustration (e.g., were insubordinate or disruptive) were likely to have physically fought ($r = .61$ for girls; $r = .58$ for boys), or to have either have harassed others (e.g., verbally abusive, destroyed property), or physically fought ($r = .80$ for girls; $r = .65$ for boys). Also, those with lower grade point averages were more likely to have physically fought ($r = -.18$ for girls; $r = -.28$ for boys). Therefore, in sixth grade, boys and girls who were showing signs of frustration with academics (e.g., insubordinate, disruptive), were angrily harassing others and were physically fighting more with peers. Between 6th and 8th grades physical fighting was moderately stable for boys ($r = .50$) and for girls ($r = .61$). Being off track in high school was predicted uniquely by physical fighting in 6th grade (for boys only) and by grade point average in 6th grade (for both boys and girls).

Frustration with academic work and/or peer relationships, experienced on a daily basis may heighten daily irritability and stress, making young adolescents particularly vulnerable to provocation. Aggression may be directed at the perceived source of frustration, such as teachers, peer competitors, or toward school property in the form of vandalism.

Pain and Discomfort

Consistent with the CNA theory of emotional aggression noted earlier, is the proposition that any physical pain or discomfort, such as heat, cold, or loud noises increases negative affect and the likelihood that negative affects such as anger may be inflamed by higher order cognitive processes (Berkowitz, 1993; Anderson & Bushman, 2002). Whereas anger is typically cited as central to this theory, any transient negative emotional experience related to anger (e.g., shame or jealousy) may theoretically relate to aggression as well.

A 50-year history of research relating temperature and criminal violence has repeatedly demonstrated a positive association between the two. The shape of the association (i.e., linear or curvilinear), and the situations in which the relation might hold or not hold (e.g., daytime vs. nighttime) remain under continuing investigation. An empirical test of the hypothesis that increased temperatures over time related to increases in interpersonal violent crime, but *not* property crimes, was provided by a study of those age 15 and older for the years 1950 through 1995 in the United States (Anderson, Bushman, & Groom, 1997). In that study, violent crime was represented by police reports (FBI data) of both aggravated assault and homicide, and temperature in different parts of the country was measured according to the temperature of the nearest city. Results of the study showed that violent crime was positively related both to temperature ($r = .46$) and the hotness (days over 90 degrees) of summer days ($r = .38$). The ability of temperature to predict violent crime held both with and without inclusion of the 15- to 29-year-old age group; property crime was unrelated to temperature. Increased discomfort translated into violence toward people but not to increased crime in general.

As developmental psychology advances our understanding of anger and related emotions during adolescence, the appearance of two complex and composite forms of angry emotion, shame and jealousy, have also been linked with anger and angry aggression. Shame and jealousy can also be considered nuanced variants of anger that are more transient and situation-specific than trait anger in that intense discomfort is triggered by specific threats to the individual's self-esteem or security.

Research concerning both the dark side and constructive side of anger, in relation to shame, has been explored in adolescents from grades 7 through 11 (Tangney et al., 1996). The presence of anger, according to this line of research, may lead to maladaptive coping mechanisms such as physical aggression, verbal aggression, displaced aggression, and anger "held in." Anger also may lead to adaptive responses such as verbal discussions with the target person, doing nothing, or cognitive re-appraisal of the roles of respondent and/or the target. Typically, the adaptive forms of coping with anger are more common among adults and adolescents than children. Exploration of the antecedents of maladaptive and adaptive coping with anger, in this study, led to the examination of the roles of shame-proneness and guilt. In terms of subjective experiences, shame refers to the reactions that are a more global and enduring feature of the entire self, a painful and negative evaluation in which one feels, at that moment, worthless, powerless, and wishes to escape into the floor and disappear before a real or imagined audience. Guilt, however, is seen as more focused on a specific failure, such as regret or remorse over a bad act rather than discomfort spreading throughout the total self. Tangney and colleagues' research with adolescents found that shame-proneness related positively with anger arousal ($r = .21$), physical aggression ($r = .18$), verbal aggression ($r = .18$), and displaced physical aggression ($r = .27$), once guilt-proneness was factored out. However, guilt-proneness was negatively correlated with physical aggression ($r = -.39$), verbal aggression ($r = -.18$), and displaced aggression ($r = -.36$), once shame-proneness was factored out.

The lives of adolescents may potentially contain many situations in which the experience of shame might be experienced as traumatic, including being humiliated in front of one's friends, peers finding out about test failures, and so on, incidents that could foster a shame-anger-aggression linkage.

The second anger- and discomfort-related emotion concerned jealousies and rivalries among young adolescents, a prominent part of the competition for friends and status among middle schoolers having to cope with re-shuffled peer networks. One important study of friendship jealousy among those grades 5 through 9, involved the creation of twenty-seven short vignettes. The vignettes were hypothetical social situations to which respondents were asked to imagine their reactions to the interference in their friendship relationship by an interloper (Parker, Low, Walker, & Gramm, 2005). Friendship jealousy was described as that which "stems from interpersonal threat, creates uncertainty, and involves a blended array of strong emotions" (p. 240). Consistent with the research cited earlier by Tangney et al. (1996), friendship jealousy may lead to adaptive coping responses (e.g., enhanced communication with the friend, increased interest, efforts to improve the relationship), to maladaptive passive aggression (e.g., sulking, "silent treatment"), or to outright aggressive intimidation (e.g., verbal or physical assault). A measure of friendship jealousy completed by non-friend peers (i.e., peer nominations, employing items such as "possessive of their friends" and "gets jealous if you try to be friends with their friends"), related positively with a measure of verbal/physical harassment of others (e.g., "hits and pushes others around," and "makes fun of people") (r = .49 for boys; r = .77 for girls). Girls evidenced greater friendship jealousy than boys. Friendship jealousy decreased from 5th to 9th grade, consistent with the trend toward increased aggression in middle school.

These important studies of powerful emotional experiences, which are likely to be highly discomfiting, relatively transient, and situation specific suggest the importance of situational emotions in common forms of aggression. Yet adolescents who had developed methods of coping with discomfort, or who had experienced less discomfort were less likely to act aggressively.

Alcohol and Drug Use and Abuse

The relation between alcohol and drug use and aggression or violent behavior during adolescence has been particularly well studied because both forms of risk behavior are relatively common at that time. Estimates, based on nationally representative samples of adolescents in the United States, 1994 to 1995 (Add Health), for the prevalence of drinking alcohol on one or more occasions was found to be 45%, and binge drinking (five or more drinks on one occasion) was 24%, for the past year and for grades 7 though 12 (Maney, Higham-Gardill, & Mahoney, 2002). Slightly higher estimates were found to be 52% having consumed alcohol in the past 30 days, and 33% having consumed five or more drinks in a row in the past 30 days, based on the Youth Risk Behavior Study (YRBS) responses of students grade 9 through 12 (USDHHS, 2006b). Moreover, nationally representative data from both Add Health and YRBS data sets show linear increases of alcohol consumption with grade level and average age of onset at 13.4 years (National Longitudinal Study of Adolescent Health [Add Health] data) or during middle school (YRBS). For males, prevalence and frequency of binge drinking was greater than that for females in both data sets. African Americans in both data sets showed lower prevalence rates and approximately half the prevalence rate for binge drinking, in contrast to Whites and Hispanics. Fortunately, there has been a downturn in the prevalence of alcohol consumption (i.e., 51% to 43%), and binge drinking (31% to 26%) from the years 1991 to 2005 (USDHHS, 2006b).

The research to be reviewed has been more supportive of a relation between alcohol's immediate effects (frequency of use, intoxication) rather than its chronic effects (e.g., White & Hansell, 1998; Chermack & Giancola, 1997). Reviews of the effects of alcohol on aggression have also been limited by heavy reliance on laboratory research with adults, while such research with adolescents would be legally and ethically forbidden. One recent review of laboratory studies with adults has supported the association between alcohol use and aggression in the following ways: (1) some studies show that alcohol may influence aggression by affecting personality vulnerabilities such as negative mood states, high dispositional aggressiveness, or individual expectancies that alcohol use increases aggression; (2) alcohol has been found to have direct effects on the individual by disrupting cognitive functioning, such as by impairing attentional processes, abstract reasoning, and planning and self-monitoring abilities; and (3) alcohol effects can be moderated by contextual influences that increase or decrease the likelihood of aggression (e.g., public vs. private settings), greater perceived threat or provocation, social pressure towards increased aggression, and the kind of relationship such as a partner, friend, or stranger (Chermack & Giancola, 1997).

Consistent with the studies of acute alcohol effects on aggression, the following review of studies on adolescent substance use will focus on the following: (1) studies in which adolescents who consume alcohol, versus other illegal drugs, evidence greater aggression than those who do not, and those who consume greater amounts versus lesser amounts will evidence greater aggression; (2) those who consumed alcohol and who perceived that alcohol inebriation leads to aggressive acts will be more likely to be aggressive than those who do not hold this belief; (3) those who consume greater amounts of alcohol, versus lesser amounts, are also likely to commit a violent crime; (4) the association between alcohol and aggression in relation to social and developmental context; and (5) alcohol consumption contributing unique effects on aggression beyond the influence of other factors.

There are three important studies of alcohol use and aggression among representative samples of adolescents, two in the United States (Bachman & Peralta, 2002; Swahm, Simon, Hammig, & Guerro, 2004) and one in Norway (Rossow, Pape, & Wickstrom, 1999). The first was a nationally representative sample of high school seniors (n = 2,643 from 139 high schools) a part of the Monitoring the Future (MTF) study (Bachman & Peralta, 2002). This study found that 43% of seniors had engaged in one or more of three forms of frequent or heavy alcohol use in the past year: (1) drinking on more than six occasions; (2) became drunk during most of those occasions; and (3) used alcohol in the last 2 weeks. Consistent with MTF research, aggression and violence was defined as self-reports of any of fifteen aggressive behaviors (e.g., fight at work or school, gang fighting, threatened someone with a weapon). For both boys and girls, results showed that frequent or heavy alcohol use predicted significantly to aggression, and did so beyond the effects of controls for race, urban locale, parent education level, two parent household, religion, grades in school, and other drug usage. The odds ratio for the unique contributions of alcohol use was 2.3 for boys and 1.8 for girls; frequent or heavy use of alcohol doubles the likelihood of aggression.

The second large-scale study in the United States of alcohol and aggression, using a nationally representative sample of 12 to 21 year olds (n = 18, 924) was part of the 1995 data for Add Health (Swahn et al., 2004). The focus here was only on adolescent drinkers, that is, those who had at least one alcohol drink in the last year (n = 8,885; 47% of the entire sample). One measure of alcohol consumption was its frequency, meaning less than 1 day per month, 2 to 8 days per month, and 9 to 30 days per month, all in the past year. The second measure was binge drinking frequency, and was measured as less than 1 day versus 2 to 30 days per month (in the past year). Three measures of aggression and violence were fighting in the past year, injured in a fight in the past year, and injured others in a fight in the past year. Overall analysis showed that both frequency of drinking alcohol and frequency of binge drinking alcohol contributed significantly to all three aggression-violence outcomes. Perhaps more revealing was the increase in each form of aggression-violence with each level of frequency and binge drinking frequency increase. Specifically, the prevalence of fighting went up 30% (i.e., to 1 day), up 32% (to 2–8 days), and up 44% (9–30 days), with each of the three levels of alcohol drinking frequency. The increase in self-injury went up 134%, 48%, and 49% for each level of increased frequency of drinking. The results for binge drinking were more dramatic. For the two levels of binge drinking, fighting prevalence was 54% greater, self-injury 137% greater, and injury to others 82% greater.

A study of more than 10,000 Norwegian adolescents was a cross-sectional research design of 12 to 20 year olds (Rossow et al., 1999). The measure of alcohol intoxication was the number of times they had gotten drunk in the past year. The measure of aggression and violence was the number of times they had "beaten or threatened to beat someone" and whether they had "taken part in a fight using a weapon," both in the past year. Results of the overall analysis showed that the frequency of intoxication predicted to the frequency of violent behaviors beyond the influence of control variables (i.e., gender, sex role identity, age, problem behaviors, frequently drinking friends, frequently intoxicated parents, and parent supervision). Perhaps more striking, yet similar to the linear trends noted in the Swahn and colleagues study of U.S. adolescents, was the linear increase in prevalence of violent behaviors with the frequency of intoxication. The prevalence of fighting with a weapon went from 1.4% to 2.6% (an increase of 186% with an increase from zero to one instance of intoxication), to a high of 15.5% (an increase of 1,114% from baseline to those who had been intoxicated more than fifty times in the past year). As a basis of comparison, two additional Norwegian surveys, representing over 24,000 youths from ages 15 to 20 were presented in which physical fighting under the influence was examined. Across both surveys, the prevalence of physical fighting or physical fighting under the influence of alcohol went up 46% from 0 to 1–4 occasions of intoxication, up 171% from 1–4 to 5–10 occasions of intoxication, up 195% from 11–50 to 51+ occasions of intoxication.

The strong evidence for a linear relation between alcohol consumption, aggression, and violence was more recently refined in relation to the developmental and social context within which alcohol consumption takes place. A recent longitudinal study has shown that alcohol consumption in middle to early high school years was more closely related to aggression than in later high school years (Huang et al., 2001). This was a study of 14, 15, 16, and 18 year olds (n = 808; boys r = 412) who were interviewed in each of 5 subsequent years, and were assessed with their parents on seven risk factors at age 10. Aggression (defined as throwing rocks at people, picking a fight, and hitting to hurt another) was highly correlated for adjacent years (r = .59 − .72), as was alcohol use (defined as frequency of use in the past month, quantity drunk on typical occasion, and how often they got drunk when they drank) (r = .63 − .74). Consistent with grade trends presented earlier (in Chapter 1 this volume), aggression in all forms decreased with grade from ages 14 to 18, based on cross sectional data. Also, alcohol consumption increased in all forms from ages 14 through 18, again based on cross sectional data. Most striking was the correlation between an index of alcohol consumption and an index of aggression, at age 14 the correlation was r = .53, age 15 was r = .38, age 16 was r = .27, and age 18 was r = .23. One likely interpretation was that alcohol consumption at age 14 was less common than at age 18, making the former more pathognomonic. Also, as adolescents progressed toward adulthood they are likely to have had more experience with alcohol, greater overall maturity and self-control, which may have contributed to a weaker relation between alcohol consumption and aggression and violence.

Findings from a study of 8th graders in Sweden showed that excessive alcohol consumption, meaning either large quantities consumed or drinking to intoxication, tripled the probability of violent behaviors such as fighting, robbery, or aggravated assault (Eklund & Klinteberg, 2005). These data showing that early alcohol consumption is particularly problematic for aggression and violence, also are consistent with previous analysis in the Report of the Surgeon General of the United States (USDHHS, 2001), and the results of the Lipsey and Derzon (1999) meta-analysis presented in Chapter 2, both of which concluded that early alcohol use was more predictive of violence in adolescence than alcohol use at a later age.

The social context within which drinking takes place is also a significant moderator of alcohol consumption by adolescents. The cross-sectional study of Norwegian adolescents (Rossow et al., 1999), noted earlier, also found that significant contributors to the frequency of violent behaviors in the past year were having frequently drinking friends, frequently intoxicated parents, and involvement in other problem behaviors (e.g., property crimes, other substance use, and truancy). However, the precise influence of having "wet friends," "wet parents," and other problem behaviors depended on the age and gender of the adolescent. Similar findings regarding the drinking social context have been reported for U.S. adolescents as well, based on Add Health data for 12 to 21 year olds (Swahn et al., 2004). In the Swahn and colleagues study, drinking frequency, binge drinking frequency, drinking with peers, and drinking until drunk or results in negative consequences (i.e., with school, family, or friends) all contributed uniquely to the three forms of violence, namely, fighting, self-injury, and other injury. Drinking with peers increased fighting prevalence by 27%, self-injury by 71%, and injury to others by 52%. However, drinking alone also contributed significantly to fighting by increasing prevalence rates by 42%, and injury to others by 57%. Thus the data also suggested there are both asocial drinkers and social drinkers, both of whom are at greater risk for aggression and violence. Further research will be needed to disentangle the important predictors of aggression by subgroup of adolescents, and account for cultural differences as well.

Studies of alcohol consumption by incarcerated adolescents also have shown correlations despite the homogeneity of the individuals. Alcohol use and use of other illegal substances were explored in relation to violence among a group (n = 290) of Australian offenders ages 15 to 19 (Lennings, Copeland, & Howard, 2003). Among this group, 70% admitted to violent crimes. In response to interviews, 65% said that use of alcohol or cocaine had made them violent at some time. Of this group (acknowledging violence following substance use), 78% also admitted committing a violent crime. Both alcohol use and cocaine use discriminated between violent versus non-violent offenders.

Another study of incarcerated male juvenile offenders (n = 312) found that it was alcohol that was more strongly associated with violent offenses such as (self-reported) injury to victims, physical attack on an instructor or parents, or a serious physical fight, than was use of heroin or marijuana (Dawkins, 1997). Violent offenses were predicted by criminal history (28%), by any substance use (5%) beyond the contribution of criminal history, and by race (2%).

In sum, alcohol use is common among both middle and high school adolescents, and pertaining to measures of prevalence, frequency, and frequency of intoxication, related consistently, positively, and in linear fashion, to both aggressive and violent behaviors. Increasing frequency and amount of alcohol consumption also increases the risk of a variety of aggressive and violent behaviors. Both male and female adolescents are affected by alcohol consumption. Variations in the impact of alcohol consumption on aggression and violence by adolescent age, ethnicity, and social context offer intriguing areas for future research.

Incentives

An incentive refers to a potential reward delivered before a behavior is expected, that is clearly understood, and sustains or energizes (i.e., motivates) the behavior toward a goal (Cofer & Appley, 1964). Although incentives are quite varied from person to person, three types of motivations for aggression have been identified as the following: (a) controlling the behavior of the target person; (b) gaining retribution or justice, and (c) promoting or defending one's self-image (Tedeschi & Felson, 1994; Felson, 2002). The interpersonal context within which these three kinds of incentives guide behavior may be an ongoing dispute between individuals or a predatory-unprovoked situation (Felson, 2002). Previous discussion of dispute-related conflict is exemplified by a bully/victim's motivation to stop current victimization by others and discourage future teasing by aggressively promoting an image of toughness (i.e., deterrence), vigilante justice to revenge disrespect (retribution for a wrongful act), or aggressively humiliating someone who has insulted you or your group (saving face by retaliating). These three examples of dispute-related aggression are similar in many ways because they are exaggerated responses that are "over the top," they are hot in the sense of being emotion fueled (e.g., by shame, anger/rage), and all involve violations of codes of conduct held to be important to reputation within the subculture. Predatory violence has more in common with property crime in that it is "colder," planned, and designed to achieve a desired outcome. Predatory violence can also be motivated by variants of the same three incentives as were dispute-related violence. Examples of predatory violence would be non-verbal stares or direct verbal threats to make someone get out your way (to coerce or compel), robbing someone of their sneakers and leather coat (to redistribute or restore equity, in the absence of perceived unfairness), or beating up someone weaker to enhance one's reputation as tough (i.e., self-image promotion). Of course, violent acts also may have both predatory and dispute-related components and multiple motives incentivizing the same acts.

The alternative conceptualization to dispute-related violence as motivated toward achieving over-arching goals, is that aggression and violence are largely impulsive (e.g., Berkowitz, 1993). This point of view deals primarily with emotional aggression but also acknowledges that some aggression may be predatory and cold and motivated toward some rewarding ends. From this CNA perspective, emotional aggression originates in frustration, or any conditions of discomfort that produce negative affect, which later leads to affixing blame on particular individuals, and to high-order cognitive processes that amplify and exacerbate anger, sometimes ending in aggressive behavior.

Unfortunately, we do not have a complete "natural history" of aggression (Archer & Brown, 1989), and our understanding of the motivational basis of aggression remains incomplete. Yet, we have some clues as to which situations incentives operate to increase the likelihood of aggression, and those situations in which aggression appears more impulsive and takes little account of motivation toward maximizing personal gain.

There are data suggesting that increases in common forms of physical fighting follow developmental trends from early to late adolescence that increase as a response to either destabilizing shifts in school settings, or puberty-related physical and physiological changes (e.g., in size, strength). As shown in

Chapter 1 (this volume), increases in everyday fighting among young adolescents increases and bullying increases in early adolescence and decreases in later adolescence; predatory forms of violence, including criminal violence increase more gradually throughout middle and later adolescence. These two patterns of developmental change suggest that impulsive, emotion-based aggression or dispute-related motives are likely to explain aggression during early adolescence, but that more predatory motivational processes increase gradually during and after this period. Such predatory motivation was described earlier as characteristic of a rather small, qualitatively distinct set of life-course-persistent (LCP) offenders who start on a childhood path toward later violence in adolescence. It is important to keep clearly in mind these two sets of aggressive behaviors as we consider incentives operating, because various forms of violence may have different motivational goals, or little clear goals in mind at all.

Research data collected from middle and high school students as part of Add Health in 1994–1995 (2006) suggest impulsive or dispute-related incentives versus predatory motivational processes. The responses from home interviews of 20,745 middle and high school students (50% male; from 13% to 19% of sample in each of grades 7 through 12) were gathered in 1994–1995. Broad shifts in motivational processes were suggested by grade level responses to questions as to where their most recent physical fight took place, and with whom the fight took place. Students were specifically asked the following: (a) "the last time you were in a physical fight, where did it occur?"; and (b) "the last time you were in a physical fight, with whom did you fight?" Fifty-nine percent of the sample acknowledged they had been in a physical fight. Among those identifying a place where they physically fought, 42% said in school, 18% in their neighborhood, 14% at home, 1% at work, and 25% someplace else (likely to be gathering places such as malls, parties, etc.). Consistent with developmental trends noted in Chapter 1, as well as in other studies presented thus far, differences in the places in which fights took place indicated that the prevalence of fighting in school rose 25% from grades 7 to 10, before declining 60% from grades 10 through 12. Younger students disregarded the costs of getting caught, and valued more the reputational rewards, or simply reacted impulsively to threat and challenges offered by peers, which were likely to have been hotter conflicts. Thus fighting increased for middle schoolers in more highly monitored settings in which students were more likely to get in trouble (e.g., with school authorities), and in which dispute-related motivations were prominent; responding to provocation, appearing tough, warding off peer attacks, and emotion-based impulsive responses were also likely to be prominent. However, the same data set showed that although a smaller percentage of fights took place "someplace else," there was a 300% increase in fighting in those settings from grades 7 through 12. For older adolescents there is a shift toward predatory violence. This may reflect greater time spent with peers, and greater time in unsupervised settings, in which "cooler" acts that are planned outside the reach of surveillance are more motivating. Acts of criminal, predatory violence may increase throughout adolescence. Crime victimization data, for victims less than 18 years of age, also showed that violent crime increased dramatically at 3 P.M. to school dismissal, a 250% increase in victimizations when compared with 1 P.M. (Snyder & Sickmund, 1999), a time when students are beyond school supervision. Motivations for common, everyday forms of violence are dispute related and emotional, whereas more predatory violence occurs where situational constraints and possible observation are less likely.

The Add Health data concerning the person with whom the individual physically fought also suggests a shift in motivational processes from dispute/impulsive to predatory forms of aggression and violence. Among those who acknowledged having physically fought, 46% fought with a friend or acquaintance, 27% with a stranger, 2% with a boyfriend/girlfriend or date, 11% with a family member, 11% with someone not listed above, and 3% with more than one person. In all, among those acknowledging a physical fight, 59% fought with someone they had a relationship with (i.e., family, friend, acquaintance), thus suggesting "hotter" disputes with those whom the respondent had an ongoing relationship. When examined by grade level, fighting with a friend or someone they knew increased 25% from grade 7 to grade 10, and then declined 20% by grades 11 and 12. However, fighting with strangers, with whom they had no relationship, increased 50% from grades 7 through 12. Crime victimization data also demonstrate that for the year 1996, and for juveniles ages 12 through 17 who were victims of a serious crime, 64% of the victims knew their assailant (i.e., 18% an acquaintance, 34% a friend, 11% a relative, versus 36% a stranger) (Snyder & Sickmund, 1999). The inference regarding motivational processes being made here is, again, that more impulsive and emotional aggression (emotions of anger, jealousy, etc.), or dispute-related motivations increase and then decrease, whereas fighting that is predatory is likely to increase throughout adolescence.

A subset of aggression toward peers that is motivated largely by predatory processes (i.e., designed to coerce or compel, redistribute equity, and promote self-image) is the "pure bully" noted earlier. By definition, bullies choose situations in which they can victimize weaker opponents (e.g., out of the awareness of teachers and parents) and do so without any noticeable anxiety or insecurity (Olweus, 1991). An extreme version of the bully whose primary purpose is to promote a self-image as tough, develop a "large" reputation as a "crazy/wild" killer, was studied as a feature of the ecology of danger present in poverty areas of New York City (Fagan & Wilkinson, 1998). As one young killer put it, when he killed someone he "got a stripe." A further exaggeration of bullying was described by Toch (1992) regarding incarcerated violent men. Among incarcerated men it was the offenders who would kill for no reason who were accorded the most respect among violent men. One of the personality types of violent men was the bully who enjoyed hurting victims, particularly when they begged for mercy, and by virtue of the time and place selected to attack a peer, never gave a victim an even chance. Common to bullies is attention to planning the attack, impression management, and enjoyment of aggression toward weaker peers, all of which are powerful incentives for repeatedly victimizing others.

Aggressive Cues

Behavioral approaches in psychology have long held that sights, sounds, and more complex sequences and patterns of stimuli can come to remind people to behave in certain ways. The written reminders we construct before going to the grocery store, or palm pilot date reminders are some everyday cues that evoke or guide behavior at a certain time and place. Aggression and violence also may be cued by particular sights and sounds, such as seeing a real-life or play fight between other individuals, a cue for highly aggressive youth to join in, or performance of some novel form of violence we have never before personally witnessed (as in a book, televised violence, video-game violence). The cue may be as simple as the sight of a weapon, or as complex as a lengthy confrontation between two or more individuals. Two cues have been studied more extensively in relation to aggression and violence, violent media, and exposure to weapons, both of which set off aggressive responses.

The mechanisms by which observation of violent imagery, such as weapons, and violent media stimulate aggression have been the subject of considerable scientific investigation, and the subject of intense scientific and public debate. Early research on the impact of televised violence relied on theories of observational learning, such as that proposed by Dr. Albert Bandura. The theory stated simply that the observation of sequences of real-life or televised aggressive behavior could lead to imitation, given a prestige-full model and the right conditions under which the individual might perform what was learned. Recent cognitive approaches have suggested that violent objects or actions might prompt the recall of aggression related concepts in memory, thereby facilitating an increase in aggressive behavior (Anderson & Bushman, 2002).

Regardless of which theoretical explanations are utilized to explain why certain violent images relate to aggressive behavior, the research evidence itself has been conclusive. That greater exposure to media violence stimulates increases in aggression is supported by meta-analyses of 217 studies, yielding an average correlation size of $r = .31$ (Paik & Comstock, 1994). The $r = .31$ correlation between media violence and aggression found by Paik and Comstock, was comparable to the relation between smoking and lung cancer shown by Wynder and Graham (1950; as reanalyzed by Bushman and Anderson, 2001). Moreover, a variety of field studies investigating places in North America that received television for the first time, and countries around the world that had newly received programs such as the World Wrestling Federation shows, had demonstrated aggression increases similar to what was being found in smaller, naturalistic, and laboratory studies (Centerwall, 1993).

Research also has begun to show that time involved in violent video games cues similar increases in aggressive behavior. Research involving college students (averaging 18.5 years of age) in which real-world aggressive behavior, defined as "hit or threatened to hit other students," or "attacked someone with the idea of seriously hurting or killing him/her," have been positively related with both time spent playing video games ($r = .20$) and long-term violent video game exposure ($r = .46$) (Anderson & Dill, 2000). A meta-analysis of thirty-five studies of violent video games, involving 4,262 individuals, half of whom were below the age of 18, showed a combined correlation between time spent playing and aggression of $r = .19$ for non-experimental and experimental studies (Anderson & Bushman, 2001). Interestingly, violent video game play also increased feelings of anger and hostility ($r = .18$), and physiological arousal ($r = .22$) (Anderson & Bushman, 2001).

Research also has addressed the cueing effects of gun use and access to guns in relation to different forms of aggressive and violent behavior. One study involved male and female middle school students ($n = 334$, 6th through 8th grades) in upstate New York (Ding, Nelsen, & Lassonde, 2002). The researchers determined which students had access to guns and used guns (e.g., questions were ". . . anyone in home own a gun?" and "how many times have you gone hunting for wild game?"). Students also rated themselves on whether they were more or less likely to vent anger and frustration in violent ways (e.g., "I get violent if I don't get my way"), and whether they had been more frequently aggressive (e.g., "hit a friend," "suspended from school for fighting"). Those students who both had access to guns and used guns were more likely to vent frustration angrily (r = .24), and were more frequently aggressive (r = .30).

Adolescents may own guns for different reason, and the reasons suggest some have a greater propensity to react to gun cues. One study examined the attitudes toward aggression and guns in relation to gun ownership of boys and girls (n = 1, 619) in grades 3 through 12 (Shapiro et al., 1997). Fifty five of the students owned their own guns. Using a sixty-one-item measure of attitudes toward guns and aggressive behavior, the researchers found that attitudes clustered into four categories: *aggressive response to shame* (e.g., "if somebody insults you, and you don't want to be a chump, you have to fight"); *comfort with aggression* (e.g., negatively scored, "I don't like being around people with guns because someone could end up getting hurt"); *excitement* (e.g., "it would be exciting to hold a loaded gun in my hand"); and *power/safety* (e.g., "carrying a gun makes me feel powerful and strong"). Those students with the lowest score on this measure had a 1 in 125 chance of owning a gun, whereas those with the highest scores had a 1 in 3 chance of owning a gun.

A large-scale study of gun ownership and its correlates among a sample (n = 6,263) of predominantly African-American 5th through 7th graders, found positive associations between the reasons for gun ownership and bullying behavior (Cunningham et al., 2000). More than 46% of the students reported owning a gun or guns, including 30% BB guns, 14% rifles, 9% handguns, and 4% other types. Almost 60% of those students who were high-risk gun owners, defined as those who owned guns to get respect or to fight others, were classified as frequent bullies. In addition, those students who were high-risk gun owners (vs. those who were moderate and low risk) were more likely to take part in violence toward others (i.e., fighting, hurting others, or using weapons against others) and to bully teachers.

Violent Episodes in Middle and High Schools

Ethnographic research on violent episodes can both illustrate how many of the situational factors reviewed in the preceding pages play into the genesis and maintenance of physical aggression and also tell us which of the situational influences appear most influential or prominent. Unfortunately, there are few examples of the analysis of violent episodes, or examples of violent episodes in widely varying settings (e.g., urban, rural, poverty, middle class). Yet careful analysis of violent episodes, when data are also shown to be relatively consistent with nationally administered survey and interview data such as presented earlier, can be helpful in understanding how conflicts begin and end in real-life settings.

A theoretical model that lends itself well to understanding violent episodes describes regularities in patterns of interpersonal relatedness, or cognitive "scripts" that individuals acquire in childhood and adolescence (Baldwin, 1992). One well-known script often used for illustrative purposes is ordering food at a restaurant, which begins with looking over the menu, ordering from the server, eating, and paying for the meal. Germane to aggression is a script such as "I insult him, then he clenches his fist, then I turn and run" (Baldwin, p. 468). One may learn scripts through personal experiences, such as encounters with others in the past, but may also acquire aggressive scripts by observing sequences of aggressive behaviors on television, found to increase aggressive behavior in adolescence and adulthood, above the initial levels of aggression (Huesmann, Moise-Titus, Podolski, & Eron, 2003). Scripts may include thoughts, feelings, and motivation observed in one's self, or in the other (i.e., awareness of one's inner state and the inner state of the other). For example, one's goal of hurting the other person may be accompanied by evaluation of the other's behavior as annoying, and awareness of the other's angry emotion. Other important features of cognitive scripts is that they may, if the pattern is encountered repeatedly, be overlearned, so that they function automatically, leading to inappropriate application in certain situations. Scripts might include expectations about how an episode will unfold and biases that distort perception of the other's ambiguous behaviors as hostile (in this cognitive system referred to as a "schema"). Interviews of middle and high school students about recent violent incidents will serve to illustrate how goals, emotions, and perceptions follow during violent episodes.

Research on 250 violent episodes taking place among middle and high school boys ($n = 70$) and girls ($n = 40$) living in a high crime area in a southern U.S. city, can serve as a useful example of aggressive cognitive scripts and schema (Lockwood, 1997). The perspective taken was a social interactionist one, which seeks explanation of violent episodes by analysis of interaction among people. This study relied on hour-long interviews about violent incidents in which they had been involved. Owing to the urban-poverty setting in which the respondents lived, the results showed a very broad range of violent behaviors, ranging from relatively common "kicking-biting-hitting with a fist" (in 67% of the incidents) to "beat up" (in 21% of incidents) to use of a gun (in 5% of incidents). Only 10% of incidents occurred during a crime (1% related to illegal drugs; the remaining 9% were robberies, thefts, and use of a gun).

Descriptive information concerning the relationships between antagonists, place of violent incidents, other people present, and estimated duration of the episode are presented in Table 4.1.

TABLE 4.1. *Descriptive information relating to 250 violent episodes among middle and high school students*

---

1. **Relationships of Antagonists**: 58% acquaintances, 16% friends, 15% family members (mostly siblings or cousins), 11% strangers.
2. **Place of Incident:**
   (a) *45% school locations* (18% classroom, 9% hall or stairs, 5% school bus, 5% physical education gym, locker room, or playing fields, 3% cafeteria, 2% outside school, on grounds, 2% other locations in school, 1% school recreation room, 1% school bathroom)
   (b) *23% home locations* (18% inside home, 5% outside home and on property)
   (c) *30% public areas* (17% sidewalk or street, 3% outside public basketball court, 3% other area of park such as playground pool, 2% outside store, mall, etc., 2% travel to school, 3% other public locations)
   (d) *2% other* (church recreation room, summer camp, social work recreation room)
3. **Others Present:** 60% others present (common roles of those present were to "encourage violence, to join in out of loyalty, only 4% attempted to mediate); 40% were one to one (note: police present in 18% of incidents; 50% of adults in charge found out about incidents).
4. **Duration of Incident:** 70% lasted 15 minutes or less; 20% took an hour or longer from the initial provocation to end of combat.

Source: Lockwood (1997).

Comparisons with Add Health 1994–1995 data presented earlier show settings for violence that are both similar and different. Place of violent incident in Lockwood's sample was 68% at home plus school, comparable to Add Health 56% at home plus school. The person with whom they were most likely to fight was 89% acquaintance, family, or friend, in the Lockwood sample, as compared with 59% for Add health friend, acquaintance, or family. The current episodes clearly involved fewer fights with strangers, and much more fighting with acquaintances than in the Add Health data. The use of fist-kick-bite at 67%, versus 5% of incidents in which a gun was used, is roughly similar to the rarity of weapons use nationally in the YRBS data (USDHHS, 2006b). Data from the YRBS surveys in the early 1990s (Brenner et al., 1999) also showed there were 138 violent incidents per year among high school per 100 students (1.38 per student), but there was less than the 250 per 110 students (or 2.2 per student) in the Lockwood group, which were middle school students in a high crime area.

The most enlightening analysis of the "scripts" for the 250 episodes concerned the initiation, maintenance, sequencing, and goals of the violent encounters. First, the number of incidents per student was the same for both boys and girls. Boys fought primarily with boys, and girls fought equally with boys and girls. Second, in 70% of incidents the antagonist, not the respondent was said to make the "opening moves" or provocation. This proportion assigning blame to the other was consistent with other research concerning 254 fighting episodes reported by college students, the majority of whom blamed the opponent for starting the altercation (Marcus & Reio, 2002). Third, in 62% of episodes there was a "working agreement" to fight in which invitations or challenges to fight were offered and accepted. Fourth, and consistent with earlier discussion of the importance of trait and situational anger, anger was experienced in 62% of incidents, fear in 14% (largely those involving guns). Fifth, and also consistent with earlier discussion of verbal arguments association with aggression, initiations, or "opening moves," were verbal in about 44% of incidents (divided into 10% requests to do something, 9% backbiting, 9% verbal teasing/rough physical play, 7% insults, and 3% threats of physical harm). Moreover, opening moves were physical in about 43% of incidents (including 13% offensive touching, 13% interference with possessions, and 3% physical or nonverbal gestures). In less than 10% of the time was an opening move followed by an attempt to avoid violence (e.g., by taking evasive action). Sixth, and consistent with earlier discussion of motivation for violence, the following aims were given: 40% said retribution/punishment for something the other did; 22% said to get the other to desist from offensive action ("compliance"); 21% said defense of one's self or defense of others; and 8% said promotion of self-image (i.e., saving face, defending honor, or enhancing one's reputation).

Students offered both justifications and excuses for their violence that clearly showed violence to be an acceptable strategy or script for handling differences with others. Eighty-four percent of incidents individuals offered "justifications" in which they accepted responsibility for being violent, but denied the actions were wrong. Examples of this justification for violence (and consistent with the "aims" noted earlier) included 29% who said they were retaliating for harm, 18% that the other's behavior was offensive, 14% for self-defense, and 1% to promote their self-image. These justifications were similar to the earlier noted vigilante and honor-related motivations noted in interviews of adolescents about seriously violent behaviors (Lopez & Emmer, 2002). The small percentage who gave as their justification self-promotion suggests that this may be much less common here than shown in other ethnographic research among inner city, minority youth whose use of guns was primarily image promoting, and served to advance an image of toughness and dangerousness in order to protect themselves (Fagan & Wilkinson, 1998). The dominance here of attribution of blame to others, was consistent with theories putting blame on the other as a cornerstone of anger and aggression, and also may be consistent with a hostile attribution bias in which neutral behaviors of others are seen as hostile and worthy of retaliation.

Excuses were given for the remaining 16% of incidents. Excuses were statements in which the respondent denied responsibility for violence, but admitted that the action was wrong. Among the excuses given were impairment by anger (7%) impairment due to alcohol (1%), or pushed into it by the antagonist (6%). The infrequency with which alcohol impairment was given as an excuse was inconsistent with the much larger percentage of college students acknowledging that self and opponent were intoxicated (Marcus & Reio, 2002; Marcus & Swett, 2003), and the large body of literature reviewed earlier linking alcohol use and both aggression and violence. It is possible that in poorer communities such as in the current analysis, adolescents' ability to purchase alcohol is more limited, or, possibly, that despite intoxication it was other excuses or justifications that were more salient or more readily acknowledged, prompted possibly by a hyper-masculinity motivation that they are in charge of their actions.

Summary

Table 4.2 is a summary of developmental risk factors (Chapter 2), personality risk factors (Chapter 3), and situational risk factors (Chapter 4) for aggression and violence. Although empathy is typically considered a protective factor for aggression and violence, this personality trait is considered here as a risk factor when it is absent or minimal. The research process by which, for example, developmental or personality risk factors may be discovered as associated with aggression and violence will likely bring new variables to the model. The model is intended as testable, although inclusion of all variables in a single study would require huge sample sizes and abundant instrumentation. More limited testing of six to ten variables, and focus on relative influence of each, is more feasible for future research on aggression and violence in adolescence.

TABLE 4.2. *Developmental, personality, and situational risk factors for aggression and violence in adolescence*

Developmental Influences	Personality Influences	Situational Influences
Early Risk Factors (< age 12)	*Sensation-seeking*	*Provocation*
1) General offenses	1) Impulsivity	1) Hostile attribution bias
2) Substance use	2) Thrill and adventure	2) Assignment of blame
3) Male gender	seeking	3) Verbal
4) Aggression	3) Fight-seeking	argumentativeness
5) Minority race		4) Bully/victim status
6) Antisocial parents	*Negative Affect*	
7) Problem behavior	1) Trait anger	*Frustration*
8) Low IQ	2) Poor anger control	1) Dis-identification with
9) Medical/physical	3) Poor anger coping	school
10) Psychological condition	4) Anger "out"	2) Peer rejection
11) Poor school attitude/grades	5) Depressed Mood/	
12) Poor parent–child	Clinical Depression	*Pain/Discomfort*
relationship		1) Hot temperatures
13) Other family characteristics	*Empathy*	2) Shame/Jealousy
14) Poor social ties	1) Low emotional	
	empathy	*Alcohol/Drug Use*
Late Risk Factors (ages 12–14)	2) Low cognitive	1) Frequency of use and
1) Poor social ties	empathy	intoxication
2) Antisocial peers		2) Developmental-
3) General offenses		context
4) Male gender		3) Social context: alone;
5) Age (Middle school:		with peers
aggression; high school:		
violence)		*Incentives*
6) Physical violence		1) Low cost situations
7) Aggression		2) Close relationships
8) Low IQ		3) Low monitored
9) Psychological condition		situations
10) Poor school attitude/grades		4) Pure bullying status
11) Antisocial parents		
12) Broken homes		*Aggressive Cues*
13) Low family S.E.S.		1) Televised and video
		violence
		2) Gun possession/
		accessibility

5

Aggression and Violence in Romantic Relationships

Close relationships change dramatically from the elementary school years to the middle and high school years, presenting many new challenges as human development proceeds toward adulthood. Interpersonal styles of moving toward or with significant others or, conversely, of moving against them have been learned and practiced for many years prior to the entry to adolescence. Aggression is primarily an interpersonal process. Once adolescence is reached, the challenges of getting along with heterosexual partners in close relationships are no less difficult than relating to the same gender friends and acquaintances, and the likelihood of aggressive behavior between romantic partners may appear as early as do romantic relationships. Taboos against physically hurting the one you love may not be strong enough to overcome aggression learned over the previous 12 years. The developmental contexts provided by childhood and adolescent close relationships, within which aggression and violence arises, and the forms and prevalence of partner aggression and violence in adolescence are explored in this chapter. The origins of dating aggression seen both in differences among individual partners and among couples that appear to foster dating partner aggression also are the major focus of this chapter.

Consider the following example of dating partner aggression as a prototype for adolescent relationship aggression. George and Sarah, he a 12th grader and she a 10th grader, have been dating for 2 years. One day, an argument flares up because one of the partners has discovered the other to have been unfaithful, violating their implicit agreement of exclusivity. An argument escalates and for the first time the conflict results in pushing, slapping, and verbal threats to further harm one another. What was unthinkable at the beginning of their relationship, when love was new, making good impressions important, and they could not talk with or see one another sufficiently, has now deteriorated into episodes of breaking up and getting back together. The break-ups were now punctuated by verbal and physical aggression, sometimes spilling over into their friendship and family relationships, and possibly to future romantic relationships as well.

The significance of such violent encounters between George and Sarah rests on the associations between various close relationships, the impact of good or poor quality romantic relationships on the individual, and the remarkable prevalence of aggressive and violent behaviors when romantic relationships begin in middle school. Close relationships with parents, friends, and romantic partners all constitute an important context within which human development takes place. Close relationships appear to be both unique and redundant with one another in quality and impact on the individual adolescent (Collins, 2003). Increased time spent with friends rather than parents may herald a growing potency of friends. Parent–child and friendship relationships also may serve as an emotional safety net, ready to catch the individual should the romantic relationship fail (Zimmer-Gembeck, 2002). Yet it is abundantly clear from recent research that the establishment of good quality or poor quality relationships with parents and friends provides emotional scaffolding to romantic relationships (Collins & Laursen, 2004). It would be difficult to imagine that a conflict-ridden and aggressive relationship between the adolescent and parents or friends would not shadow the adolescent's romantic relationships or, conversely, that highly conflicted romantic relationship with a romantic partner would not spill over into parent–child relationships. This has led some to propose that close relationships operate in a system or network, and that maintaining ties to all and negotiation among the three close relationships requires great skill (Zimmer-Gembeck, 2002).

Recent research has shown that success or failure in romantic relationships can have a profound and unique impact on the adolescent, and both their current and future development. For example, it is clear that relationship break-ups can trigger the onset of a future major depressive episode (Monroe, Rhode, Seeley, & Lewinsohn, 1999). In addition, a recent review has provided research evidence that an early start to any dating relationships is associated with adolescent behavior problems, alcohol use, and school difficulties, and, conversely, that successful and happy romantic relationships are related to many measures of individual well-being (Collins, 2003). On the more positive side, a recent study has shown that those in mid-adolescence whose romantic relationships provide greater intimacy and love experiences, greater passion and lowered self-consciousness, are also further along the road toward the achievement of a major developmental task of adolescence; a clearer psychosocial identity (Montgomery, 2005). By definition, romantic relationships present repeated opportunity for continued conflict or conflict resolution, as contrasted with disputes with same gender peers, which can more easily be terminated, or parent–child conflicts that can simply be avoided.

Romantic relationships in adolescence also may rival other sources of aggression and violence in the lives of adolescents, and dating aggression begins as early as do dating relationships. As noted earlier (in Chapter 1, Table 1.3), 45% of 9th graders reported having been in at least one physical fight with anyone in the past year; and 5% suffered an injury as a result of a physical fight. Dating partner aggression and violence have been explored in two separate studies of 8th and 9th graders. Both studies showed that from 15% to 21% of boys, and from 28% to 42% of girls had perpetrated some form of physical aggression (e.g., slapping, pushing) *or* physical violence (e.g., beat up, hit with a fist, choked) toward their current dating partners (Arriaga & Foshee, 2004; Foshee, 1996). Moreover, this same pair of studies found that physical violence alone had been perpetrated toward dating partners by 11% to 17% of girls, and from 4% to 15% of boys. That such high rates of dating aggression and violence would occur at the earliest stages of dating experiences, at rates rivaling dispute related physical fighting in general, indicates a significant danger in close relationships. Moreover, early dating aggression affords girls an opportunity to partake in a form of aggression and violence at or beyond the level of boys, and suggests an urgent need to examine prevalence of dating partner aggression and violence and the correlates of aggression in early romantic relationships.

Normative Changes in Adolescent Social Relationships

Perhaps the most dramatic shift in close relationships from childhood to adolescence is the shift from same-gender and parent–child relationships to mixed gender and romantic relationships, a transition beginning as early as middle school. There is a shift in peer relationships from primarily same-gender relationships in pre-adolescence, to mixed-gender associations and the beginnings of romantic relationships in middle school. Finally, there is a movement toward spending increasing amounts of time in romantic relationships during the high school years. By middle school, only about 6% of students take part exclusively in same-gender activities, whereas 82% "hang around" with both boys and girls (Connolly et al., 2004). Moreover, 24% to 31% participate in dating activities and 21% acknowledged having a girlfriend or boyfriend. Interviews of a nationally representative sample of adolescents from the United States (the National Longitudinal Study of Adolescent Health [Add Health]) have shown that from three age spans, namely, early to middle to late adolescence, 26%, 39%, and 54%, respectively, they were seeing less of other friends while spending more time with romantic partners (Carver, Joyner, & Udry, 2003). Moreover, at age 12, at least 26% of boys and girls had indicated they were in a romantic relationship, whereas at age 18 at least 69% of boys and girls reported that they were in a romantic relationship. Romantic relationships, therefore, acquire greater prominence as development moves toward later adolescence.

As it has become clearer that adolescent romantic relationships have significance for later development, models by which we can describe the major features of adolescent romantic relationships have been proposed. Collins (2003), for example, has proposed five features that are useful for describing what is known about romantic relationships, and can here serve as a model for organizing what is known about aggression and violence in romantic relationships. The five features of romantic relationships in adolescence are the following: (1) *involvement* – whether or not adolescents date, the age at which they begin dating, and the consistency and frequency of dating; (2) *partner-selection* – whom they select as partners (e.g., older versus same age, same or different race or socioeconomic status); (3) *content* – what it is adolescent partners do together, the diversity of shared activities, and situations avoided when together; (4) *quality* – the extent to which **relationships** provide beneficent experiences such as intimacy, affection, and nurturance, versus irritation, antagonism, and high conflict and controlling behaviors; and (5) *cognitive and emotional processes* – the extent to which **partners** evidence emotionally destructive emotional responses, perceptions, expectancies, schema, and attributions regarding the self and partner. Following a detailed normative description of the development of romantic relationships in adolescence, and examination of the prevalence and forms of dating aggression and violence, the five domains will be used to address correlates of dating violence.

Normative Changes in Adolescent Dating Relationships

Studies of the normative changes in romantic relationships during adolescence typically have been limited by the use of small, unrepresentative samples of adolescents, with the exception of data from Add Health Wave I, 1995 (n = 11, 973, ages 12 through 18), and follow-up interviews one year later in Wave II, 1996 (n = 947 adolescents re-interviewed about their relationships) (Carver, Joyner, & Udry, 2003). Using a confidential, home interview method that allowed respondents to record their responses on a laptop computer, a sample representative of adolescents in the United States, was asked key questions about their romantic relationships. Romantic relationships in the Add Health study were those with whom respondents, in the previous

18 months, had "special romantic relationships," or those non-family members they held hands with, kissed on the mouth, and told they liked or loved them. Importantly, the Add Health data has greatly advanced our understanding of developmental changes in romantic relationships from middle through high school years.

The results of the Add Health interviews have yielded many important insights into developmental changes in the quality of romantic relationships during adolescence. Overall, 65% of middle and high school students reported having had a special romantic relationship. Romantic relationships increased in intimacy and commitment with advancing age. Relationships lasted a median of 16 months during adolescence. Duration ranged from a median of 5 months for 12 to 13 year olds, to 21 months for those ages 16 and older, a four-fold increase in relationship duration from middle school to the end of high school. Whereas there was relative consistency in some relationship qualities from middle through high school years, such as in partners thinking of the pair as a couple (approximately 81%), and telling partners they loved each other (approximately 68%), there were dramatic changes in other dimensions of relationship quality. Specifically, from middle school (<14 years of age) to later high school (16+ years), there were increases in going "out together alone" (38% to 76%), giving partners presents (42% to 66%), and seeing less of other friends (26% to 54%). Also, from middle school to the later high school years, increases in sexually intimate behaviors such as touching "each other under clothing" (28% to 66%), touching "each other's genitals" (20% vs. 61%), and having sexual intercourse (8% vs. 50%) also suggested growing intimacy in romantic relationships.

Non-representative studies of adolescents, with smaller samples, have allowed for more detailed measurement of intimacy, in relation to changes in other relationship emotions and beliefs. The development of intimacy is more complex than increases in duration, time alone, and sexual activity would suggest. One such study of middle school, high school, and college students examined changes with age in intimacy and a number of aspects of dating such as love experiences, and affective intensity of relationship (i.e., passion, attraction, jealousy) (Montgomery, 2005). Findings showed that developmental changes are complex, including the following: (1) early adolescent girls experienced lower intimacy than did older girls, whereas no developmental change in intimacy was observed for boys; (2) early adolescent boys reported being in love more times than older boys; (3) early adolescents, more than older adolescents, believed love finds a way to overcome problems and differences between partners; and (4) affective intensity and intimacy increased modestly with age. Although age was positively correlated with intimacy, when all variables were entered in one model predicting to intimacy, age dropped out as a major, unique predictor, and was overshadowed by stronger predictors such as gender, dating experience, romantic beliefs, and a clearer sense of personal identity. In all, intimacy may increase with age during adolescence, but intimacy also was better predicted by other complex relationship beliefs and emotions during adolescence, as well as changes that may be gender specific.

The Add Health interview data (Carver et al., 2003) also tells us that accompanying changes in intimacy and commitment, from middle to later high school years, were dramatic increases in verbal, psychological, and physical abusiveness toward partners. As relationships "heat up," in terms of intimacy and emotional involvement, so does the likelihood that abusiveness will appear. The following increases were noted in abusive behaviors toward partners from early to later adolescence: "partner insulted you in front of others" (6% to 14%); "partner swore at you" (8% to 22%); "partner threatened you with violence" (0% to 4%); "partner pushed or shoved you" (4% to 9%); "partner threw something at you" (2% to 3%). Similar developmental increases in verbal or physical abusiveness also have been found in other national (U.S.) surveys. The data collected from the Youth Risk Behavior Survey (YRBS) (USDHHS, 2006b), which began collecting data on dating partner aggression in 1999, also yielded a picture of development change for high school students. The results of the YRBS also showed a 50% increase in dating aggression behaviors such as being "hit, slapped, or physically hurt on purpose" by their boyfriend or girlfriend in the past 12 months (i.e., 8% for 9th graders to 12% for 12th graders) and (in 2001) a 30% increase in being "physically forced to have sexual intercourse when they did not want to" (7% for 9th gradeers to 9% for 12th gradeers). In sum, and contrary to earlier noted age trends in YRBS data (Chapter 1) – particularly those showing increases in common aggressive behaviors with peers such as physical fighting in middle school followed by decreases to grade 12 – aggression toward romantic partners appears in middle school and continues to increase with advancing age.

There are other important differences, and also some similarities, between trends noted in dispute-related aggressive behaviors in Chapter 1 and relationship aggression during adolescence, namely those regarding gender and race differences. For example, Add Health dating aggression data for 1996 showed that boys and girls reported similar rates of being "pushed or shoved" by partners (boys: 8%; girls: 8%). Similar rates for boys and girls in YRBS data (for 1999) for being "hit, slapped, or physically hurt on purpose" (boys: 8%; girls: 9%), also were reported. There was clearly gender symmetry in some forms of dating aggression. However, the YRBS for 2001 revealed that girls were more likely than boys to report they were "physically forced to have sexual intercourse when they did not want to" (boys: 5%; girls: 10%). Therefore, with the important exception of forced sexual intercourse, boys and girls reported similar prevalence rates for dating aggression, a trend far different from the overwhelming male versus female imbalance noted for other aggressive behaviors in the national surveys of all other forms of aggression and violence noted in Chapter 1.

Similar to demographic differences in aggressive and violent behaviors noted in Chapter 1, violent dating behaviors were not spread out evenly among racial groups. Add Health dating aggression data (for 1996) showed that the prevalence for being "pushed or shoved" by a boyfriend or girlfriend was lowest for White adolescents (7%), followed in order of increasing prevalence by Hispanic (8%), Asian (12%), and African-American (13%) adolescents. Similar trends for 1999 YRBS data were shown for romantic partners being "hit, slapped, or physically hurt," with the lowest prevalence rates found for White adolescents (7%), followed in increasing order of prevalence by Hispanic (9%), Other (10%), and African-American (12%) adolescents. Regarding partners being "forced to have sexual intercourse," the rates were lowest for Whites (7%), followed in increasing order of prevalence by Hispanic (9%), African American (10%), and Other (11%). Therefore, race differences follow patterns for dating violence that are similar to those noted for other forms of aggression and violence noted in Chapter 1.

Prevalence and Forms of Dating Violence in Adolescence

The last 20 years has revolutionized our understanding of dating partner aggression and violence, in verbal, emotional, sexual, and physical forms within adolescent dating relationships. Early research studies had focused on the surprisingly common appearance of aggression and violence in adolescent relationships, just as earlier studies had discovered the prevalence of dating aggression in early adulthood and abusiveness in marital relationships (Marcus, 2005). Research on prevalence then spurred on a search for better understanding of the correlates of dating aggression and violence. Also, we began to understand more about the patterning and constancy of aggression and violence in relationships over time, and searched for improved measurement of dating aggression. For example, recent research has both supported the validity of self-reported dating aggression, but has also demonstrated that more frequent monitoring revealed even greater prevalence, and stronger correlation with partner emotional responses to aggression than did less frequent monitoring, the latter being more subject to forgetting over time (Jouriles et al., 2005). The following discussion explores that first step in the progression of our understanding, namely, description and prevalence of the various forms of aggression and violence in adolescent dating relationships.

To study the various forms of dating aggression, research studies have relied on the selection of smaller, non-representative samples of adolescents, but have used instruments that are richly detailed and allow for self-reports of both perpetrated and received aggressive and violent behaviors. Table 5.1 presents the data from three studies (two from the United States and one from Canada) using two well-standardized and well-researched, self-report measures of dating violence; the Conflict Tactics Scale (CTS) (Straus, 1979), and the Conflict in Adolescent Dating Relationship Inventory (CADRI) (Wolfe et al., 2001). These data are the ratings of adolescent boys and girls who were assessing their current dating relationship or their most recent dating relationship. The ratings are not time-limited (as is the case with ratings by young and married adults) because romantic relationships in adolescence may change frequently and a year time span may not yield any improved accuracy of measurement. Prevalence rates for "any" aggression in dating relationships are uniformly higher than for national surveys since there are many different behaviors reported, and ratings of specific behaviors may prompt memory for those behaviors.

Generalizations that can be made, given some overlap but lack of identical items for the CTS and CADRI measures, and differences in respondent ages, should therefore be made conservatively. First, except for forced sexual activity, in which case perpetration by boys is more prevalent than perpetration by girls, the data show that girls perpetrate more aggression and violence toward dating partners than do boys. This gender difference in favor of females is consistent with a meta-analysis of eighty-three studies of partner aggression, using mainly the CTS with diverse age samples, in which female perpetration in heterosexual relationships was found to be slightly greater than male perpetration (Archer, 2000). It should be added, however, that Archer also found that for more serious violent behaviors, such as injury requiring medical attention, that it was females who suffered greater injury than males. Since, typically, administrations of the CTS and CADRI to high school students do not include scales measuring injuries; it is unclear whether this trend toward greater injury by girls would hold for adolescent dating partners.

The second conclusion that can be drawn from these three studies is that in light of perpetration of "any" dating aggression by boys (i.e., ranging across studies from 22.5% to 39.1%), and any perpetration of aggression by girls (i.e., ranging from 37.8% to 43.6%), partner aggression is not a rare occurrence. Generally, from one fifth to two fifths of high school students report aggressing

TABLE 5.1. *Prevalence of perpetrated partner physical aggression among high school dating individuals using the Conflict Tactics Scale (CTS) and the Conflict in Adolescent Dating Relationship Inventory (CADRI)*

	O'Keefe (1997) n = 939: ages 14–20 CTS		Cascardi et al. (1999) n = 1,156: ages 14–18 CTS		Wolfe et al. (2001) n = 1,019: ages 14–16 CADRI	
	Boys	Girls	Boys	Girls	Boys	Girls
1. Threw something at partner	16	27	7	15	6	14
2. Physically restrained	–	–	14	12	–	–
3. Pushed, grabbed, shoved (shook on the CADRI)	28	32	14	28	2	15
4. Slapped (or pulled hair on the CADRI)	12	26	4	18	2	11
5. Kicked, bit, hit with fist	10	19	6	17	3	17
6. Choked	–	–	3	2	–	–
7. Beat up	3	3	2	4	–	–
8. Threatened with knife/gun	1	3	1	2	–	–
9. Hit or tried to hit with something	10	17	–	–	–	–
10. Forced sexual activities	13	3	–	–	3	2
11. Any 1. through 10.	39	44	23	38	–	–

Note: Prevalence rates (percentages) are rounded off.

toward their partners. Comparable figures regarding "any" aggression, for a group of high risk students in a drop-out prevention program (ages 14 to 19), reveal higher prevalence rates for any perpetrated physical aggression than that displayed in Table 5.1 (i.e., any girl: 68%; any boy: 33%) (Chase et al., 1998). Prevalence rates for perpetration of "any" dating aggression for 8th and 9th grade students, found for 42% of girls and 21% of boys at the end of the school year (Arriaga & Foshee, 2004), were lower than the high-risk high school students, but were comparable to the one fifth to two fifths prevalence rates noted for the high school samples.

A third generalization that may be drawn from Table 5.1 is that less serious perpetrated aggression, i.e., that which is less likely to seriously harm the partner, such as "push, grabbed, and shoved" on the CTS is more common. Less serious perpetrated aggression ranged from 14% to 32% of partners. More serious violent behaviors, such as "threaten with a knife or gun," are approximately one tenth the prevalence rate for less serious aggression, ranging from 1% to 3% of partners on the CTS. Yet, as suggested in earlier analyses of "any" perpetrated aggression by partners, more serious aggressive behaviors, such as threatening a partner with a weapon are dangerous and, although uncommon, neither are they rare in adolescent dating relationships.

Relationship Differences and Individual Differences in Dating Aggression

Relationship Differences
There is a small but growing body of research findings that has examined the correlates of partner aggression, focused mainly on the relative presence *in the relationship* of beneficent emotional experiences such as intimacy, affection, and nurturance, as contrasted with irritation, antagonism, and high conflict/controlling behavior. The focus of these investigations is on the couple rather than on the individual partners in the relationship.

Considering the five-fold increase in the median duration of romantic relationships from middle to high school (Carver et al., 2003), relationships later in adolescence are more likely to become increasingly unique and reflective of the imprint of the individual partners. Also, as relationships increase in duration in late adolescence so does the importance of the relationship quality of good or poor intimacy, along with increased pressure from family or friends to remain together or to break-up, and the added pressure arising from the failure and termination of more serious intimate relationships. This increasing uniqueness of more mature relationships with the passage of time has led some theorists on relationship development to propose that interactions between two people come to reflect the unique pattern that is the relationship shared by the two individuals; the couple dyad itself should therefore be the main focus of analysis (Hinde, 1997). Moreover, this theory proposes that relationship development is a dialectical process of continuing creation, change, or degradation that occurs as the partners interact, and "the tendency toward violence may be more a part of the relationship than either participant as an individual" (Hinde, p. 189). This theory posits different routes by which relationships may become violent. One possible developmental route to relationship violence would be for partners high on dispositional aggression to choose one another (sometimes referred to as "assortative" partnering), with subsequent escalation of aggressive tactics to solve conflicts. Or, alternately, an aggressive partner may confirm an aggressive perception of self by selecting and dominating a more passive partner. Yet the theory holds that both partners are changed by the developmental process. Other writers have proposed a similar relationship development model regarding dating in mid-adolescence, one in which coercive and counter-coercive interaction constitute an "aggressive 'background noise' to interactions . . . initial acts of physical aggression are likely to occur more rapidly and more frequently . . . (resulting in) a violent dynamic (which is) differentiated by its potential for rage-related injurious violence" (Wekerle & Wolfe, 1999, p. 438). Given the relative ease of ending a dating relationship (as versus marital relationship), and the availability of a pool of opposite-gender friends in school, it is surprising that aggression in adolescent dating relationships would ever escalate to the point of injuriousness, but the dyadic emotional processes may help to explain this puzzle.

Evidence that adolescent romantic couples become more unique with increased duration, seriousness, and intimacy, and that relationship violence varies with those dyadic features, is growing. Whereas dating relationships in the early adulthood years have clearly been shown to increase in aggression with increasing duration and seriousness of the relationship, and shown that aggression is less common in couples in which there is greater positive emotion, emotional intimacy, and empathy (see review by Marcus & Swett, 2003a), the study of aggressive high school romantic relationships has only begun to focus on couple dynamics. Possibly, more frequent changes in relationship partners, less prevalence of more severe aggressive behaviors in dating relationships than seen in adult abusive relationships, and less pressure on adolescents to marry, may have kept research on a violent couple dynamic off the radar screen at this point in time. More generally, adolescent romantic relationships, so often portrayed dramatically in literature, may not be taken as seriously as are later romantic relationships.

Studies of adolescent romantic relationships have begun to show that duration and seriousness relate positively with the prevalence of relationship aggression and violence in those relationships. Relationships that are longer in duration are those in which partners are more likely to report sustaining verbal and physical aggression from their partners (Giordano, Manning, & Longmore, 2005; O'Keefe & Treister, 1998), and to report perpetrating aggression toward partners (O'Keefe & Treister, 1998). When combined with a number of other predictors of sustained aggression, relationship duration continues to contribute uniquely to sustained verbal and physical forms of partner aggression (Giordano, Manning, & Longmore, 2005), or to received verbal, but not physical, aggression from partners (Roberts, Auinger, & Klein, 2006). Seriousness of the relationship also has correlated positively with both perpetrated and received physical aggression as rated by boys, but not girls (O'Keefe & Treister, 1998), or to perpetration as a unique contributor for girls only (O'Keefe, 1997). Recently, the investigation of two additional indicators of seriousness and emotional involvement of partners, namely, being in a "special romantic relationship," and the presence of sexual intercourse with the partner were found to be the strongest predictors of both verbal and physical aggression received from partners for both males and females in a nationally representative sample of 10 to 18 year olds (Roberts, Auinger, & Klein, 2006). For males in particular, the unique contribution of sexual intercourse with a partner increased the likelihood of sustaining physical aggression from their partners by 2.24 times, beyond the contribution of others factors (i.e., age, duration, age differences), and involvement with a partner who has become pregnant increased physical aggression from girl partners by 2.44 times.

Whereas it is conceivable that aggression might be entirely initiated by one partner alone, with no antecedent conflict over some issue, that is, a predatory, single perpetrator preying on one helpless victim, the self-report instruments used to study aggression have almost entirely focused on both partner's perceptions of couple styles of resolving disputes. As noted earlier, the gold standards for assessing dating aggression and violence by dating partners, the CTS (Straus, 1979) or its new version, the CTS-2 (Straus et al., 1996), and the newer CADRI (Wolfe et al., 2001), are measures in which the respondent is asked in what manner they and their partners resolve inevitable differences or arguments. The directions for both measures specify resolution of conflicts as the context within which aggression may occur. Therefore, since partner aggression is viewed as one way in which disputes are either resolved or not, it is not surprising that various measures of overall conflict within the relationship have been studied in relation to dating aggression.

One study measured the conflict in the relationship and used a rating of both the frequency and seriousness of the problems in the relationship, in relation to the amount of violence perpetrated toward partners in the relationship (O'Keefe & Treister, 1998). The findings of that study showed that, for both boys and girls, the correlation between conflict and perpetration was positive and moderate. The researcher's previous examination of a different group of high school students, using the same measure of relationship conflict, had shown that perpetrated physical violence toward partners was uniquely predicted by relationship conflict (O'Keefe, 1997). In that study, conflict in the relationship uniquely predicted perpetrated partner aggression for *girls*, beyond the contribution of the belief that female-to-male violence is justifiable, the belief that male-to-female violence is unjustifiable, the seriousness of the relationship, the receipt of violence from the partner, and frequency of alcohol or drug use in the past year. This study also found that conflict in the relationship uniquely predicted perpetrated partner aggression for boys, beyond the influence of witnessing inter-parental violence, a belief that male-to-female dating violence is justifiable, being the recipient of dating violence from the partner, and frequency of alcohol or drug use.

More recently, a study of high school students explored the relation between a measure of perpetrated aggression toward partners (i.e., in both milder and more severe forms), a measure of the frequency of arguments with partners, and the number of arguments had with the partner in the previous month (Kinsfogel & Grych, 2004). Moderate and positive bivariate correlations for girls and boys showed that perpetrated aggression toward partners related to both conflict frequency and number of conflicts per month. Moreover, strong and positive correlations between a measure of negative communication (i.e., insulting or ridiculing in front of others, using a hostile tone of voice) and conflict frequency for boys and for girls, suggested that the tenor of daily conflict was likely to include highly negative verbal and non-verbal communication between partners. Couple emotional dynamics in the form of greater and more negatively valenced emotional conflict within the relationship is an important predictor of dating partner aggression.

Another way to conceptualize the conflict between partners is the extent to which both boy and girl partners are likely to use physical violence toward one another as a conflict tactic intended to resolve their disagreements. Because of the paucity of studies of intact dating couples during adolescence, we must rely on single partner reports of perpetration and victimization, rather than the independent reports of both partners. Specifically regarding high school dating partners, the positive association between individual partner ratings of physical aggression perpetrated and received is substantial. One study of high school students showed that boys' and girls' estimates of perpetrated and received physical violence were highly positively related (O'Keefe & Treister, 1998). Moreover, in that study, 48% of boys and 41% of girls indicated that the most common pattern of dating aggression was that both initiated aggression. There was moderate agreement on whether one partner was the primary initiator of aggression, when mutual initiation of aggression was not endorsed. Boys estimated that 28% was started by them and girls indicated 39% was started by boys. Of those reporting that girls initiated aggression, girls estimated 20% was initiated by them and boys estimated that 24% was initiated by girls. Yet another study found that 70% of dating violence perpetrators also report being victims, and 72% of dating violence victims were also perpetrators (Malik et al., 1997). Dating violence perpetration among adolescent dating partners is clearly a bidirectional process.

At the end of adolescence, the issue of whether dyadic relationship qualities (as versus individual partner characteristics) maintain aggression is particularly important because of its significance for the prediction of aggression into the early years of marriage. In late adolescence, the option of continuing the relationship and progressing toward marriage arises, especially for those who have dated for years. Two longitudinal studies of partner aggression in late adolescence and early adulthood suggest that both couple relationship processes and individual partner personality play a role in maintaining patterns of dating aggression over time. In the first study of 105 at-risk boys (i.e., were drawn from city areas with higher delinquency and were predominantly Euro-American), they and their partners were followed from ages 18 through the early 20s (Capaldi, Shortt, & Crosby, 2003). Approximately one third of both boys and girls reported perpetrating aggression toward their partners. Of those who stayed with the same partner for 2 1/2 years, 60% of young men and 68% of young women had again physically aggressed at the second assessment. Consistent with studies reported earlier, those who had been together longer had reported greater partner aggression at the second assessment, beyond statistical control for aggression at the initial assessment. Authors interpreted that finding to mean that there were continuing and unresolved conflicts between partners that increased the risk for dating aggression. More important was the discovery that for those who stayed together, but not those who acquired new partners, aggression was moderately correlated across the 2-year span. Moreover, and over time, boys reported increases in their aggression toward their partners, and both male and female partners altered their levels of aggression in the direction of one another. Couple dynamics, in the form of unresolved conflicts and inter-partner aggression, appeared to predict to the stability of dating aggression within intact and troubled romantic relationships.

The second longitudinal study involved dating young adults (who were not dyadic partners in the same relationship) who were followed from ages 21 through 26 as part of the Dunedin, New Zealand study (Robins, Caspi, & Moffitt, 2002). That study also yielded findings regarding the continuance or desistance of partner aggression. The findings from that study showed that of those who stayed with the same partners, but not those who established new relationships, physically aggressive behaviors (i.e., both minor and severe) were moderately correlated from time one to time two. Surprisingly, the presence of physical aggression at the beginning of this period was unrelated to breaking up during the 5-year span, a finding similar to the majority of couples in the Capaldi and colleagues study. The results of the Dunedin study showed that physically aggressive behaviors were related to the frequency of conflict in the relationship, as well as partner "negative emotionality" (as a personality trait measure). However, conflict in the relationship and physical aggression in the relationship declined significantly for those who terminated the old relationships and began new ones. In addition, individual partner negative emotionality, assessed at age 18 predicted to both conflict in the relationship, and physical aggression perpetrated toward the partner in both the old and new relationships. As the authors entitled their research study, "It's not just who you're with, It's who you are . . . ," individual partner personality, as well as couple continuity both contributed to dating partner aggression.

Individual Differences

Differences among partners in areas of motivation, personality, and social behaviors have been among the most frequently studied correlates of dating aggression. The motivational processes of individual partners found related to dating aggression, for example, are similar to those motivators of non-dating adolescent aggression and violence. Partner anger, jealousy, alcohol/drug use, attitudes of acceptance of aggression, and attempts to control the behavior of one's partner are among the most frequently researched differences associated with dating violence.

Overt anger, or individual styles of getting mad and yelling at the partner, use of sarcasm, or getting mad and walking away, was one dimension resulting from a statistical factor analysis of the CTS with high school students (Feldman & Gowen, 1998). Anger in romantic relationships is largely an accusatory or "you message," a provocative display in which one partner blames the other partner for something. Overt anger, as a conflict resolution strategy, was found to be highly and positively associated with a combination of both mild physical and verbal aggression (e.g., pushed, shoved, grabbed, hit), and moderately negatively related with less confrontational conflict tactics such as use of compromise, and seeking social support from others (Feldman & Gowen, 1998). Overt anger functions as an assertion of power over the partner, and appears to replace more conciliatory approaches to resolving conflicts. Important because of its reliable association with peer aggression noted in Chapter 3, other research has found that anger as a general personality trait, rather than a method of conflict resolution, also has related positively and moderately with measures of verbal and mild physical abusiveness toward partners and the frequency of conflict in dating relationships, for both boy and girl dating partners (Kinsfogel & Grych, 2004).

Anger that follows a perceived threat to the relationship, or jealousy, also appears to be an important emotional vulnerability related to dating partner aggression, similar to the way that friendship jealousy associated with peer aggression as noted earlier (in Chapter 4). Reminiscent of the conflict scenario of George and Sarah introduced earlier, when victims of dating partner violence were asked to select from among thirteen possible motives behind their partner's aggression, high school girls first said their partners were jealous, and second that their partners were angry; boys first said their partners were jealous, and second said that their partners wanted to "get back" at them (O'Keefe & Treister, 1998). A study using the CTS with high school students, also showed that jealous actions, such as in those acknowledging jealousy and suspicion of their partner's friends related moderately and positively with perpetrated physical aggression toward partners. Also, jealous actions related moderately with control tactics designed to regulate the partner's behavior, such as when the partner tries to keep the romantic partner from seeing or talking to their families (Cascardi et al., 1999). It is likely that jealousy reactions to one's partner, as with dating aggression itself, is less likely to appear at the beginning of relationships, when the relationship is new and expectations are positive, but more likely to appear at the middle or end of relationships, when partner seriousness and emotional intensity are greater. However, there is insufficient research specifically pointing to the appearance of jealousy and jealous strategies at various stages of relationship development among adolescents. That high school students most frequently selected jealousy as their most common reason for partner aggression, however, was consistent with jealousy motivations given for dating aggression by college students (Sugarman & Hotaling, 1989).

Closely related to jealousy and anger as antecedents of dating partner aggression, is the concept of rejection sensitivity in adolescent girls. Those girls who anxiously expect rejection in close relationships have been found to overreact to perceived rejection with hostile and aggressive behaviors (Downey, Bonica, & Rincon, 1999). Related to rejection sensitivity, in the sense of being an individual vulnerability, but somewhat less explored in high school relationships, are partners who are insecure about their relationships. Such partners experience a heightened vulnerability to aggressive over-reaction. Research has shown for high school girls, but not high school boys, that having a less secure, anxious attachment to their best friends (but not their current partner) predicted to perpetration of physical aggression toward their partners (Feiring et al., 2002). Clearly a few partner emotional vulnerabilities, noted particularly in girls, may increase the risk for dating aggression, but this area will require more intensive investigation before this complex association is more clearly understood.

Attitudes of acceptance of aggression toward partners, that it is acceptable or justifiable to physically aggress toward one's boyfriend or girlfriend, has been firmly established as one of the most important motivational precursors of dating violence. One measure of acceptance of partner aggression, the

"Attitudes about Aggression in Dating Situations" measure, (Slep, Cascardi, Avery-Leaf, & O'Leary, 2001), consisted of twelve items describing acts of physical dating aggression within specific contexts. Specifically, five items described a male aggressing toward a female partner, five items described a female aggressing against a male partner, and two items described aggression toward a same gender peer. Name calling in front of friends, arguments over a partner's wish to see another person, and discovery of infidelity, are examples of situations portrayed in which a partner loses control and slaps, pushes, or hits, in response. It is important to note that these scenarios are similar to those threats to the relationship noted early as a correlate of partner aggression. Dating partner ratings of agreement with the partner who loses control is the measure of acceptance of partner aggression. Using the measure of acceptance of aggression toward partners, girls and boys who were more accepting of aggression have been found to physically aggress toward their current partners (Slep et al., 2001).

Other studies have supported the association between acceptance of violence toward dating partners and future dating aggression, but have also revealed nuance depending on partner gender. In one study, for example, dating violence was found to be stable over a 1-year time span (Wolfe et al., 2004). Attitudes of acceptance of violence toward partners, however, were related to dating violence for boys at initial assessment and later assessment, but not for girls at either time period. Also, initial attitudes toward dating violence did not predict to later dating violence for either boys or girls once combined with other factors.

Acceptance of aggression toward one's partner also has been evaluated for its unique contribution to dating aggression, in conjunction with other predictors. The major difference in that study was the separate assessment of both the male-to-female and female-to-male direction of aggression, and both acceptability and unacceptability of both forms of aggression. In that multivariate research, a large number of contextual influence on dating partner aggression in addition to the justifiability of male-to-female and female-to-male dating aggression (including witnessing inter-parental violence), and a number of situational influences (e.g., alcohol/drug use, receipt of violence from partner, seriousness of relationship) were assessed (O'Keefe, 1997). For boys, five factors significantly predicted to their own perpetrated dating violence: (1) witnessing inter-parental violence; (2) belief that male-to-female violence is justifiable; (3) being the recipient of dating violence; (4) alcohol/drug use; and (5) greater conflict in the dating relationship. For girls, seven variables related to their own perpetrated violence toward partner: (1) the belief that female-to-male violence is justifiable; (2) the belief that male-to-female violence is unjustifiable; (3) the greater conflict in the relationship; (4) a more serious relationship; (5) being the recipient of dating violence; (6) alcohol/drug use; and (7) African-American race. Clearly there are common predictors of perpetrated dating aggression for both boys and girls, such as amount of conflict in the relationship, receipt of partner violence, and alcohol/drug use. However, there remains a need to explore gender-sensitive models that predict somewhat differently for boys and girls, and that take into account which partner is the aggressor and which is the victim.

The final set of individual partner predictors of dating violence concerns the broader network of relationships within which the dating partner(s) may be found, including the parent–child relationship (past and present), the peer relationships one has now, and the dating relationships of one's friends. Generally, that body of research findings shows that witnessing others who use aggression as a strategy in close relationships, that is, a coercive-counter-coercive interpersonal dynamic, relates positively with the use of such strategies with one's own dating partner.

Research has been abundant on the issue of exposure to parents who have been violent with one another, and its influence on dating aggression of their adolescent offspring, but the research findings have also been inconsistent regarding the effects of such exposure on boy versus girl daters. The evidence clearly shows that boys exposed to inter-parental aggression have been found more likely than boys not exposed to parental aggression, to aggress toward dating partners (Kinsfogel & Grych, 2004; Malik, Sorenson, & Aneshensel, 1997; O'Keefe & Treister, 1998; Wolfe et al., 1998). For boys, observing inter-parental aggression also has related to higher levels of anger or hostility (Kinsfogel & Grych, 2004; Wolfe et al., 1998) and positive attitudes toward aggression toward girls or aggressive teasing directed toward girls (Kinsfogel & Grych, 2004; Wolfe et al., 1998). The research results for girls have been less consistent. Whereas one study did find inter-parental aggression related both to girls' aggression to partners and girls' aggression received from partners (O'Keefe & Treister, 1998), another study found that it mattered which parent was the aggressor. Observation of female-to-male inter-parental aggression, but not male-to-female inter-parental aggression, was uniquely related to perpetration of dating aggression for both boys and girls, beyond the influence of the boys' and girls' substance use, demographics, family structure, acceptance of violence, and exposure to community violence (Malik et al., 1997).

The evidence for the impact of earlier child abuse on later dating aggression has shown even more complex associations than that relating dating aggression to observation of inter-parental aggression, largely because of the former's gender specificity. Child maltreatment, defined broadly as a combination of child physical abuse, child sexual abuse, or witnessing inter-parental aggression prior to adolescence, has been found positively associated with a combination of physically, sexually, and psychologically aggressive behavior perpetrated toward dating partners by boys, whereas maltreatment predicted to being a victim of dating partner abuse for girls (Wolfe et al, 1998). Wolfe et al. (1998) also found that perpetration of abusive/coercive behavior toward dating partners was related specifically to childhood sexual abuse by parents. Over a 1-year period, child maltreatment for both boys and girls predicted to increases in dating violence by virtue of its mediation by symptoms of emotional trauma related to maltreatment; those more traumatized by abuse were those who became more aggressive toward dating partners. However, whereas other studies have shown that violence by parents toward children (e.g., kicking, beating up, threatening the child) related to later dating violence perpetration and victimization for both boys and girls (O'Keefe & Treister, 1998), others have not found child abuse experiences to be related to dating violence perpetration. Instead, child abuse experiences were related to victimization once demographic exposure to community violence, and personality mediators (e.g., personal norms of acceptance, purposes in life, substance abuse) were controlled (Malik et al., 1997). Although earlier child abuse may relate to later dating violence, its effects are mediated by the individual's mental health and personality characteristics, as well as important attitudes toward partner violence (e.g., acceptance of violent solutions to conflicts). When the weight of the evidence for child abuse effects on dating violence becomes clearer, it will likely have many qualifications based on differential impact on girls versus boys, victimization versus perpetration, and the specific impact the abuse has had on personality.

The most consistent and convincing findings regarding relationship between the individual's social network and dating aggression have been with regard to their past and contemporary relationships with both same and opposite gender peers. Dating aggression has correlated well with many dimensions of relationships with peers, as one would predict given earlier noted increased time spent with peers rather than parents (noted in Chapter 2). Moreover, the negative influences of coercive and counter-coercive peer relationships are experienced as soon as dating has begun! As early as middle school, those males and females who bully peers have been shown to have a poorer quality of relationships with friends (i.e., lower in self-disclosure, lower in affection, lower in commitment, and higher in dominance by use of power); and bullies also perpetrated more aggression with dates (Connolly et al., 2000). A recent examination of bullies and partner violence from 6th through 12th grades again demonstrated that bullying was primarily a problem that permeated various peer relationships (Pepler et al., 2006). In that follow-up study, bullies were more likely than non-bullies to sexually harass same and opposite gender peers, to socially aggress against dating partners (e.g., by passing rumors, social exclusion), and to show physically violent behaviors toward dating partners (e.g., ranging from slapping and kicking to threatening with a knife). Bullies appeared to establish the same relationship dynamics across various peer relationships.

A second important correlate of peer relationships and dating violence was who their friends were. High school students who were physically aggressive to their dating partners were also more likely to have friends who aggressed against their partners (Kinsfogel & Grych, 2004), and had either known someone who had been injured, or had themselves been injured in a physical fight with peers (Malik et al., 1997). Those who self disclose more to peers have been found more likely to be victimized by dating aggression (Giordano et al., 2005). Those who seek more social support from others (e.g., peers, parents) as a strategy of coping with relationship conflicts, are also more likely to be violent toward partners (Feldman & Gowen, 1998). It remains unclear at this time whether increased social connectedness to peers precedes or follows dating violence, or whether bidirectional influences provides the best explanation for dating violence.

The relative influence of both having friends who are aggressive toward their dating partners and having observed inter-parental aggression, has been tested in relation to perpetration of dating violence in a longitudinal study of 8th and 9th graders (Arriaga & Foshee, 2004). Assessment of only those who had been on a date showed that during a six-month period during the school year, the prevalence of perpetrated dating aggression by boys went up (from 11% to 21%), as did the perpetration of dating aggression by girls (from 28% to 42%). Interestingly, perpetration of severe violence (e.g., assault with knife, and beat up the other) also increased for boys (i.e., from 5% to 11%), and for girls (i.e., from 11% to 17%). As early as middle school, severe dating violence was not rare, and dating aggression and violence perpetrated by girls was greater than that by boys. The most important of their findings was that witnessing inter-parental violence significantly increased the likelihood of the partner's own perpetration of dating violence at initial assessment by 1.75 times. Having a friend involved in dating violence increased the likelihood of violence perpetration by 3.03 times at initial assessment. Observing inter-parental violence appears to lose its predictive significance for future dating violence, when contrasted with friend's involvement. For those who were not dating violence perpetrators at the initial assessment, but who later reported perpetrating dating violence at the second assessment, having friends who were involved in dating violence increased their likelihood of initiating perpetration by 1.85 fold. However, having witnessed inter-parental violence was unrelated to onset of new perpetration at the second assessment. Evidently, establishing patterns of coercive relationships with peers, as in the case of bullies, having friends who are involved in violent interaction with their peers, or having friends who are more specifically involved in violent dating relationship, all increase the risk for dating violence perpetration. In this second decade of life, it is the influence of friends' behavior that appears to be a more consistent and potent influence than having observed inter-spousal violence at an earlier period in time.

Summary

Dating partner aggression rivals other forms of aggression in adolescence in the prevalence of its less and more serious forms. Neither non-dating nor dating aggression is rare in the lives of adolescents. Both are experienced by about a third or more of adolescents. Dating aggression appears as early as dating begins, and is a sizeable problem for all ethnic and racial groups, although more so among minorities. Some individual risk factors for dating aggression were those also common to non-partner aggression, including elevated anger, attitudes of acceptance of aggression, alcohol and drug use, and historical and contemporary associations with others who are abusive to others.

However, individual dispositions represent only one set of risk factors for dating aggression, the other being features of the dating relationship itself. Dating relationships, from early to late adolescence, grow in terms of intimacy, duration, seriousness, sexual involvement, and emotional intensity. Previous research on relationship qualities has classified heterosexual relationship dynamics as either relatively "open" or closed (Marcus & Swett, 2003a). Relationships that were systemically "open," and characterized by a predominance of positive emotions (e.g., positive affect, empathy, intimacy, self-disclosure), were found less vulnerable to aggression. Relationships that were relatively "closed," were characterized by a predominance of negative emotions (e.g., jealousy, anger, negative affect, anxiety), were more vulnerable to aggression. Dating relationships in adolescence also varied in systemic qualities. Relationships in which there was greater duration and seriousness, greater conflict tinged with negative affect, and greater aggression used by both partners, there was likely to be greater dating aggression and violence. Unfortunately, these are the same dyadic emotional qualities that also increase steadily throughout adolescence. Thus, and contrary to earlier noted findings regarding reduced non-relationship aggression during adolescence, the trend is for dating aggression to increase with development of relationships in adolescence. The later stages of adolescence present one of the most serious challenges to post-adolescent development-continuity of dating aggression in stable but unhappy relationships.

The research reviewed here on adolescent dating aggression also diverges from non-dating aggression in other important ways. First, dating aggression appears not to be a reason for ending relationships, particularly in later adolescence and early adulthood, presenting another paradox of greater importance: adolescents are likely to remain in relationships in which there is repeated aggression, and perhaps serious forms of aggression, committed by partners with whom they have strong emotional bonds. Future research will need to investigate possible reasons for chronic partner aggression. It may be that partners provide a more benevolent interpretation of the other's aggression (e.g., she hits me because she loves me), there may be pressures to stay with the partner once there has been considerable investment of time and emotions, or there may be a lack of available alternative partners.

There may be other ways to resolve the paradox of continuity of aggression in dating relationships. Clearly there are gender differences in dating partner aggression, and differences in the predictors of dating partner aggression for boys and girls. It may be that girls respond with greater aggression toward boys because they believe boys will not hurt them or hit back (i.e., it is socially unacceptable). Yet boys who are taught to hit back when struck may eventually violate taboos against hitting girls, their size and strength then more likely to produce injuries. Also, it may be that girls value relationships more highly than do boys, are therefore more willing to remain in failing relationships, and are also more seriously stung by partner rejection. Girls also may be more vulnerable to partner rejection because of the predominance of affective disorders (e.g., depression) among adolescent girls, which places them at greater risk for aggression in response to partner rejection. Yet, it is clearly important to further understand both aggressiveness by girl and boy dating partners, given dating partner reciprocity and possible continuity of aggression into the years of early adulthood.

6

Primary, Secondary, and Tertiary Prevention of Aggression and Violence

The last 30 years have witnessed the development of hundreds of prevention programs purporting to thwart the appearance of aggression and violence, or simply reduce their frequency once they have appeared. However, of the successful programs that have been developed for children and adolescents, many programs overlap in content and methods of delivery. Programs also have been entitled as violence prevention programs but have been more broadly directed toward antisocial behavior, delinquency, or substance abuse in adolescence; worthy goals but not the focus of the present volume. Other programs may have been intended to decrease aggression but have actually increased it (see Dodge, 2006 for a review), or have been simply ineffective in reducing aggression or violence. The current review identifies criteria for effective programs, and examples of programs that have met those standards. Some redundancy among goals, content, or methods presented here may not be superfluous if it helps clarify which ingredients help to make programs most effective.

The current presentation cannot hope to thoroughly review all the excellent and effective programs targeting aggression and violence developed over the past 30 years. The current review can present programs designed for various subgroups of children and adolescents that have, by various creative means, reduced aggressive or violent behavior, or reduced major risk factors for both, and may allow the reader a taste of what has been possible. The goal of this current survey of programs is to add to public awareness of what is possible rather than to exhaustively review all varieties of effective programs. Particular emphasis will be on programs that target risk factors noted in previous chapters, including developmental, personality, and situational risk factors. For example, programs reducing aggressive behavior, increasing empathy, and improving anger management are of key interest. The initial discussion will center on a review of the scientific standards that have been used to judge the effectiveness of prevention programs. Briefly, holding programs to standards of effective implementation, reliable and valid measurements of change, and a body of studies replicating expected outcomes is basic to establishing a body of effective programs. Following the discussion of research standards, the results of a meta-analysis of school-based programs will help to identify which kinds of programs have been most effective in achieving the goal of reduced aggression or violent behavior. Next, we will present specific programs designed to reduce aggression or violence for all children and adolescents, programs designed for children at-risk and with special needs, and programs for children and adolescents who are already violent. The major thrust of the current examination will be to identify what is possible, and what has worked, but not all programs that have done so.

Scientific Standards for Prevention Programs

The early 1990s was a time of rising violence rates by adolescents in the United States, and a time in which various scientific organizations began to lend their resources and expertise toward solving the problems facing the nation. First, a blue ribbon commission established by the American Psychological Association (APA, 1993) generated a set of five seminal recommendations based on extant evidence at the time for the scientific evaluation of prevention efforts, and a rationale as to why particular programs were most likely to be effective. Eight years later, a commission established by the Surgeon General of the United States (USDHHS, 2001) presented its recommendations for standards guiding the scientific evaluation of prevention programs, and added its important elaborations of standards specific to the quality of program research. Recommendations from both commissions were echoed most recently in a National Institutes of Health State-of-the-Science Conference Statement (NIH, 2006), and the publication of a report of the State-of-the-Science Violence Prevention Conference (Tuma, Loeber, & Lochman, 2006). All three commissions represented the view of practitioners and researchers deeply involved in the creation of violence prevention programs and evaluation of those programs, and represented many disciplinary perspectives.

The APA blue ribbon commission made the following five recommendations: (1) programs should draw on our understanding of risk factors, and use "theory-based intervention strategies with known efficacy in changing behavior, tested program designs, and validated, objective measurement techniques to assess outcomes"(p. 53–54); (2) in relation to the timing and content of programs, was the important suggestion that intervention should "begin as early as possible to interrupt the trajectory toward violence" (p. 54), specifically with regard to programs that reduced early aggressive behavior and ameliorated risk factors such as poor school achievement and inconsistent parenting practices; (3) interventions should address aggression as well as related problem behaviors, such as cognitive biases and deficits, and poor interpersonal relationships; (4) because aggression is often consistent across social contexts, it was important that interventions reinforce or bolster one another across the contexts of home, school, peer group, media, and community in order to produce lasting effects; and (5) programs should take advantage of developmental "windows of opportunity" by presenting programs at transition points such as the beginning of elementary school and adolescence.

Eight years later, the Surgeon General's Report on Youth Violence (USDHHS, 2001) affirmed the need for the highest scientific standards as recognized in rigorous experimental designs (i.e., assignment to experimental and control groups), reliable and valid measurement of program outcomes, and a sound theoretical basis for intervention strategies. Beyond these essential scientific standards, the Report suggested additional criteria were needed for programs directed at violence reduction, or modification of risk factors for violence. First, they suggested that our confidence in programs would be enhanced if they demonstrated both "efficacy" in controlled, experimental settings as well as "effectiveness" when applied to natural settings such as homes, schools, or communities. It was deemed important that programs be replicated in both controlled and real-life settings. The latter was an important test of whether a program would work when, for example, the training of school personnel to implement the program, the workings of school schedules and complexities of school environments, limitations of parent work schedules interfering with attendance at training sessions, and many other real-life exigencies were present. Second, the Report added that prevention programs should be able to demonstrate reductions in the prevalence or rate of violent behaviors (i.e., pre- to post-experiment differences), or a delay in the onset of violent behavior. Third, the Report recommended that programs should be able to demonstrate long-term effectiveness or sustainability of improvements. The standard offered here was that effects should be demonstrated for at least 1 year after the end of the project. Fourth, the Report suggested that attrition rates should be low because high drop-out rates would suggest problems in the implementation of the program. Fifth, program results should be replicable in various trials with different sets of participants. Programs meeting all five criteria were designated as "model" programs.

Features of violence prevention programs that were effective and ineffective were summarized in a Conference Statement published by the NIH

State-of-the-Science independent panel of health professionals and public representatives (NIH, 2006). This report followed a systematic review of violence prevention research studies. The Conference Statement recognized the following ten characteristics of programs that worked: (1) "they are derived from sound theoretical rationales;" (2) "they address strong risk factors;" (3) "they involve long-term treatments, often lasting a year and sometimes much longer;" (4) "they work intensively with those targeted for treatment and often use a clinical approach;" (5) "they follow a cognitive/behavioral strategy;" (6) "they are multi-modal and multi-contextual;" (7) they focus on improving social competence and other skill development strategies for targeted youth and/or their families;" (8) "they are developmentally appropriate;" (9) "they are not delivered in coercive institutional settings;" and (10) "they have the capacity for delivery with fidelity."(p. 463). Briefly, the programs they judged as not working were characterized by the following: (1) they aggregated youth to yield an iatrogenic effect; (2) programs used scare tactics or toughness strategies (e.g., boot camps, scared straight); (3) they lectured at youth; and (4) the programs had unclear guidelines and staff were not held accountable for outcomes.

A separate report, based on the NIH State-of-the-Science Conference on Violence Prevention (Tuma, Loeber, & Lochman, 2006) represented a more global set of personal observations and implications drawn by key conference participants. The focus of that response, however, was on helping practitioners to use, and the public to understand what was known about prevention programs that worked. Similar to the conclusions of the APA (1993) commission, that panel of conference experts presented their four recommendations concerning when or which programs were most successful: (1) programs "helping young parents to cope with stress and use healthy discipline, conflict management, and monitoring skills" (p. 454); (2) "When health care providers support parents to use effective communication skills, anger and depression management, problem solving between adults, set up predictable homework routines, and build collaborative relationships with teachers" (p. 454); (3) when "teachers receive guidance on classroom management and interactive teaching, and parents are assisted with family management and communication to create a positive learning environment" (p. 454); and (4) "when teenagers with a history of chronic and severe criminal behavior are provided a structured and therapeutic living environment with: intensive supervision at home, in school, and in the community; clear and consistent limits; positive reinforcement for appropriate behavior; a relationship with mentoring adults; and separation from delinquent peers" (p. 454).

The recommendations by the NIH researchers bolstered the APA (1993) panel findings, and had come full circle, by suggesting that a major focus of prevention programs should be on building healthy parenting practices, teaching skills to children and adolescents with demonstrated positive impact, a focus on ameliorating key early risk factors for violence, and promoting collaboration across settings of home and school. The NIH recommendations, however, added the importance of meeting the special needs of already violent adolescents in a humane, treatment-focused manner, and when possible in their home settings.

Following the presentation of the results of a meta-analysis of school-based prevention programs, the remainder of the chapter will focus on specific programs using the Surgeon General Report's designations of primary, secondary, and tertiary prevention. Primary prevention refers to programs directed toward younger, mainstream children, in order to prevent the onset of aggression or violence. Such programs, for example, might involve social skills training for children, parent management training, or programs to help teachers manage classrooms effectively. Secondary prevention programs reduce the risk for later aggression or violence by addressing the needs of "at-risk" children or adolescents. At-risk children, for example, would be those who come from high-crime areas, children who are already aggressive or are bullying others, or children who have been physically abused. Tertiary prevention programs refer to those that lower the likelihood that an adolescent who is already violent will behave violently at a later point in time. Where possible, the current review will focus mainly on programs identified in the Surgeon General's (USDHHS, 2001) report as promising and model programs, and on defining programs and updating research on those programs already judged in the report to be exemplary programs.

Meta-Analysis of Prevention Programs Targeting Aggression and Violence

Expert analysis of program effectiveness, as in the earlier noted scientific commission findings, can be further enhanced by a rigorous meta-analysis of 221 studies completed since 1960. These studies were school-based programs that specifically targeted aggressive or violent behavior (Wilson, Lipsey, & Derzon, 2003). Important to that statistical meta-analysis of studies was its focus on pre- versus post-test differences, and studies that assigned children to experimental versus control groups. The studies in the meta-analysis included over 56,000 children ranging in age from less than 5 years old through the high school years, and programs that had a primary, secondary, and tertiary prevention focus. Moreover, the programs were of seven different kinds: social competence training; behavioral and classroom management techniques; therapy or counseling services; academic or educational services; peer mediation; separate schooling (i.e., separate classrooms with smaller teacher–pupil ratios); and multi-modal services (i.e., combining three or more prevention methods). The main results of that statistical analysis had first shown that there were significant, moderate effects for all programs taken together in lowering aggression; those receiving no programs demonstrated no change. Authors noted that effect size for the reduction in aggression within demonstration projects (i.e., those set up for experimental examination rather than those part of usual school routines), were large enough to yield an approximately 50% reduction if applied to Youth Risk Behavior Study (YRBS) rates for prevalence of physical fighting on school grounds! Although the programs in general held out considerable promise for reducing aggression and violence, it also became clear from the analysis that not all treatments yielded equal effects, nor did all groups of children benefit equally. Specifically, those children age 5 and under, and those 14 and older benefited more than participants at other ages. Primary prevention programs, in which children were not selected because of special risk factors (i.e., individual or environmental), benefited least from prevention programs; those who were already aggressive benefited most from prevention programs.

A finding of considerable importance for our current review of prevention programs pertained to which school-based programs yielded the greatest decrement in aggressive behavior. When implemented in special demonstration programs, those that emphasized behavioral and classroom management techniques, or therapy and counseling services yielded the greatest decrement in aggressive behavior. Behavioral and classroom management approaches were those that used rewards, token economies, and other behavioral methods to modify children's behavior. Those that provided therapy or counseling services were those offering group or individual counseling or case management. The third most effective prevention programs, only slightly less effective than classroom management or therapy and counseling services, were programs focused on social competence training. Social competence training refers to methods designed to teach children to understand and resolve interpersonal conflicts by using improved communication and conflict resolution skills, or programs using cognitive methods of controlling anger and resolve conflicts, for example, practice, relaxation, and self statements. Multi-modal and peer mediation programs produced the smallest effects on aggression. In sum, programs that focused on individual therapeutic needs, skills that built social competence, and those that improved classroom behavior, appeared most effective in reducing aggressive behaviors. One important qualification to these findings was that prevention programs that were part of the ongoing school programs were less effective. That suggested that when well-designed programs were applied to the school environment over a longer period of time, programs may suffer from decrements in fidelity, dosage, loss of training effects, or some other real-life influences that reduced the program's effectiveness (see also Hennrich, Brown, & Aber, 1999).

Primary Prevention Programs

Primary prevention programs have proliferated for many reasons. First, developmental psychologists have been aware for at least the last 60 years that young children show considerable individual differences in "readiness" for school on entry to kindergarten. Some children lacked emotional self-control and ability to follow teacher commands, aptitude and motivation for schoolwork, and social competence. Moreover, as a consequence of longitudinal research studies on the development of chronic aggression noted earlier (Chapter 2) some have suggested that prevention programs should address those individual differences at the earliest possible point in the trajectory toward violence in adolescence (Tremblay, 2006). A second reason for starting early was that young children as a group, due to many societal changes in the United States, have actually lost ground in terms of emotional intelligence (Goleman, 1995). Emotional intelligence refers to children's abilities to know what they feel and monitor changes in emotion, to regulate emotional states, to use emotions to motivate themselves, to recognize and respond to emotions in others (i.e., empathy), and to effectively use emotions in interactions with others. This has highlighted the necessity of schooling the emotions. Whether conceived of as helping many of those young children not quite ready for school, or of helping all children to compensate for ground lost over the past 40 years, the rationale for primary prevention is a potent one.

One important, model program for primary prevention has been Promoting Alternative Thinking Strategies (PATHS) (Greenberg & Kushe, 2006). The theoretical rationale for this program comes from many different disciplines focused on the needs of young children. More specifically, this program derives its conceptual rationale from the following five principles of cognitive, social, and emotional development of young children: (1) the child's ability to cope and self-regulate is dependent on their ability to gradually integrate unpleasant emotion with emotion language (i.e., labeling and communicating emotions), and with increased ability to take the role of others, plan ways to solve social problems (e.g., by generating alternative plans to solve disputes), and to consider the consequences of their actions; (2) the creation of real-life opportunities to use these abilities within "healthy, caring and responsive classrooms" (p. 399); (3) to enhance early brain development (i.e., cortex control) by practicing methods of self-control within nurturing teacher–child–peer interactions; (4) to promote the gradual internalization by the child of positive social values (e.g., good manners and their consequences); and by (5) developing children's abilities to "accurately process the emotional content of the situation and effectively regulate his or her emotional arousal so that he and she can think through the problem"(p. 400).

The PATHS program is a school-based intervention that entails teacher training in workshop format. Its child programs include twelve lessons that emphasize readiness skills and basic self-control, fifty-six lessons focused on teaching emotional and interpersonal understanding and emotional intelligence, and thirty-three lessons on interpersonal cognitive problem solving. Lessons typically take 20 to 30 minutes per day (for the Kindergarten through 5th grade version), three times per week, with homework assignments to promote generalization of skills. Curriculum methods include puppets, use of children's literature, pictures and classroom posters, and an allegorical story about a turtle who learns self-control when distressed. The program can be implemented over a 5-year period. The PATHS program has been recognized as a promising model for aggression prevention, lacking only evidence on sustainability (USDHHS, 2001; Henrich et al., 1999). Also, PATHS builds on the successes of earlier programs designed to teach interpersonal cognitive problem solving, yielding reductions in children's aggression (e.g., the Interpersonal Cognitive Problem Solving program of Shure, 2001). Research using the PATHS program with three different populations of children (i.e., deaf impaired, regular education, and special education) has demonstrated improvements in children's ability to recognize and understand emotions, improved social problem solving skills, improved self-control, improved ability to tolerate frustration, and reductions in aggressive and disruptive behaviors (Greenberg & Kusche, 2006; Greenberg, Kusche, Cook, & Quamma, 1995; Kam, Greenberg, & Kusche, 2004).

Another widely used and well-researched primary prevention program, but with a broader range of application from Kindergarten through 9th grades, is the Second Step Violence Prevention Curriculum (Fitzgerald & Edstrom, 2006; Frey, Hirschstein, & Guzzo, 2000). Second Step makes use of what is known about the development of children's prosocial skills and research concerning cognitive behavioral skills that contribute to prosocial behaviors. Trained teachers, in addition to school counselors and psychologists, conduct twenty-two to twenty-eight lessons for preschool and elementary school students in which social dilemmas are depicted. Lessons for elementary school students use video clips, puppets, and so on. Lessons for middle school/junior high school children emphasize group discussions, classroom activities, homework, and videos (Fitzgerald & Edstrom, 2006).

The three major focii of the Second Step prevention program are empathy, social problem solving, and anger management (Frey, Hirschstein, & Guzzo, 2000). Empathy development involves the recognition of physical, facial, verbal, and situational cues to six emotions, and practice focuses on role playing, communicating, and interpreting emotional expressions. The children's practice includes responses to stories, changes in feelings over time, different emotional responses to the same situation (i.e., by different children), and recognizing different perspectives. Social problem solving refers to the following: (1) identifying problems using story and context clues; (2) brainstorming possible solutions to a problem; and (3) evaluating solutions in terms of principles of safety, fairness, peoples' feelings, and effectiveness of the proposed solution. The anger management unit helps students to recognize anger cues in their bodies, use positive self statements and other stress-reduction techniques (e.g., counting backwards) in order to diminish less controlled angry behavior. Controlling anger involves identifying one's personal triggers, cues that arouse intense anger and then learning practiced strategies to inhibit responding. Practicing self-talk in order to cool down, reflect on, and evaluate responses are employed in response to many stressful situations, such as responding to criticism.

Second Step lessons require practice two times a week with teachers or counselors, and photo cards of common situations used to guide group discussion. For middle school students, Second Step shifts more to beliefs and attitudes about aggression and uses other audio-visual materials used to guide discussions. Teachers are trained to use the program, and instructional strategies include discussion, role play, and help in generalizing skills modeled by instructors. Techniques used to help children to remember the skills were those provided by teachers who used reminding, reinforcing, and who pointed out instances of the children's use of target skills. Frey and colleagues point out that schools making long-term commitments to implementation, and in which the school principals make long-term commitments, are important to the program's success. A family guide to Second Step is provided, including video models, which helps parents to understand and support program objectives.

Evaluations of Second Step have shown, for forty-nine classrooms of 2nd and 3rd grade students, that those receiving lessons two times per week, for 4 to 5 months, evidenced the following: (1) reductions in physical aggression, from autumn to spring, for experimental but not control groups; (2) reductions were greatest on the playground and lunchroom; (3) friendly comments and neutral interactions increased for experimental but not control students; (4) a 6-month follow-up showed significantly lower levels of physical aggression for experimental group children (Grossman et al., 1997). Unfortunately, teacher and parent ratings did not show evidence of short- or long-term gains by the experimental group children. The authors suggested that adults may not be fully aware of aggressive behaviors outside the classroom or with other children than their own students. Replication with 2nd through 5th graders also had shown that, 1 year after the program, students taking the Second Step program showed improvements in social competence, reduced physically aggressive behavior, and less supervision required by adults in order to help in child–child conflict situations (Frey, Nolen, Van Schoiack-Edstrom, & Hirschstein, 2005). Further replication of Second Step with 6th, 7th, and 8th grade students in the United States and Canada, over a 2-year period of time, has shown that those in the second year of the program benefited most (Van Schoiack-Edstrom, Frey, & Beland, 2002). Results for the middle school study showed that girls in the first year of the program became less accepting in their attitudes toward aggression, and perceived less difficulty in social interactions (e.g., fewer problems keeping anger under control, generating solutions to problems, saying "no" to friends). During the second year, students in the Second Step program showed less acceptance of physical aggression, derogation of others, and social exclusion. Unfortunately, the replication with middle school students did not include measures of actual physical aggression. The program for middle school students also differed from that presented to younger children. The middle school version included scripted lessons led by trained adults, and discussion of videotaped vignettes, newspaper events, or stories. Discussions for middle school students also were designed to promote perspective taking and possible strategies for dealing with those situations.

Bullying prevention programs have been widely disseminated, and estimates of bullying prevention program effectiveness has been widely debated over the past 30 years. One recent critical review of bullying prevention programs distinguished between programs designed to change the rules and consequences for bullying, that is, systemic changes, versus programs designed to build on problem solving approaches to bullying, that is, individual changes (Rigby, 2006). The review concluded that outcomes of bullying prevention programs had been variable, with reductions in bullying for younger rather than older participants, and "no single method of preventing or dealing with bullying has been shown to be consistently more effective than others" (Rigby, 2006, p. 333). This critique is particularly important since increases in bullying behavior among middle school students appears to be worldwide. However, current research has tried to remedy some of the shortcomings noted in earlier research.

The oldest of the bullying prevention programs, the Olweus Bullying Prevention Program, had recently shown evidence that altering the rules and consequences for middle school students in eighteen middle schools yielded significant decreases in bullying perpetration for both boys and girls, and large decrements in bullying victimization among boys (Limber et al., 2004). Limber (2006) had recently pointed out that the challenges of applying the Olweus program to U.S. students in their 2004 study led to specific modifications deemed important to the program's success. Specifically, the following changes were made in adapting the program: (1) the development of school-wide rather than classroom rules about bullying was particularly important to middle schools because students in the United States have many teachers; (2) 2-day, intensive training, of teachers and staff, with continued, on-site monthly consultation was offered; (3) adaptation of video and other materials for U.S. schools was important; and (4) community members were encouraged to partner with schools to address bullying problems (Linder, 2006). Recommendations were made for Olweus programs around the world to adapt programs to local school character.

The critiques of the two kinds of programs have led other researchers to create programs that address both systemic and individual change, with good initial results. Recent research into the Steps to Respect: A Bullying Prevention Program (Committee for Children, 2001), incorporated training of adults, changes in systemic policies, and changes in student prosocial beliefs and social-emotional learning into a program for children in grades 3 through 6. This research study involved a matched assignment to either a schoolwide bullying prevention program or a control condition; thirty-six classrooms for each of the two conditions (Frey et al., 2005). Training for all school staff included publicizing definitions of bullying, a model for responding to bullying reports, and teacher/staff coaching for students involved in bullying. Students received skills lessons on building positive peer relationships, emotion management, and in recognizing, refusing, and the reporting of bullying behavior. Being a responsible bystander was also part of the lessons. Children's literature also provided opportunities to examine bullying related themes. Finally, parents were informed by administrators about their school anti-bullying policies, and were given suggested activities at home to support school activities. Baseline and post-test observations showed that 77% of students were involved in bullying at one point or other; 61% bullied, 48% encouraged bullying, and 75% engaged in non-bullying aggression. In 1 year, this bullying prevention program resulted in changes in beliefs about bullying. First, intervention students were less accepting of bullying, felt more responsible to intervene with friends who bullied, and reported greater adult responsiveness to incidents. Second, intervention students reported less victimization at post-test. Most encouraging were results on the playground. Observations showed that intervention students who had bullied at pre-test declined in bullying at post-test, and that program students increased in agreeable and decreased in argumentative behaviors on the playground. Pre- to post-playground observations showed 25% fewer bullying behaviors.

There have been numerous reviews of the effectiveness of bullying programs instituted around the world, including those cited earlier, but no meta-analyses suggesting which age groups may be most amenable to intervention, or whether systemic or individual changes or a combination of both approaches may be most successful. Bullying takes particularly ugly forms in middle school, as children increase in size and strength. Since bullying has been found to be the third leading cause of injury among 11 through 15 year olds (Pickett et al., 2002), it is particularly important to discover which programs work for that age group.

Secondary Prevention

Those at greatest risk for aggression or violence at elementary school, middle school, or high school ages have been the main targets of secondary prevention efforts. A concern about children who are highly aggressive in elementary school, come from a neighborhood with high crime rates, or possess angry emotions that are difficult to manage, or are simply middle school boys, has underscored a need for more intensive prevention efforts for at-risk children. Programs may simply address the adolescent who needs some help with anger management. However, since risk factors are considered additive, and the joint presence of multiple risk factors elevates the risk for serious violence, researchers have developed programs with multiple components for both children and adolescents addressing each of the risk factors simultaneously.

A recent meta-analysis of forty-four secondary prevention programs conducted in school settings has suggested which kinds of programs have been most successful and for whom their impact was greatest (Mytton et al., 2002). The programs examined in that analysis incorporated random assignment to treatment and control conditions; secondary programs in general had moderate effects in reducing both aggressive behavior and reducing the school or agency responses (e.g., detention, court contact, suspension) in response to aggressive actions. Program effects were somewhat greater for middle and high school students than for elementary school students. Aggression, defined in various studies as teacher or parent ratings of aggression or bullying/fighting incidence, was reduced both by programs that taught anger control or conflict resolution (e.g., non-response), and by programs that taught relationship skills or modified the social context (e.g., peer mediation, changing family relationships). Programs that taught non-response had a moderate impact on lowering aggressive behavior whereas those that improved relationships had a large effect on lowering aggressive behavior. Most important, despite the participants being judged to be at risk, programs yielded about a one-third reduction in aggressive behavior.

Some secondary prevention programs have demonstrated effectiveness by simply adapting and enhancing successful primary prevention methods to those children with special needs. The PATHS program, noted earlier, has been adapted for minority kindergarten and first grade children who were from greater than average crime areas. More intensive efforts were directed at the 10% of children who had the highest parent and teacher ratings of aggression (CPPSG, 1999a; CPPSG, 1999b). This adaptation of the PATHS program was called Fast Track, and provided 80% of the PATHS curriculum to one half of the 1st grade classrooms, and assessed program classrooms to control classrooms after 1 year. Lessons were provided two to three times per week by trained teachers and focused on the following areas: (1) recognizing and labeling emotions; (2) friendship skills (i.e., participation, cooperation, fair play, and negotiations); (3) self-control skills; and (4) social problem solving. The results, after one year, showed that *classrooms* receiving the modified PATHS program, as compared with control classrooms, showed lower aggression scores and a more positive classroom atmosphere. Those classrooms who received a greater number of lessons showed lower levels of aggression than those receiving fewer lessons.

Children receiving the modified PATHS program, and who were at the top 10% in ratings of aggression, were provided seven additional services addressing their special needs. These intensive services were the following: (1) twenty-two sessions of social skills training, which provided training in friendship building, self-control, and social problem solving; (2) services to parents, including those which helped parents to obtain greater compliance from their children, improve parenting practices, and adjusted parenting practices to developmentally appropriate expectations of their children; (3) cooperative parent–child structured play sessions to promote improved parenting skills; (4) tutoring in reading (i.e., thirty-minute sessions); (5) home visitation by professionals to provide support for family problem solving and coping with stressful life events; (6) "peer-pairing" session with various partners to promote friendships; and (7) intensive, phonics-based reading tutoring three times per week. The year-end assessment showed important program effects on these children at risk. Academically, these children showed significant gains in reading skills and had less need for special education services. Program children showed greater emotion recognition, emotion coping, and social problem-solving skills. Classroom observation revealed fewer aggressive behaviors, more positive peer interactions, and more peer preferences among program children. Although program parents did not differ from control parents in use of coercive practices, program parents did show warmer, more positive involvement with their children and used more appropriate and consistent discipline practices. Although the impact of Fast Track with high-risk children was deemed to be in the moderate range, the program was a multi-year program and it was expected that multi-year prevention efforts would continue to build on early gains.

The most recent evaluation of the ongoing Fast Track program for high-risk children took place when the children were in 4th and 5th grades (CPPRG, 2004). Program children continued to receive academic tutoring, home visitation, peer-pairing sessions, and a mentoring program component was added (i.e., with same gender and same race individual). Program children, when contrasted with controls, were less likely to evidence violent delinquent behaviors (e.g., carrying a weapon, coercing or attacking others), and continued to show improved social competence (i.e., less hostile attribution bias, less likely to choose aggressive responses as coping strategy). However, program children's advantages in academic and school behavior problems were not maintained.

Another promising program that was both school and community based, and instituted over a 3-year period, focused efforts on predominantly African American boys from 5th through 8th grades in Chicago (Ngwe et al., 2004). The program was called the Aban Aya Youth Project. Key to this secondary prevention program was a social development curriculum, comprised of sixteen to twenty-one lessons per year, plus a school-community program. The school community program provided parent supports to achieving curriculum goals, promoted parent–child communication, and forged links between school, parents, and agencies in the community. Results showed that the program succeeded in reducing surveyed, self-reported use of a variety of violent behaviors (e.g., weapon carrying and use, cutting or stabbing someone, or shooting at someone) whereas controls increased their violent behaviors. Second, the program also achieved reductions in some of the mediators of violent behaviors. Specifically with regard to the program's impact on mediators of violence, participation in the program reduced positive attitudes toward violence, associations with friends who were violent or who encouraged violence toward others, and intentions to perpetrate violent behaviors. Interestingly, the program was deemed ineffective among those possessing the greatest violence-related mediators. Those who had violent friends, approved of violence, and had intentions to perpetrate violence were unresponsive to the program. Thus, programs may be effective in altering, in a positive direction, attitudes and associations conducive to violence, yet those who continue to hold fast to these inclinations may not be open to change by this secondary prevention program.

Secondary prevention programs also have focused on particular risk factors for violence. Anger Management Training (AMT) has focused both on this one personality risk factor for aggression, and on anger management as part of a more intensive program for at risk adolescents. Consistent with our earlier presentation of four components of anger (i.e., as instigated, with obsessive thinking, emotional arousal, and with greater likelihood of aggressive behavior; see Chapter 3), anger management training has been designed to help adolescents reduce the intensity and duration of angry emotion (Feindler, Marriott, & Iwata, 1984; Feindler & Scally, 1998). AMT was designed as a ten-session, small group format workshop with didactic and experiential components. Participants are taught to manage anger arousal, think differently about anger and provocation, and develop prosocial skills. Group leaders model more appropriate coping strategies. Participants rehearse modes of coping with provocation in everyday situations, and then members apply these lessons in homework assignments (Feindler & Weisner, 2006). Moreover, participants learn differences between healthy and unhealthy anger, ways to calm arousal levels, recognizing triggers to their own anger, change beliefs about aggression, learn assertive (vs. aggressive) responding, and generate multiple solutions to interpersonal disputes. Despite similarities to primary prevention strategies, it is important to note that the program is tailored to individual student needs and it is focused on generalization of skills to student lives. Research on Anger Management Training has demonstrated improvement in self-control and reductions in school records of aggressive behavior for high-risk middle school children (Feindler, Marriott, & Iwata, 1984), and reductions in physical aggression incidents for adolescents with emotional problems (Kellner & Bry, 1999).

The AMT module was later included with two other components in a program for at-risk adolescents called Aggression Replacement Training (ART) (Goldstein, Glick, & Gibbs, 1998). A second component focused on improvement in social skills, such as, non-aggressive responses to teasing, and coping with the stress of being excluded. The third component fostered improved moral reasoning using prepared scenarios, those such as being asked to violate their boss's rules at work to please a friend. The social skills and moral reasoning modules, as in the case of AMT, are taught in didactic and experiential format. Discussion, demonstrations, rehearsal, and homework are each tailored to the needs of the adolescents in the group. Research using the three components of ART has shown improved in-community functioning once institutionalized adolescents returned to the community (Glick & Goldstein, 1987), and reduced anger and aggressive behaviors, with improved social behaviors among correctional inmates (Rokach, 1987).

Counseling and psychotherapy approaches have been effective when used in outpatient and school settings by reducing the likelihood that adolescents will later become violent (Wilson et al., 2003; USDHHS, 2001). Cognitive behavioral methods have shown large effects in reducing aggression, according to a meta-analysis of twelve studies (Robinson, Smith, Miller, & Brownell, 1999). Cognitive behavior modification, as used in school-based studies, has increased self-control by "teaching students to use or modify covert self-statements to control behavior along with traditional behavioral approaches" (p. 197). Behavioral methods have included use of instructor modeling and positively reinforcing desired improvements. Such methods may fit well within self-contained special education classes, or they can be used with specially formed groups for at-risk adolescents. As with AMT or ART, the use of didactic and experiential methods fits well within a school setting, and can make good use of incidents occurring within the context of the school environment. Adolescents learning effective social skills for coping with provocation by peers, or with the frustration introduced by social and academic tasks, may not be all that is necessary to ensure greater emotional and behavioral self-control for those with more serious personal difficulties.

Counseling and psychotherapy, when used to resolve problems relating to aggression, but problems also linked to family issues, mood-related problems, and so on, may not easily fit within the confines of a school setting. School settings may not be able to provide the confidentiality, the considerable investment of professional time, or allow for the family participation that can be offered in private clinical settings. Earning the trust of an adolescent who is involved in a number of serious aggressive incidents may take considerable time and therapeutic skill; getting just the "tip of the iceberg" may not be sufficient information to fully help adolescents. Despite the psychotherapist looking carefully into multiple sources of information from juvenile services, parents, and teachers, psychotherapy may require enormous time and energy, and does not ensure that the young adolescent will be willing to entrust the adult with sensitive issues.

One particular approach to psychotherapy that is well researched, and is also consistent with the Cognitive Neo-Associationist theory of angry aggression noted earlier, is Emotion-Focused Therapy (EFT) (Greenberg, 2002). The use of EFT specifically with adolescents has not yet been fully explored. EFT recognizes three problems with anger: (1) not knowing one is angry; (2) recognizing but not being able to express anger (i.e., due to fear); and (3) "too much intensity . . . getting carried away into destructive blaming or attacking . . . being chronically angry and over-reactive" (Greenberg, 2002, p. 230). EFT is not focused on venting anger, but on providing the recipient with an emotion coach who will help the client with the following: (1) "to validate feelings and produce change in the meanings they show." (p. 235); (2) "to fully experience, express, and work through (. . . unresolved feeling of) . . . disappointment with parents" (p. 235); (3) to evaluate whether anger is a healthy, primary anger directed at loved ones who have done something wrong or frustrated them; (4) to talk about one's feelings with others rather than engage in outbursts or rage; (5) to express one's anger when justified, for example, to protect one's boundaries; (6) to cope with anger that is unhealthy, such as that which comes from a history or witnessing or having been victimized by violence, to cope with overwhelming emotion associated with rage and "contact other feelings, often fear or grief caused by an unsatisfied need to be loved" (p. 152); and (7) to recognize when anger is a secondary emotion and therefore anger "removes awareness of other feelings, such as fear or hurt, that can be more uncomfortable than anger . . . (or) masks the shame of loss of self-esteem or fear of a fragile self . . . or shame when they are rejected or humiliated" (p. 157). From the perspective of EFT, anger is not simply to be removed or lessened, but understood as covering up other feelings such as shame or humiliation. This approach, as contrasted with the cognitive behavioral perspective, represents a humanistic perspective on counseling and psychotherapy. EFT may be particularly useful to adolescents who have been both bullies and victims, those with a history of peer rejection or violence by peers, and those adolescents who have developed an exaggerated sense of injustice, and a need to avenge. Relief from these complex forms of anger and rage, as well as serious mood disorders, may require therapeutic intervention in clinical settings where the individual feels safe and confidentiality is assured.

One final approach to secondary prevention concerns alterations in the school environment itself so as to increase the likelihood of students' safety. The literature refers to this domain as safe school planning. Unfortunately, modifications made to schools as a result of school shootings have led to improvements in school security procedures or crisis plans which have demonstrated little or no evidence of effectiveness. A recent survey of school personnel in Colorado, following the Columbine shootings, showed that 65% had improved school security procedures and 20% had produced school crisis plans (Crepeau-Hobson, Filaccio, & Gottfried, 2005). Whereas the elements of school safety planning, those such as assessment of school safety needs, alterations of school planning and school procedures (e.g., minimizing school entrances, removing walls that block visual surveillance, creating an emergency plan) make good sense (Stephens, 1998), they do not have a body of research demonstrating their effectiveness in increasing student safety. Others have reasoned that since serious school violence is a rare event, embedded in ongoing social interactions rather than loner activities, and a dynamic and changing risk situation, safe school planning requires ongoing risk assessment rather than merely static assessment (Douglas & Skeem, 2005; Mulvey & Cauffman, 2001). Moreover, the risk of stigmatizing individuals, and excessive spending on police monitoring and metal detecting devices, may make schools much less like the institutions of learning they were designed to be (Mulvey & Cauffman, 2001). Instead, the placement of school resources into staying in contact with groups and individuals known to engage in conflict with others and monitoring the situations in which they do so may be more effective. Also, monitoring for changes in the daily interactions with fellow students, and putting more effort into creating a more positive school climate (e.g., by creating a sense of fairness of rules, promoting healthy and respectful behaviors between all school members) may ultimately be the best form of change in the school environment (Mulvey & Cauffman, 2001).

Tertiary Prevention

Working with violent adolescents is a daunting enterprise. At the risk of over-simplification, and of stereotyping, a prototypical violent 15-year-old adolescent may help to illuminate the task of tertiary prevention. This 15-year-old has had ten years in which to escalate aggressive behavior along the path toward serious violent behavior, including a history of violent acts leading up to the one for which he is now facing criminal justice penalties. He now has a set of charges against him for both minor and major criminally violent acts. He is about 3 years behind in school, is not controllable within his home or school setting, and trusts or pays little heed to authorities in either setting. He is about 230 pounds, used to physically fighting with others, practiced at coercing and intimidating peers, and has few of the latter in the mainstream who have not long ago distanced themselves from him. His friends are likely to be in trouble with the law and facing similar penalties. He roams where he wants, sometimes not coming home at night, and is unable to maintain part time employment because work requires discipline and sustained motivation. Tertiary prevention must, of necessity, address multiple problems, in multiple settings, and more so than either primary or secondary prevention, focus on the specific needs of each individual adolescent.

Multisystemic Therapy (MST) has repeatedly demonstrated effectiveness with violent juvenile offenders. MST has been shown to reduce the likelihood that chronic and violent juvenile offenders will be re-arrested for violent and serious crimes in a 4-year follow-up study (Borduin et al., 1995). This same group of 12 to 17 year olds, approximately half of whom had been convicted of at least one violent crime (e.g., sexual assault, aggravated assault, and average four felony arrests) when interviewed at follow-up over 13 years later, showed significantly fewer re-arrests for violent offenses and fewer number of violent offenses, when compared with those having received individual therapy (i.e., an eclectic set focused on support and feedback, insight, building close relationships, or behavioral approaches) (Schaeffer & Borduin, 2005).

The focus of MST is different than that of individual therapy, the latter focused on more general personal, family, and academic issues faced by the juvenile. In contrast, MST is focused on changing intrapersonal (e.g., cognitive) and multiple systemic (i.e., family, peer, and school) factors specifically associated with the adolescent's violent and non-violent criminal behavior. Moreover, MST is described as a home- and community-based model of service delivery in which therapists collaborate with parents to provide them with skills and resources to empower parents to resolve unique problems associated with their own child's problems (Schaeffer & Borduin, 2005). The role of the therapist in addressing the adolescent's difficulties and strengths in individual, family, and extra-familial domains is guided by nine principles (Henggler et al., 2002). For example, during approximately 4 months of treatment, and 15 hours of contact per therapist each week (including 24-hour on-call services), therapist, adolescent, and parents define problems objectively, work to identify links between the youth's problems and the systemic context, and design interventions to promote responsible behaviors and decrease irresponsible behaviors.

A case example of Jonathan, a 14-year-old Caucasian male may help to illustrate the main features of MST (Cunningham, 2006). Jonathan was brought to an emergency room by police after having chased his mother with a bat, threatening harm to himself, and having a history of threats of harm to teachers, peers, and self. Because of homicidal threats and suicidal threats a plan was initiated to ensure the safety of Jonathan, his family, classmates, and school personnel. The safety plan required the signature and assent of Jonathan, his mother, and his therapist. The safety plan included the following elements: provided for cognitive-behavioral methods to help Jonathan walk away from challenging situations; called for his mother to monitor his whereabouts every 2 hours; also his mother was to search him and his bedroom for weapons and relocate a handgun (with trigger lock and lockbox) to his aunt's house; his therapist was to notify police of any threats to kill his mother or another youth. The therapist and family members worked to identify system strengths and weaknesses. Systemic strengths were identified as the following: Jonathan sought out and responded well to adult attention (individual); Jonathan's mother was motivated to obtain helping services (family); neighborhood peers participated in prosocial activities (peer); a positive bond was present with a school guidance counselor (school); and there was a recreation center near the home (community). Identified system needs (or weaknesses) were the following: Jonathan's depression, mood lability, and irritability (individual); parent substance abuse (family); unknown peers who were verbally provocative (peer); there was no relationship or an adversarial relationship between the family and school (school); and Jonathan lived in a high crime neighborhood (community). Specific therapeutic actions taken, for example, specified who was going to do what and when they were going to do it (e.g., use of "time out" by family members during escalating conflict), and building better communication among participants and therapist.

Research has shown that MST is most effective when it enables families to function more effectively (i.e., improved family cohesion and monitoring of the adolescent), and when the family helps the youth disengage from delinquent peers (Huey et al., 2000). Moreover, therapists were more effective when they gained the trust of the family and the therapist successfully encouraged family members to work on problems every day.

Psychopharmacological approaches also have been tailored to the specific needs of the individual violent adolescent, and some general recommendations for effective medications have been found. However, the application of drugs to specific individuals, with specific disorders and symptoms, has not proved to be an easy task. Despite early enthusiasm regarding the use of pharmacological interventions about 20 years ago, a recent review of psychiatric treatments for aggressive youth (Connor et al., 2006) concluded that research did not carefully define the "type of aggression being treated (nor) define the aggression subtype frequency, and severity as primary outcome measures" (p. 815). Connor and colleagues noted that the aggression in adolescence may be mediated or moderated by "impulsivity, negative emotions such as hostility, irritability, fear and acute stress; and/or lack of empathy for the suffering of others" (p. 813). Consistent with earlier noted differences between reactive and proactive aggression in previous chapters, Connor and colleagues indicated that psychopharmacology appears more effective for reactive types of aggression. Moreover, they further recommended that psychiatrists administering medication treat the primary disorder first before adopting a target symptom approach. That is, medication can be targeted at the underlying psychiatric disorder, such as a bipolar disorder or major depression, before using the symptom-target approach regardless of the underlying disorder. Also, they recommended treating co-morbid conditions, such as ADHD (attention deficit hyperactivity disorder) or depression, which are known to be responsive to medication, and the medication may then reduce aggressive behaviors as well. Interestingly, they recommend that the target symptom approach should only be used after other psychological therapies, such as MST, skill-building, and parent management have failed.

Randomized, controlled trials have shown robust effects for treatment of aggression for second generation anti-psychotic medications such as risperidone for a variety of psychiatric diagnoses (e.g., conduct disorder, disruptive behavior symptoms, and mental retardation), according to Connor and colleagues. Second, lithium and devalproex sodium, classified as mood stabilizers, also have been effective in reducing aggression in adolescents. Since, as noted above, the literature has shown that maladaptive aggression is associated with ADHD, research on the use of stimulant medications has shown that methylphenidate, has been successfully used to reduce aggression in ADHD patients. The use of antidepressants in order to treat aggressive adolescents with major depressive disorder has not been supported in clinical trials. Finally, the use of clonidine in the case of ADHD co-morbid with conduct disorder and aggression, has shown some initial evidence of effectiveness in lowering aggression.

The realities and complexities of pharmacological treatment within a hospital setting, as noted in the case of a particular 15-year-old boy, can dispel any notion of "magic pills" representing a panacea for violence. "CJ," a 15-year-old boy, was admitted to a psychiatric hospital due to his expression of serious sexual and violent fantasies, a psychotic appearance to his outpatient therapist, and an expressed inability to keep from acting on these thoughts

(Villani & Sharfstein, 1999). He had been admitted to that hospital on three prior occasions due to fire setting, aggressive behaviors, and suicidal behaviors (including wrist cutting and attempts at hanging himself). CJ's behavior in the hospital included starting physical fights with peers. His initial diagnosis at admission was ADHD and a Depressive Disorder. The initial medication provided CJ was methylphenidate for ADHD with valproic acid for mood stabilization. Due to continued aggression and violent fantasies, CJ was then given respiridone, which was later discontinued due to extrapyramidal side effects. Despite the introduction of fluvoxamine to help dampen obsessive thought, provocative sexual comments and behavior continued. During the third week of hospitalization, both methylphenidate and fluvoxamine were discontinued because of their potential dis-inhibiting effects, and paroxetine treatment begun to address underlying depression. Valproic acid was stopped due to side effects, and CJ was switched from paroxetine to clomepramine. CJ was discharged to a residential treatment center after four months in the hospital, and showed mild improvement and fewer escalatory episodes requiring quiet room or locked door seclusion.

Villani and Sharfstein raised a number of sobering issues regarding the hospital treatment of CJ. First, they noted that "finding the optimal combination that minimizes aggressive thoughts and actions, yet permits and even facilitates learning, without significant side effects, can be a laborious process" (p. 462). They further added that hospital stays have been drastically reduced because managed care insurance provider protocols typically use criteria of medical necessity focusing primarily on acute symptoms. This reality of constraints imposed on treatment collides with the fact that medications often need to be added one at a time, with adequate trial periods of four to six weeks to determine their effectiveness. The authors noted that MST could not be accessed through the mental health system, and could only be obtained through the juvenile justice system. In sum, although psychopharmacological approaches have shown promise in clinical trials, medications require time to work in order to judge their effectiveness, and clearly not all medications work equally well with all patients. Some violent behavior requires more immediate response than medication can provide, even when the particular medication does indeed eventually prove effective.

Summary

There are many primary, secondary, and tertiary prevention programs that have met the rigorous scientific standards developed for violence prevention research. Primary prevention programs have the longest history of use, owing in part to observations of considerable difference in children's readiness for the social and academic demands of school entry. Successful programs for the broadest array of young students, focus on the following: (1) children's abilities to recognize and cope with or manage unpleasant emotions; (2) social problem-solving skills, those such as generating alternative solutions to conflict with others, taking the role of the other person, and evaluating the quality of chosen solutions; (3) increasing children's empathy skills; (4) increasing anger management by identifying personal triggers or cool down strategies; (5) changing school-wide knowledge about bullying and ways to deter bullying, and individual strategies for stopping or coping with peer bullying.

Successful secondary prevention programs, those for children or adolescents who are at risk, appear first to capitalize on important features of primary prevention programs that work. However, the instruction in anger management, replacement for aggressive behaviors, friendship development skills, and counseling or therapeutic approaches are more intensive. Workshop practice and homework assignments are common among secondary prevention programs. Most important, the focus on secondary prevention efforts is more directed, than primary prevention, at the needs of the individual child's or adolescent's needs or problems. Counseling and academic tutoring are important methods of prevention. Equal in importance to individualization of focus, is that of building nurturing, structured environments that support development across home, peer, school, and community systems, and provide adults with skills to effect this change. Finally, multi-year efforts appear to sustain the initial effects of the prevention program, although some initial advantages may be lost over time (as with Fast Track).

At the level of tertiary prevention programs, we find the greatest degree of individualization in order to reduce the likelihood of further violence. MST focuses on efforts toward promoting the safety of all, and assessment of multi-systemic strengths and weaknesses. Interventions are specifically designed to reduce the likelihood of a particular adolescent's violent behavior. Psychopharmacological interventions also target individual disorders and symptoms, with some success, and promote optimally safe environments when hospitalization is possible.

The recommendations of three scientific panels appeared to be nearly unanimous regarding their conclusions about program effectiveness. Prevention efforts were most likely to be effective if they started as early as possible, so as to avert a cascade of negative effects, and tend to build the skills of those who provide for children's needs in various settings. Also, addressing multiple deficits, such as in academic, cognitive, and social skill domains, and demonstrating pre- to post-changes in these skills, as well as changes in aggressive or violent behavior was important. NIH (2006) and USDHHS (2001) also note that ineffective programs not only fail to deliver the aforementioned improvements, but they permit counter-productive and violent practices by peers and supervisors in institutions (e.g., harsh and punitive practices, fear evoking, threats), that contaminate any hope for tertiary prevention benefits.

7

Closing Comments

The prevention programs reviewed in Chapter 6 have met rigorous scientific standards and have addressed many of the key distal and proximal correlates of aggressive and violent behavior in adolescence. A complete review of all meritorious prevention programs was well beyond the scope of this volume, specifically programs targeting children prior to age 5 and juvenile justice services. Yet identified programs clearly addressed individual, family, school, and community risk and protective factors.

Prevention Programs Addressing Key Risk and Protective Factors

Among the distal correlates of violence in adolescence addressed by secondary prevention programs were those directed at children who were highly aggressive and rejected by peers in elementary school. By early elementary school these children had begun on an escalatory path toward more serious outcomes. An ambitious, multi-year program, known as Fast Track, developed friendship building groups, skills training, and relationship enhancement interventions for parents and teachers, intensive academic enrichment services, and mentoring services for older elementary school children. Other secondary prevention programs have successfully addressed cognitive deficits and biases, children's antisocial and bullying behaviors prior to middle school by effectively altering individual, family, and school risk and protective factors.

Proximal risk and protective factors have been effectively modified for most, but not all key personality risk factors. All primary and secondary prevention programs reviewed had successfully increased anger management skills by children and adolescents and increased empathic mediation of aggressive behavior. Other programs had successfully reduced other mediators of aggressive and violent behavior, such as acceptance of aggression and intention to behave violently, leading to a reduction in serious violent behaviors at a later point in time. All of the primary prevention programs, through various and creative means, and largely relying on teachers as intervention agents, had improved children's social and social problem-solving skills. Subsequently, primary prevention programs reduced conflict with peers and increased positive social interactions within playground and school settings.

Risk Factors Not Addressed by Programs

Some proximal risk factors reviewed have not been addressed. There are some personality and most situational risk factors that have not been the target of prevention programs. Prevention programs for adolescents appear not to have successfully reduced a propensity for thrill and adventure seeking. The impulsivity component of sensation-seeking disposition had been partly addressed by the many anger management programs and components, and prevention programs typically promote better emotional control. However, there appears to be little mention in the research literature of methods of reducing, redirecting, or somehow building mediation mechanisms for thrill and adventure seeking that might reduce its impact on both aggressive and violent behavior. As research reviewed earlier had shown, sensation-seeking disposition may be a major well-spring for many adolescent risk-taking behaviors.

There are also many situational influences prompting or facilitating aggressive or violent behavior that have received very little emphasis in prevention research. Early exposure of children to violent imagery and hyper-stimulating experiences may increase receptivity and heighten aggressiveness in response to later violent imagery when presented in videogames, movies, and TV programs targeted at adolescent audiences. It remains unclear whether it is possible to reduce access to violent imagery or build mediational buffers for violent imagery. It might be possible to simply reduce trait anger or reduce attitudinal acceptance of violence, thereby building protective mechanisms. It might also be possible to enhance moderators of violent imagery by illuminating its consequences or punishing outcomes. However, it is also unclear whether there is any serious and credible movement toward reducing the endless flow of novel violent imagery to which children and adolescents are exposed; the marketplace appears to be the determining factor of exposure at this point in time. The second important situational influence, for which we have found few ways to reduce risk or enhance protective factors specifically for adolescents, is alcohol use by younger adolescents. Early adolescence is a point of greatest vulnerability to alcohol and its behavioral effects. Efforts to reduce access to alcohol by minors, or to alter the mediators, motivators, or moderators of alcohol use, have not met with success at this time.

School and Community Adoption of Prevention Programs

Primary prevention programs should be built into the ongoing education of children, and secondary and tertiary prevention programs should be available to communities struggling with high rates of aggressive and violent behavior. Objections to ongoing primary prevention programs, because they may distract from the main academic mission of schooling, are countered by an analysis of over 300 such programs. Those students enrolled in social and emotional learning programs also have earned achievement test scores 10 percentile points higher than those not enrolled (Weissberg, 2005). Primary prevention programs typically cost little per student and returns in terms of later behavioral improvement suggest they are the most cost-beneficial types of programs (USDHHS, 2001). Whereas teachers and parents may initially be resistant to the imposition on their time of primary prevention programs, they usually develop greater enthusiasm when children become less dependent on them for assistance, resolve more of their peer conflicts independently, and display less "off-task" behavior. Younger children may be more motivated to earn the respect and praise of peers and adults, more so than the violent 15-year-old who has fallen seriously behind academically and is much less open to any aspect of the school enterprise. Early prevention appears to be effective as well as popular with a myriad of program users and developers.

Primary prevention programs, with their broad messages for all children, may not be important for the youngest children alone; re-tooling with similar messages also may be useful for middle school and high school students. Messages such as showing respect for oneself, for one's peers, and for adults and other authorities, finding solutions to interpersonal conflicts that are acceptable to all parties, and learning how to assert one's rights without becoming aggressive, are also prescriptions needed by adolescents. Whereas in the 1940s and 1950s in the United States, there may have been a clearer, top-down hierarchical power structure in homes and schools, and the problems noted by teachers were those such as running in the halls, talking out of turn, and gum chewing, today's problems are different (*U.S. News and World Report*, November 8, 1993). Today, problems are more likely to be weapon carrying and fighting on school grounds, which are more serious and which require greater emphasis on prevention. Age-appropriate messages of respect and successful conflict resolution strategies can surely be packaged for adolescents in the same way consumer messages are sold in the marketplace. The messages are clearly important at all ages.

Secondary prevention efforts may be needed by communities for many reasons, and can supplement ongoing primary prevention programs. At-risk communities overwhelmed by violence among their middle and high school students, those in which there may be a greater proportion of children who may not have learned well in elementary school, and who have a greater proportion of parents who are struggling for everyday survival, may need programs that help children at risk. A society dependent on a highly educated and well socialized populace pays a large price when these students slip through the system without needed skills. Programs such as Fast Track, as one example, need to be enhanced by longer term follow-up and study, and then distributed more broadly within the country to help ensure meaningful integration of individuals into the society.

Perhaps no subject has as sharply divided the citizens of the United States as has how to deal with adolescents who have become violent. The issues swirling around this debate extend far beyond what can be addressed here. At the risk of over-simplification, the choice comes down to approaches that focus primarily on punishing adolescents and protection of the public (i.e., by taking them out of circulation), and treatment which also includes protection of the public. The punishment perspective, no doubt fueled by intense public rage directed at the audacious adolescent violent offender, has led to the adoption of boot camp programs with military style treatment, and programs designed to "scare" the adolescent into compliance with the law. Neither approach has successfully reduced further violent behaviors or recidivism among youth. Newspapers have consistently presented stories about "get tough" programs yielding injury and death among adolescent inmates; the latest being the death in Florida of a 14-year-old boot camp participant in which seven adults were charged. There should be no illusions about the difficulty of controlling adolescents who are violent, who have a callous disregard for others, and have developed a well-practiced set of coercive behaviors; they are also survivors. They have weathered experiences such as gang fighting and growing up in a toxic neighborhood. Given the presence of many of the personal risk factors noted in earlier chapters, they may regard with pride their survival skills under pressure. I counseled a 13-year-old who stated, after being frightened to tears by a judge who left him in a jail cell by himself, between neighboring cells occupied by adult detainees, that he would never again violate the law. Within a few days after release he had been re-arrested for breaking in and entering another house. He had concluded that he had, by virtue of the judge's punishment, survived all the system could "throw at him," and felt more antisocially empowered, invulnerable, and omnipotent than before his brief stint in jail. This reaction was certainly not the interpretation the judge wanted.

The alternative to a facility devoted to facilities designed to coerce and punish, is one in which treatment is the primary focus. Programs such as Multisystemic Therapy (MST), which treats the adolescent who remains in the home and community, or Aggression Replacement Training, provided within an institutional setting, have successfully reduced recidivism and future arrests for violence and promoted improved adjustment in the community. The cost for an average four-month MST treatment is $8,000, much less than the tens of thousands of dollars required to fund a year in a youth detention facility. Society's willingness to provide successful services may earn it the respect of other nations for attempting to resolve one of its most difficult problems: violence and aggression in adolescence.

References

Achenbach, T. M., & Edlebrock, C. S. (1987). *Manual for the Youth Self-Report and Profile*. Burlington, VT: University of Vermont.

Add Health (2006). Wave I. Full data set. National Longitudinal Study of Adolescent Health. Unpublished raw data. Chapel Hill, NC: Carolina Population Center.

American Psychiatric Association (2000). *DSM IV-TR*. Washington, DC: American Psychiatric Association.

American Psychological Association (1993). *Violence & Youth: Summary Report of the American Psychological Association Commission on Violence and Youth, Volume 1*. Washington, DC: American Psychological Association.

Anderson, C. A., & Bushman, B. J., (1997). External validity of "trivial" experiments: The case of laboratory aggression. *Review of General Psychology*, 1, 19–41.

Anderson, C. A., & Bushman, B. J. (2002). Human Aggression. *Annual Review of Psychology*, 53, 27–51.

Anderson, C. A., Bushman, B., & Groom, R. (1997). Hot years and serious and deadly assault: Empirical tests of the heat hypothesis. *Journal of Personality and Social Psychology*, 73, 1213–1223.

Anderson, C. A., & Dill, K. E. (2000). Video games and aggressive thoughts, feelings, and behavior in the laboratory and real life. *Journal of Personality and Social Psychology*, 78, 772–790.

Ang, R., & Woo, A. (2003). Influence of sensation seeking on boys' psychosocial adjustment. *North American Journal of Psychology*, 5, 121–137.

Angold, A., Costello, E., Messer, S., Pickles, A., Winder, F., & Silver, D. (1995). Development of a short questionnaire for use in epidemiological studies of depression in children and adolescents. *International Journal of Methods in Psychiatric Research*, 5, 251–262.

Archer, J. (2000). Sex differences in aggression between heterosexual partners: A meta-analytic review. *Psychological Bulletin*, 126, 651–680.

Archer, J. (2004). Sex differences in aggression in real-world settings: A meta-analytic review. *Review of General Psychology*, 8, 291–322.

Archer, J. (2006). Testosterone and human aggression: An evaluation of the challenge hypothesis. *Neuroscience & Biobehavioral Reviews*, 30, 319–345.

Archer, J. & Browne, K. (1989). Concepts and approaches to the study of aggression. In J. Archer & K. Browne (Eds). *Human Aggression: Naturalistic Approaches* (pp. 3–29). London: Routledge.

Arnett, J. (1999). Adolescent storm and stress, reconsidered. *American Psychologist*, 54, 317–326.

Arriaga, X., & Foshee, V. (2004). Adolescent dating violence: Do adolescents follow in their friends', or their parent's, footsteps? *Journal of Interpersonal Violence*, 19, 162–184.

Bachman, R., & Peralta, R. (2002). The relationship between drinking and violence in an adolescent population: does gender matter? *Deviant Behavior: An Interdisciplinary Journal*, 23, 1–19.

Baldwin, M. (1992). Relational schema and the processing of social information. *Psychological Bulletin*, 112, 461–484.

Baron, R., & Kenny, D. (1986). The moderator-mediator variable distinction in social psychological research: Conceptual, strategic, and statistical considerations. *Journal of Personality and Social Psychology*, 51, 1173–1182.

Berkowitz, L. (1993). *Aggression: Its causes, consequences, and control*. New York: McGraw-Hill.

Berkowitz, L., & Harmon-Jones, E. (2004). Toward an understanding of the determinants of anger. *Emotion*, 4, 107–130.

Beyers, J., & Loeber, R. (2003). Untangling developmental relations between depressed mood and delinquency in male adolescents. *Journal of Abnormal Child Psychology*, 31, 247–266.

Bierman, K., & Wargo, J. (1995). Predicting the longitudinal course associated with aggressive-rejected, aggressive (nonrejected), and rejected (nonaggressive) status. *Developmental Psychology*, 7, 669–682.

Bjorkqvist, K., Osterman, K., & Kaukiainen, A. (2000). Social intelligence-empathy aggression? *Aggression and Violent Behavior*, 5(2), 191–200.

Bogg, T., & Roberts, B. (2004). Conscientiousness and health-related behaviors: A meta-analysis of the leading behavioral contributors to mortality. *Psychological Bulletin*, 130, 887–919.

Borduin, C. M., Mann, B. J., Cone, L. T., Henggeler, S. W., Fucci, B. R., Blaske, D. M., & Williams, R. A. (1995). Multisystemic treatment of serious juvenile offenders: Long-term prevention of criminality and violence. *Journal of Consulting and Clinical Psychology* 63, 569–578.

Boulton, M. J. (1991). A comparison of structural and contextual features of middle school children's playful and aggressive fighting. *Ethology and Sociobiology*, 12, 119–145.

Brener, N. D., Billy, J. O., & Grady, W. R. (2003). Assessment of factors affecting the validity of self-reported health-risk behavior among adolescents. *Journal of Adolescent Health*, 33, 436–457.

Brener, N. D., Grunbaum, J., Kann, L., McManus, M., & Ross, J. (2004). Assessing health risk behaviors among adolescents: The effect of question wording and appeals for honesty. *Journal of Adolescent Health*, 35, 91–100.

Brener, N., Kann, L., McManus, T., Kinchen, S. A., Sundberg, E. L., & Ross, J. G. (2002). Reliability of the 1999 youth risk behavior survey questionnaire. *Journal of Adolescent Health*, 31, 336–342.

Brener, N., Lowry, R., Barrios, L., Simon, T., & Eaton, D. (2004). Violence-related behaviors among high school students-United States, 1991–2003. *JAMA*, 292, 1168–1169.

Brener, N., Lowry, R., Barrios, L., Simon, T., & Eaton, D. (2005). Violence-related behaviors among high school students-United States, 1991–2003. *Journal of School Health*, 75, 81–93.

Brener, N. D., Simon, R. R., Krug, E. G., & Lowry, R. (1999). Recent trends in violence-related behaviors among high school students in the United States. *JAMA*, 282, 440–446.

Brezina, T., Piquero, A., & Mazerolle, P. (2001). Student anger and aggressive behavior in school: An initial test of Agnew's macro-level strain theory. *Journal of Research in Crime and Delinquency*, 38, 362–386.

Broidy, L., Nagin, D., Tremblay, R., Bates, J., Brame, B., Dodge, K., Fergusson, D., Horwood, J., Loeber, R., Laird, R., Lynam, D., Moffitt, T., Pettit, G., & Vitaro, F. (2003). Developmental trajectories of childhood disruptive disorders and adolescent delinquency: A six-site, cross-national study. *Developmental Psychology*, 39, 222–245.

Broidy, L., Cauffman, E., Espelage, D., Mazerolle, P., & Piquero, A. (2003). Sex differences in empathy and its relation to juvenile offending. *Violence and Victims*, 18, 503–516.

Bryant, D. (1982). An index of empathy for children and adolescents. *Child Development*, 53, 413–425.

Buchanan, C. M., Eccles, J. S., & Becker, J. B. (1992). Are adolescents the victims of raging hormones? Evidence for activational effects of hormones on moods and behavior at adolescence. *Psychological Bulletin*, 111, 62–107.

Bureau of Justice Statistics, United States Department of Justice. (2000). National Crime Victimization Survey, 1992–1998 [Electronic data set] Ann Arbor, MI: The Inter-University Consortium for Political and Social Research (ICPSR), Producer and Distributor.

Bushman, B., & Anderson, C. (2001). Media violence and the American public: Scientific facts versus media misinformation. *American Psychologist*, 56, 477–489.

Buss, A. J., & Perry, M. (1992). The aggression questionnaire. *Journal of Personality and Social Psychology*, 63, 452–459.

Butcher, J. N., Graham, J. R., Williams, C., & Kammer, B. (1992). *Minnesota Multiphasic Personality Inventory-Adolescent*, Minneapolis, MN: University of Minnesota.

Byrnes, J., Miller, D., & Schafer, W. (1999). Gender differences in risk taking: A meta-analysis. *Psychological Bulletin*, 125, 367–383.

Cano, A., Avery-Leaf, S., Cascardi, M., & O'Leary, K. (1998). Dating violence in two high school samples: Discriminating variables. *Journal of Primary Prevention*, 18, 431–446.

Capaldi, D., & Gorman-Smith, D. (2003). The development of aggression in young male/female couples. In P. Florsheim (Ed). *Adolescent romantic relations and sexual behavior: Theory, research, and practical implications* (pp. 243–278). Mahwah, NJ: Erlbaum.

Capaldi, D., Shortt, J., & Crosby, L. (2003). Physical and psychological aggression in at-risk young couples: Stability and change in young adulthood. *Merrill-Palmer Quarterly*, 49, 1–27.

Carver, K., Joyner, K., & Udry, J. (2003). National estimates of adolescent romantic relationships. In P. Florsheim (Ed). *Adolescent romantic relations and sexual behavior: Theory, research, and practical implications* (pp. 23–56). Mahwah, NJ: Erlbaum.

Cascardi, M., Avery-Leaf, S., O'Leary, K. D., & Smith-Slep, A. (1999). Factor structure and convergent validity of the conflict tactics scale in high school students. *Psychological Assessment*, 11, 546–555.

Caspi, A., Begg, D., Dickson, N., Harrington, H., Langley, J., Moffitt, T., & Silva, P. (1997). Personality differences predict health-risk behaviors in young adulthood: Evidence from a longitudinal study. *Journal of Personality and Social Psychology*, 73, 1052–1063.

Centers for Disease Control and Prevention. (2006). *Youth risk behavioral surveillance-United States-2005*. Washington, DC: U. S. Department of Health and Human Services.

Centerwall, B. (1993). Television and violent crime. *Public Interest*, 111, 56–71.

Chase, K., Treboux, D., O'Leary, K., & Strassberg, Z. (1998). Specificity of dating aggression and its justification among high-risk adolescents. *Journal of Abnormal Child Psychology*, 26, 467–473.

Chermack, S., & Giancola, P. (1997). The relation between alcohol and aggression: An integrated biopsychosocial conceptualization. *Clinical Psychology Review*, 17, 621 649.

Chlopan, B., McCain, M., Carbonell, J., & Hagen, R. (1985). Empathy: Review of available measures. *Journal of Personality and Social Psychology*, 48, 635–653.

Clark, L. (2005). Temperament as a unifying basis for personality and psychopathology. *Journal of Abnormal Psychology*, 114, 505–521.

Cofer, C., & Appley, M. (1964). *Motivation: Theory and research*. NY: Wiley.

Coggeshall, M. B., & Kingery, P. M. (2001). Cross-survey analysis of school violence and disorder. *Psychology in the Schools*, 38, 107–116.

Cohen, D., & Strayer, J. (1996). Empathy in conduct-disordered and comparison youth. *Developmental Psychology*, 32, 988–998.

Coie, J. D., & Dodge, K. A. (1998). Aggression and antisocial behavior. In W. Damon & N. Eisenberg (Eds.) *Handbook of Child Psychology, Volume 3: Social, Emotional and Personality Development* (pp. 779–862). New York: Wiley.

Cole, D., & Martin, N. The longitudinal structure of the Children's Depression Inventory: Testing a latent trait-state model. *Psychological Assessment*, 17, 144–155.

Cole, D., Tram, J., Martin, J., Hoffman, K., Ruiz, M., Jacquez, F., & Maschman, T. (2002). Individual differences in the emergency of depressive symptoms in children and adolescents: A longitudinal investigation of parent and child reports. *Journal of Abnormal Psychology*, 111, 156–165.

Collins, W. (2003). More than myth: The developmental significance of romantic relationships during adolescence. *Journal of Research on Adolescence*, 13, 1–24.

Collins, W., & Laursen, B. (2004). Changing relationships, changing youth: Interpersonal contexts of adolescent development. *Journal of Early Adolescence*, 24, 55–62.

Colman, A. (2001). *A dictionary of psychology*. Oxford, UK: Oxford University Press.

Conduct Problems Prevention Research Group. (1999). Initial impact of the Fast Track prevention trial for conduct problems. I. The high-risk sample. *Journal of Consulting and Clinical Psychology*, 67, 631–647.

Conduct Problems Prevention Research Group. (1999). Initial impact of the Fast Track prevention trial for conduct problems: II. Classroom effects. *Journal of Consulting and Clinical Psychology*, 67, 648–657.

Conduct Problems Prevention Research Group. (2004). The effects of the Fast Track program on serious problem outcomes at the end of elementary school. *Journal of Clinical Child and Adolescent Psychiatry*, 31, 650–661.

Connolly, J., Craig, W., Goldberg, A., & Pepler, D. (2004). Mixed-gender groups, dating, and romantic relationships in early adolescence. *Journal of Research on Adolescence*, 14, 185–207.

Connolly, J., Pepler, D., Craig, W., & Taradash, A. (2000). Dating experiences and romantic relationships of bullies in early adolescence. *Child Maltreatment*, 5, 299–310.

Connor, D., Carlson, G., Chang, K., & Daniolos, P. and eleven members of the Stanford/Howard/American Academy of Child and Adolescent Psychiatry Workgroup on Juvenile Impulsivity and Aggression. (2006). Juvenile maladaptive aggression: A review of prevention, treatment, and service configuration and a proposed research agenda. *Journal of Clinical Psychiatry*, 67, 808–820.

Cook, P., Lawrence, B., Ludwig, J., & Miller, T. (1999). The medical costs of gunshot wounds. *Journal of the American Medical Association*, 282, 447–454.

Cooper, M., Wood, P., Orcutt, H., & Albino, A. (2003). Personality and the predisposition to engage in risk or problem behaviors during adolescence. *Journal of Personality and Social Psychology*, 84, 390–410.

Cornell, D., Peterson, C., & Richards, H. (1999). Anger as a predictor of aggression among incarcerated adolescents. *Journal of Consulting and Clinical Psychology*, 67, 108–115.

Cota-Robles, S., Neiss, M., & Rowe, D. (2002). The role of puberty in violent and nonviolent delinquency among Anglo American, Mexican American, and African American boys. *Journal of Adolescent Research*, 17, 364–376.

Crepeau-Hobson, M., Filaccio, M., & Gottfried, L. (2005). Violence prevention after Columbine: A survey of high school mental health professionals. *Children & Schools*, 27, 157–165.

Cunningham, P. (2006). Multisystemic therapy approach to treating potentially violent youth. Presented at the Convention of the American Psychological Association, New Orleans, August 12.

Cunningham, P., Henggeler, S., Limber, S., Melton, G., & Nation, M. (2000). Pattern and correlates of gun ownership among nonmetropolitan and rural middle school students. *Journal of Clinical Child Psychology*, 29, 432–442.

Davis, M. (1980). A multidimensional approach to individual differences in empathy. JSAS Catalogue of Selected Documents in Psychology, 10, 85.

Davis, M., & Franzoi, S. (1991). Stability and change in adolescent self-consciousness and empathy. *Journal of Research in Personality*, 25, 70–87.

Dawkins, M. (1997). Drug use and violent crime among adolescents. *Adolescence*, 32, 395–406.

del Barrio, V., Aluja, A., & Garcia, L. (2004). Relationship between empathy and the Big Five personality traits in a sample of Spanish adolescents. *Social Behavior and Personality*, 32, 677–682.

del Barrio, V., Aluja, A., & Spielberger, C. (2004). Anger assessment with the STAXI-CA: Psychometric properties of a new instrument for children and adolescents. *Personality and Individual Differences*, 37, 227–244.

de Castro, B., Merk, W., Koops, W., Veerman, J., & Bosch, J. (2005). Emotions in social information processing and their relations with reactive and proactive aggression in referred aggressive boys. *Journal of Clinical Child and Adolescent Psychology*, 34, 105–116.

De Los Reyes, A., & Prinstein, M. (2004). Applying depression-distortion hypotheses to the assessment of peer victimization in adolescents. *Journal of Clinical Child and Adolescent Psychology*, 33, 325–335.

Denham, S., & Almeida, M. (1987). Children's social problem-solving skills, behavioral adjustment and interventions: A meta-analysis evaluating theory and practice. *Journal of Applied Developmental Psychology*, 8, 391–409.

Derzon, J. (2001). Antisocial behavior and the prediction of violence: A meta-analysis. *Psychology in the Schools*, 38, 93–106.

DiLiberto, L., Katz, R., Beauchamp, L., & Howells, G. (2002). Using articulated thoughts in simulated situations to assess cognitive activity in aggressive and non-aggressive adolescents. *Journal of Child and Family Studies*, 11, 179–189.

Ding, C., Nelsen, E., & Lassonde, C. (2002). Correlates of gun involvement and aggressiveness among adolescents. *Youth & Society*, 34, 195–213.

Dodge, K. (2006). Professionalizing the practice of public policy in the prevention of violence. *Journal of Abnormal Child Psychology*, 34, 475–479.

Dodge, K. A., Bates, J., & Pettit, G. (1990). Mechanisms in the cycle of violence. *Science*, 250, 1678–1683.

Dodge, K. A., & Coie, J. D. (1987). Social and information processing factors in reactive and proactive aggression in children's peer groups. *Journal of Personality and Social Psychology*, 53, 1146–1158.

Dodge, K. A., Coie, J. D., & Lynam, D. (2006). Aggression and antisocial behavior in youth. In N. Eisenberg (Ed.) *Handbook of Child Psychology, Volume 6: Social, Emotional, and Personality Development* (pp. 719–788). NY: Wiley.

Dodge, K. A., Price, J., Bachorowski, J., & Newman, J. (1990). Hostile attribution biases in severely aggressive adolescents. *Journal of Abnormal Psychology*, 99, 385–392.

Dolan, M., & Rennie, C. (2006). Reliability and validity of the psychopathy checklist: Youth version in a UK sample of conduct disordered boys. *Personality and Individual Differences*, 40, 65–75.

Douglas, K. S., & Skeem, J. (2005). Violence risk assessment: Getting specific about being dynamic. *Psychology, Public Policy, and Law*, 11, 347–383.

Downey, G., Bonica, C., & Rincon, C. (1999). Rejection sensitivity and adolescent romantic relationships. In W. Furman, B. Brown, & C. Feiring (Eds.). *The development of romantic relationships in adolescence* (pp. 148–174). New York: Cambridge University Press.

Duan, C., & Hill, C. (1996). The current state of empathy research. *Journal of Counseling Psychology*, 43, 261–274.

Eisenberg, N. (2005). The development of empathy-related responding. In C. Gustavo, C. & C. Edwards (Eds). *Moral motivation through the life span*, Vol. 51 of the *Nebraska Symposium on Motivation* (pp. 73–117). Lincoln: University of Nebraska Press.

Eisenberg, N., Cumberland, A., Guthrie, I., Murphy, B., & Shepard, S. (2005). Age changes in prosocial responding and moral reasoning in adolescence and early adulthood. *Journal of Research on Adolescence*, 15, 235–260.

Eisenberg, N., Spinrod, T., & Sadofsky, A. (2006). Empathy-related responding in children. In M. Killen & J Smetana (Eds.) *Handbook of moral development* (pp. 517–549). Mahwah, NJ: Erlbaum.

Eklund, J., & Klinteberg, B. (2005). Personality characteristics as risk indications of alcohol use and violent behavior in male and female adolescents. *Journal of Individual Differences*, 26, 63–73.

Elliott, D. S. (1994). Serious violent offenses: Onset, developmental course, and termination – The American Society of Criminology 1993 Presidential Address. *Criminology*, 32, 1–21.

Elliott, D. S., Huizinga, D., & Morse, B. J. (1986). Self-reported violent offending: A descriptive analysis of juvenile violent offenders and their offending careers. *Journal of Interpersonal Violence*, 1, 472–514.

Elliott, D., & Tolan, P. (1999). Youth violence prevention, intervention, and social policy. In Flannery, D. & Huff, C. (Eds.). *Youth violence: Prevention, intervention and social policy*. Washington, DC: American Psychiatric Press, 3–46.

Eron, L., Lefkowitz, M., Walder, L., & Huesmann, L. (1974). Relation of learning in childhood to psychopathology and aggression in young adulthood. In A. Davis (Ed.). *Child Personality and Psychopathology*. New York: Wiley, 53–88.

Eslea, M., & Rees, J. (2001). At what age are children most likely to be bullied at school? *Aggressive Behavior*, 27, 419–429.

Espelage, D., Holt, M., & Henke, R. (2003). Examination of peer-group contextual effects on aggression during adolescence. *Child Development*, 74, 205–220.

Espelage, D., Mebane, S., & Adams, R. (2004). Empathy, caring, and bullying: Toward an understanding of complex associations. In D. Espelage, & S. Swearer, S. (Eds.) *Bullying in American schools: A social-ecological perspective on prevention and intervention* (pp. 37–61). Mahwah, NJ: Erlbaum.

Fagan, J., & Wilkinson, D. (1998). Guns, youth violence, and social identity in inner cities. In M. Tonry & M. Moore (Eds.). *Youth violence: Crime and Justice, Volume 24 (Crime and Justice: A review of research, pp. 373–456)*. University of Chicago Press Journals.

Fairman, C., & Winter, J. (1973). Gonadotropins and sex hormone patterns in puberty: Clinical data. In M. Grumbach, C. D. Grave, & F. Mayer (Eds.), *Control of the onset of puberty* (pp. 32–61). New York: John Wiley.

Farrington, D. P. (1991). Childhood aggression and adult violence: Early precursors and life outcomes. In D. J. Pepler & K. H. Rubin (Eds.). *The development and treatment of childhood aggression* (pp. 5–93). Hillsdale, NJ: Erlbaum.

Federal Bureau of Investigation. (1992). Juveniles and violence. Crime in the United States – 1991. *Uniform Crime Reports*. Washington, DC: Government Printing Office.

Federal Bureau of Investigation. (2006). FBI Supplemental Reports, National Archive of Criminal Justice Data, Online Data Analysis System, http://www.ICPSR.UMICH.EDU/CGI-BIN/SDA.

Federal Bureau of Investigation. (2003). Age-specific arrest rates and race specific arrest rates for selected offenses, 1993–2001, U.S. Department of Justice.

Feindler, E., Marriott, S., & Iwata, M. (1984). Group anger control training for junior high school delinquents. *Cognitive Therapy and Research*, 8, 299–311.

Feindler, E., & Wiesner, S. (2006). Young anger management treatments for school violence prevention. In S. Jimerson & M. Furlong (Eds.), *Handbook of school violence and school safety: From research to practice* (pp. 353–363). Mahwah, NJ: Erlbaum.

Feiring, C., Deblinger, E., Hoch-Espada, A., & Haworth, T. (2002). Romantic relationship aggression and attitudes in high school students: The role of gender, grade, and attachment and emotional styles. *Journal of Youth and Adolescence*, 31, 373–385.

Feldman, L. (1995). Valence focus and arousal focus: Individual differences in the structure of affective experiences. *Journal of Personality and Social Psychology*, 69, 153–166.

Feldman, S., & Gowen, L. (1998). Conflict negotiation tactics in romantic relationships in high school students. *Journal of Youth and Adolescence*, 27, 691–717.

Felson, R. B. (2002). *Violence and gender: Reexamined*. Washington, DC: American Psychological Association.

Feshbach, N. D., & Feshbach, S. (1982). Empathy training and the regulation of aggression: Potentialities and limitations. *Academic Psychology Bulletin*, 4, 399–413.

Fitzgerald, P., & Edstrom, L. (2006). Second Step: A violence prevention curriculum. In S. Jimerson & M. Furlong, (Eds.) *Handbook of school violence and school safety: From research to practice* (pp. 383–394). Mahwah, NJ: Erlbaum.

Flannery, D., Singer, M., & Wester, K. (2001). Violence exposure, psychological trauma, and suicide risk in a community sample of dangerously violent adolescents. *Journal of the American Academy of Child & Adolescent Psychiatry*, 40, 435–442.

Foshee, V. (1996). Gender differences in adolescent dating abuse prevalence, type, & injuries. *Health Education Research*, 11, 275–286.

Frederickson, B. (2002). Positive emotions. In C. Snyder & S. Lopez (Eds.). *Handbook of positive psychology* (pp. 120–133), New York: Oxford University Press.

Frey, K., Hirschstein, M., & Guzzo, B. (2000). Second step: Preventing aggression by promoting social competence. *Journal of Emotional and Behavioral Disorders*, 8, 102–113.

Frey, K., Hirschstein, M., Snell, J., Edstrom, L., MacKenzie, E., & Broderick, C. (2005). Reducing playground bullying and supporting beliefs: An experimental trial of the Steps to Respect Program. *Developmental Psychology*, 41, 479–491.

Frey, K., Nolen, S., Van Schoiack-Edstrom, L., & Hirschstein, M. (2005). Effects of a school-based social-emotional competence program: Linking children's goals, attributions, and behavior. *Journal of Applied Developmental Psychology*, 26, 171–200.

Frick, P., Cornell, A., Barry, C., Bodin, S., & Dane, H. (2003). Callous-unemotional traits and conduct problems in the prediction of conduct problem severity, aggression, and self-report of delinquency. *Journal of Abnormal Child Psychology*, 31, 457–470.

Frijda, N. (1986). *The emotions*. UK: Cambridge University Press.

Frijda, N., Kuipers, P., & Ter Schure, E. (1989). Relations among emotion, appraisal, and emotional action readiness. *Journal of Personality and Social Psychology*, 57, 212–228.

Funder, D. (2006). Towards a resolution of the personality triad: Persons, situations, and behaviors. *Journal of Research in Personality*, 40, 21–34.

Furlong, M., Bates, M., & Smith, D. (2001). Predicting school weapon possession: A secondary analysis of the youth risk behavior surveillance survey. *Psychology in the Schools*, 38, 127–139.

Garbarino, J. (1997). Making sense out of senseless youth violence. Paper presented at the Annual Convention of the American Psychological Association, Chicago, August.

Giordano, P., Manning, W., & Longmore, M. (2005). The romantic relationships of African-American and White adolescents. *The Sociological Quarterly*, 46, 545–568.

Glick, B., & Goldstein, A. (1987). Aggression replacement training. *Journal of Counseling & Development*, 65, 356–362.

Goldstein, A., Glick, B., & Gibbs, J. (1998). *Aggression replacement training: A comprehensive intervention for aggressive youth (revised edition)*. Champaign, IL: Research Press.

Goleman, D. (1995). *Emotional intelligence*, New York: Bantam books.

Graham, K., Tremblay, P. F., Wells, S., Pernanen, K., Purcell, J., Jelley, J. (2006). Harm, intent, and the nature of aggressive behavior: Measuring naturally occurring aggression in barroom settings. *Assessment*, 13, 280–296.

Green, D., Goldman, S., & Salovey, P. (1993). Measurement error masks bipolarity in affect ratings. *Journal of Personality and Social Psychology*, 64, 1029–1041.

Greenberg, L. (2002). *Emotion-focused therapy: Coaching clients to work through their feelings*. Washington, DC: American Psychological Association.

Greenberg, M. T., Kusche, C. A., Cook, E. T., & Quamma, J. P. (1995). Promoting emotional competence in school-aged deaf children: The effects of the PATHS curriculum, *Development and Psychopathology*, 7, 117–136.

Greenberg, M. T., & Kusche, C. (2006). Building social and emotional competence: The PATHS curriculum. In S. Jimerson & M. Furlong (Eds), *Handbook of school violence and school safety: From research to practice* (pp. 395–412). Mahwah, NJ: Erlbaum.

Grossman, D., Neckerman, H., Koepsell, T., Liu, P., Asher, K., Beland, K., Frey, K., & Rivara, F. (1997). Effectiveness of a violence prevention curriculum among children in elementary school. A randomized controlled trial. *JAMA*, 277, 1605–1611.

Gurtman, M. (1992). Construct validity of interpersonal personality measures: The interpersonal circumplex as a nomological net. *Journal of Personality and Social Psychology*, 63, 105–118.

Haynie, D., Nansel, T., Eitel, P., Crump, A., Saylor, K., Yu, K., & Simons-Morton, B. (2001). Bullies, victims, and bully/victims: Distinct groups of at-risk youth. *Journal of Early Adolescence*, 21, 29–49.

Henggeler, S., Schoenwald, S., Rowland, M., & Cunningham, P. (2002). *Serious emotional disturbance in children and adolescents: Multisystemic therapy*. New York: Guilford.

Henrich, C., Brown, J., & Aber, J. (1999). Evaluating the effectiveness of school-based violence prevention: Developmental approaches. *Social Policy Report: Society for Research in Child Development*. 13, 3–19.

Henry, B., Caspi, A., Moffitt, T., & Silva, P. (1996). Temperamental and familial predictors of violent and nonviolent criminal convictions: Age 3 to age 18. *Developmental Psychology*, 32, 614–623.

Hinde, R. (1997). *Relationships: A dialectical perspective*. London, UK: Erlbaum.

Hogan, R. (1969). Development of an empathy scale. *Journal of Consulting and Clinical Psychology*, 33, 307–316.

Huang, B., White, H., Kosterman, R., Catalano, R., & Hawkins, J. (2001). Developmental associations between alcohol and interpersonal aggression during adolescence. *Journal of Research in Crime and Delinquency*, 38, 64–83.

Huesmann, L. (1984). Stability of aggression over time and generations. *Developmental Psychology*, 20, 1120–1134.

Huesmann, L. R., & Moise, J. (1999). Stability and continuity of aggression from early childhood to young adulthood. In D. Flannery & C. Huff (Eds.) *Youth violence: Prevention, Intervention, and Social Policy* (pp. 73–95), Washington, DC: American Psychiatric Press, Inc.

Huesmann, L. R., Eron, L., Lefkowitz, M. M., & Walder, L. (1984). Stability of aggression over time and generations. *Developmental Psychology*, 20, 1120–1134.

Huesmann, L., Moise-Titus, J., Podolski, C., & Eron, L. (2003). Longitudinal relations between children's exposure to TV violence and their aggressive and violent behavior in young adulthood: 1977–1992. *Developmental Psychology*, 39, 201–221.

Huey, S., Henggeler, S., Brondino, M., & Pickrel, S. (2000). Mechanisms of change in multisystemic therapy: Reducing delinquent behavior through therapist adherence and improved family and peer functioning. *Journal of Consulting and Clinical Psychology*, 68, 451–467.

Huizinga, D., Esbensen, F., & Weiher, A. (1996). The impact of arrest on subsequent delinquent behavior. In R. Loeber, D. Huizinga, & T. Thornberry (Eds.). *Program of research on the causes and correlates of delinquency: Annual report 1995–1996* (pp. 82–101). Washington, DC: Office of Juvenile Justice and Delinquency Prevention.

Ireland, J., & Archer, J. (2002). Association between measures of aggression and bullying among juvenile and young offenders. *Aggressive Behavior*, 30, 29–42.

Johnston, L. D., Bachman, J. F., & O'Malley, P. M. (2000). Monitoring the Future: A continuing study of American youth (12th – grade survey), 1998 [Electronic data set]. Ann Arbor, MI: Survey Research Center, Institute for Social Research, University of Michigan [The Inter-University Consortium for Political and Social Research (ICPSR), Producer and Distributor].

Joireman, J., Anderson, J., & Strathman, A. (2003). The aggression paradox: Understanding links among aggression, sensation seeking, and the consideration of future consequences. *Journal of Personality and Social Psychology*, 84, 1287–1302.

Jolliffe, D., & Farrington, D. P. (2004). Empathy and offending: A systematic review and meta-analysis. *Aggression and Violence Behavior: A Review Journal*, 9, 441–476.

Jolliffe, D., Farrington, D. P., Hawkins, J., Catalano, R. F., Hill, K., & Kosterman, R. (2003). Predictive, concurrent, prospective and retrospective validity of self-reported delinquency. *Criminal Behaviour and Mental Health*, 13, 179–197.

Jouriles, E., McDonald, R., Garrido, E., Rosenfield, D., & Brown, A. (2005). Assessing aggression in adolescent romantic relationships: Can we do it better? *Psychological Assessment*, 17, 469–475.

Kagan, J., & Moss, H. (1962). *Birth to maturity: A study in psychological development*. New York: Wiley.

Kann, L., Brener, N. Warren, C., Collins, J., & Giovino, G. (2002). An assessment of the effect of data collection setting on the prevalence of health risk behaviors among adolescents, *Journal of Adolescent Health*, 31, 327–335.

Kann, L., Warren, C., Harris, W., Collins, J., Douglas, K., Collins, M., Williams, B., Ross, J., & Kolbe, L. (1995). Youth risk behavior surveillance – United States, 1993. *Morbidity and Mortality Weekly Report*, 446(SS-1), 1–57.

Kam, C., Greenberg, M., & Kusche, C. (2004). Sustained effects of the PATHS curriculum on the social and psychological adjustment of children in special education. *Journal of Emotional and Behavioral Disorders*, 12, 66–78.

Kaukiainen, A., Bjorkqvist, K., Lagerspetz, K., Osterman, K., Salmivalli, C. Rothberg, S., & Ahlbom, A. (1999). The relationships between social intelligence, empathy, and three types of aggression. *Aggressive Behavior*, 25, 81–89.

Kellner, M., & Bry, B. (1999). The effects of anger management in a day school for emotionally disturbed adolescents. *Adolescence*, 34, 645–651.

Kilpatrick, D., Ruggiero, K., Acierno, R., Saunders, B., Resnick, H., & Best, C. (2003). Violence and risk of PTSD, major depression, substance abuse/dependence, and comorbidity: Results from the National Survey of Adolescents. *Journal of Consulting and Clinical Psychology*, 71, 692–700.

Kim, K., Conger, R., Lorenz, F., & Elder, G. (2001). Parent-adolescent reciprocity in negative affect and its relation to early adult social development. *Developmental Psychology*, 37, 775–790.

Kinsfogel, K., & Grych, J. (2004). Interparental conflict and adolescent dating relationships: Integrating cognitive, emotional, and peer influences. *Journal of Family Psychology*. 18, 505–515.

Knox, M., King, C., Hanna, G., Logan, D., & Ghaziuddin, N. (2000). Aggressive behavior in clinically depressed adolescents. *Journal of the American Academy of Child & Adolescent Psychiatry*, 39, 611–618.

Kolbe, L., Kann, L., & Colllins, J. (1993). Overview of the Youth Risk Behavior Surveillance System. *Public Health Report* 108, Supplement 1, 2–10.

Kosson, D., Cyterski, T., Steuerwald, B., Neumann, C., & Walker-Matthews, S. (2002). The reliability and validity of the Psychopathy Checklist: Youth Version (PCL:YV) in nonincarcerated adolescent males. *Psychological Assessment*, 14, 97–109.

Kruh, I., Frick, P., & Clements, C. (2005). Historical and personality correlates to the violence patterns of juveniles tried as adults. *Criminal Justice and Behavior*, 32, 69–96.

Ladd, G., & Profilet, S. (1996). The Child Behavior Scale: A teacher-report measure of young children's aggressive, withdrawn, and prosocial behaviors. *Developmental Psychology*, 32, 1008–1024.

Larson, R., & Richards, M. H. (1994). *Divergent realities: The emotional lives of mothers, fathers, and adolescents*. New York: Basic Books.

Leadbeater, B., & Hoglund, W. (2003). Changing contexts? The effects of a primary prevention program on classroom levels of peer relational and physical victimization. *Journal of Community Psychology*, 31, 397–418.

Lee, P., Joffe, R., & Midgley, A. (1974). Serum gonadotropins, testosterone, and prolactin concentrations throughout puberty in boys: A longitudinal study. *Journal of Clinical Endocrinology and Metabolism*, 39, 664–672.

Lennings, C., Copeland, J., & Howard, J. (2003). Substance use patterns of young offenders and violent crime. *Aggressive Behavior*, 29, 414–422.

Lerner, J., & Keltner, D. (2001). Fear, anger, and risk. *Journal of Personality and Social Psychology*, 81, 146–159.

Lerner, R., & Shea, J. (1982). Social behavior in adolescence. In B. Wolman (Ed), *Handbook of Developmental Psychology* (pp. 503–525). Englewood Cliffs, NJ: Prentice Hall.

Limber, S. (2006). The Olweus bullying prevention program: An overview of its implementation and research basis. In S. Jimerson & M. Furlong (Eds), *Handbook of school violence and school safety: From research to practice* (pp. 293–307). Mahwah, NJ: Erlbaum.

Limber, S., Nation, M., Tracy, A., Melton, G., & Flerx, V. (2004). Implementation of the Olweus Bullying Prevention program in the Southeastern United States. In P. Smith,

D. Pepler, & K. Rigby (Eds.). *Bullying in schools: How successful can interventions be?* (pp. 55–79). New York: Cambridge University Press.

Lipsey, M., & Derzon, J. (1999). Predictors of violent or serious delinquency in adolescence and early adulthood. In R. Loeber & D. Farrington (Eds.). *Serious and violent juvenile offender* (pp. 86–105). Thousand Oaks, CA: Sage.

Lochman, J., & Dodge, K. (1994). Social-cognitive processes of severely violent, moderately aggressive, and non-aggressive boys. *Journal of Consulting and Clinical Psychology*, 62, 366–374.

Lockwood, D. (1997). *Violence among middle school and high school students: Analysis and implications for prevention.* Washington, DC: National Institute of Justice Research in Brief, Department of Justice.

Loeber, R. (1982). The stability of antisocial and delinquent child behavior: A review. *Child Development*, 53, 1431–1446.

Loeber, R. & Dishion, T. (1983). Early predictors of male delinquency: A review. *Psychological Bulletin*, 94, 68–99.

Loeber, R., & Hay, D. (1997). Key issues in the development of aggression and violence from childhood to early adulthood. *Annual Review of Psychology*, 48, 371–410.

Loeber, R., Pardini, D., Homish, D. L., Crawford, A. M., Farrington, D. P., Stouthamer-Loeber, M., Creemers, J., Koehler, S. A., & Rosenfeld, R. (2005). The prediction of violence and homicide in young men. *Journal of Consulting and Clinical Psychology*, 73, 1074–1088.

Loeber, R., & Stouthamer-Loeber, M. (1998). Development of juvenile aggression and violence: Some common misconceptions and controversies. *American Psychologist*, 53, 242–259.

Lopez, V., & Emmer, E. (2002). Influences of beliefs and values on male adolescents' decision to commit violent offenses. *Psychology of Men and Masculinity*, 3, 28–40.

Luengo, M., Carrillo-de-la-Pena, M., Otero, J., & Romero, E. (1994). A short-term longitudinal study of impulsivity and antisocial behavior. *Journal of Personality and Social Psychology*, 66, 542–548.

Lynam, D., Caspi, A., Moffitt, T., Wikstrom, P., Loeber, R., & Novak, S. (2000). The interaction between impulsivity and neighborhood context on offending: The effects of impulsivity are stronger in poorer neighborhoods. *Journal of Abnormal Psychology*, 109, 563–574.

Lynch, J. P. (2002). Trends in juvenile violence offending: An analysis of victim survey data. *Office of Juvenile Justice Bulletin*, Washington, DC: Office of Juvenile Justice and Delinquency Prevention.

Malik, S., Sorenson, S., & Aneschensel, C. (1997). Community and dating violence among adolescents: Perpetration and victimization. *Journal of Adolescent Health*, 21, 291–302.

Marcus, R. F. (2005). Youth violence in everyday life. *Journal of Interpersonal Violence*, 20, 442–447.

Marcus, R. F., & Betzer, P. (1996). Attachment and antisocial behavior in early adolescence. *Journal of Early Adolescence*, 16, 229–248.

Marcus, R. F., & Kramer, C. (2001). Reactive and proactive aggression: Attachment and social competence predictors. *Journal of Genetic Psychology*, 162, 260–275.

Marcus, R. F., & Reio, T. (2002). Severity of injury resulting from violence among college students: Proximal and distal influences. *Journal of Interpersonal Violence.* 17, 888–908.

Marcus, R. F., & Sanders-Reio, J. (2001). The influence of attachment on school completion. *School Psychology Quarterly*, 16, 427–444.

Marcus, R. F., & Swett, B. (2003a). Violence in close relationships: The role of emotion. *Aggression and Violent Behavior: A Review Journal*, 8, 313–328.

Marcus, R. F., & Swett, B. (2003b). Multiple-Precursor Scenarios: Predicting and reducing campus violence. *Journal of Interpersonal Violence*, 18, 553–571.

Mayer, J., Salovey, P., Caruso, D., & Sitarenios, G. (2001). Emotional intelligence as a standard intelligence. *Emotion*, 1, 232–242.

McGee, J., & DeBernardo, C. (1999). The classroom avenger: A behavioral profile of school based shootings. *Forensic Examiner*, 8, 16–18.

McGue, M., Elkins, I., Walden, B., & Iacono, W. (2005). Perceptions of the parent-adolescent relationship: A longitudinal investigation. *Developmental Psychology*, 41, 971–984.

Mehrabian, A. (1997). Relations among personality scales of aggression, violence, and empathy: Validational evidence bearing on the risk of eruptive violence scale. *Aggressive Behavior*, 23, 433–445.

Mehrabian, A., & Epstein, N. (1972). A measure of emotional empathy. *Journal of Personality*, 40, 523–543.

Miller, P., & Eisenberg, N. (1988). The relation of empathy to aggressive and externalizing/antisocial behavior. *Psychological Bulletin*, 103, 324–344.

Miller-Johnson, S., Coie, J., Maumary-Gremaud, A., Lochman, J., & Terry, R. (1999). Relationship between childhood peer rejection and aggression and adolescent delinquency severity and type among African American youth. *Journal of Emotional & Behavioral Disorders*, 7, 137–147.

Moffitt, T. (1993). Adolescence-limited and life-course-persistent antisocial behavior: A developmental taxonomy. *Psychological Review*, 100, 701–774.

Monroe, S., Rohde, P., Seeley, J., & Lewinsohn, P. (1999). Life events and depression in adolescence: Relationship loss as a prospective risk factor for first onset of major depressive disorder. *Journal of Abnormal Psychology*, 108, 606–614.

Montemayor, R., & Hanson, E. (1985). A naturalistic view of conflict between adolescents and their parents and siblings. *Journal of Early Adolescence*, 5, 23–30.

Montgomery, M. (2005). Psychosocial intimacy and identity: From early adolescence to emerging adulthood. *Journal of Adolescent Research*, 20, 346–374.

Mouttapa, M., Valente, T., Gallaher, P., Rohrbach, L., & Unger, J. (2005). Social network predictors of bullying and victimization. *Adolescence*, 39, 315–335.

Mulvey, E., & Cauffman, E. (2001). The inherent limits of predicting school violence. *American Psychologist*, 56, 797–802.

Muris, P., & Meesters, C. (2003). The validity of attention deficit hyperactivity disorder symptom domains in nonclinical Dutch children. *Journal of Clinical Child and Adolescent Psychology*, 32, 460–466.

Mytton, J., DiGuiseppi, C., Gough, D., Taylor, R., & Logan, S. (2002). School-based violence prevention programs: Systematic review of secondary prevention trials. *Archives of Pediatric Adolescent Medicine*, 156, 752–762.

Nansell, T., Overpeck, M., Pilla, R., Ruan, W., Simmons-Morton, K. B. & Scheidt, P. (2001). Bullying behavior among US youths: Prevalence and association with psychosocial adjustment. *JAMA*, 285, 2094–2100.

National Center for Health Statistics. (2004). *10 Leading Causes of Death, by Age Group-2002*. National Vital Statistics Systems, Center for Disease Control.

National Center for Juvenile Justice. (2005). Juvenile arrest rates by offense, sex, and race. Online at http://OJJDP.NCJRS.ORG/OJJSTATEbb/crime.

National Institutes of Health. (2006). National Institutes of Health state-of-the-science conference statement. *Journal of Clinical Child Psychology*, 34, 457–470.

Ngwe, J., Liu, L. Flay, B., Segawa, E., & Aban Aya Co-Investigators (2004). Violence prevention among African American adolescent males. *American Journal of Health Behavior*, 28(supplement 1), 24–37.

Nichols, T., Graber, J., Brooks-Funn, J., Botvin, G. (2006). Sex differences in overt aggression and delinquency among urban minority middle school students. *Applied Developmental Psychology*, 27, 78–91.

Offer, J. (1969). *The psychological world of the teenager*. New York: Basic Books.

Offer, D. & Offer, J. (1975). *From teenage to young manhood: A psychological study*. New York: Basic Books.

O'Keefe, M. (1997). Predictors of dating violence among high school students. *Journal of Interpersonal Violence*, 12, 546–568.

O'Keefe, M., & Treister, L. (1998). Victims of dating violence among high school students: Are the predictors different for males and females? *Violence Against Women*, 4, 195–223.

O'Keefe, M., Mennen, F., & Lane, C. J. (2006). An examination of the factor structure for the Youth Self Report on a multiethnic population. *Research on Social Work Practice*, 16, 315–325.

Olweus, D. (1993). *Bullying in school: What we know and what we can do*. New York: Blackwell.

Olweus, D., & Endresen, I. (1998). The importance of sex-of-stimulus object: Age trends and sex differences in empathic responsiveness. *Social Development*, 7, 370–388.

Orobio de Castro, B., Veerman, J., Koops, W., Bosch, J., & Monshouwer, H. (2002). Hostile attribution of intent and aggressive behavior: A meta-analysis. *Child Development*, 73, 916–934.

Osborne, J. (2002). *Relationships between identification with academics and important academic outcomes in secondary school students*. Unpublished manuscript, North Carolina State University, Raleigh.

Osborne, J. (2004). Identification with academics and violence in schools. *Review of General Psychology*, 8, 147–162.

Paik, H., & Comstock, G. (1994). The effects of television violence on antisocial behavior: A meta-analysis. *Communication Research*, 21, 516–546.

Parke, R., & Slaby, R. (1983). The development of aggression. In P. Mussen (series ed.) & M. Hetherington (Ed.), *Handbook of Child psychology: Vol. 4. Socialization, personality, and social development* (pp. 547–641). New York: Wiley.

Parker, J., Low, C., Walker, A., Gamm, B. (2005). Friendship jealousy in young adolescents: Individual differences and links to sex, self-esteem, aggression and social adjustment. *Developmental Psychology*, 41, 235–250.

Patterson, G., DeBaryshe, B., & Ramsey, E. (1989). A developmental perspective on antisocial behavior. *American Psychologist*, 44, 329–335.

Pellegrini, A. D., & Long, J. D. (2002). A longitudinal study of bullying, dominance, and victimization during the transition from primary to secondary school. *British Journal of Developmental Psychology*, 20, 259–280.

Pepler, D., Craig, W., Connolly, J., Yuile, A., McMaster, L., & Jiang, D. (2006). A developmental perspective on bullying. *Aggressive Behavior*, 32, 376–384.

Petersen, A., Compas, B., Brooks-Gun, J., Stemmler, M., Ey, S., & Grant, K. (1993) Depression in adolescence. *American Psychologist*, 48, 155–168.

PEW Global Attitudes Project (2005). *U.S. image up slightly, but still negative: American character gets mixed reviews.* June 23, 2005.

Pickett, T., Schmid, H., Boyce, W., Simpsons, K., Scheidt, P. Mazur, J., Malcho, M. King, M., Godeau, E., Overpeck, M. Aszmann, A., Szabo, M., & Harel, Y. (2002). Multiple risk behavior and injury: An international analysis of young people. *Archives of Pediatric and Adolescent Medicine*, 156, 786–793.

Piko, B., Kereztes, N., & Pluhar, Z. (2006). Aggressive behavior and psychosocial health among children. *Personality and Individual Differences*, 40, 885–895.

Poulin, F., & Boivin, M. (2000). The role of proactive and reactive aggression in the formation and development of boys' friendships. *Developmental Psychology*, 36, 233–240.

Prinstein, M., Boergers, J., & Vernberg, E. (2001). Overt and relational aggression in adolescents: Social-psychological adjustment of aggressors and victims, *Journal of Clinical Child Psychology*, 30, 479–491.

Pulkkinen, L. (1982). Self-control and continuity from childhood to late adolescence. In P. B. Baltes & O. G. Brim (Eds.), *Lifespan development and behavior* (pp. 63–85). New York: Academic Press.

Raine, A., Moffitt, T., Caspi, A., Loeber, R., Stouthamer-Loeber, M., & Lynam, D. (2005). Neurocognitive impairments in boys on the life-course persistent antisocial path. *Journal of Abnormal Psychology*, 114, 38–49.

Raine, A., Dodge, K., Loeber, R., Gatzke, Kopp, L., Lynam, D., Reynolds, C., Stouthamer-Loeber, M., & Liu, J. (2006). The reactive-proactive aggression questionnaire: Differential correlates of reactive and proactive aggression in adolescent boys. *Aggressive Behavior*, 32, 159–171.

Ramos, E., Frontera, W., Llopart, A., & Feliciano, D. (1998). Muscle strength and hormonal levels in adolescents: Gender related differences. *International Journal of Sports Medicine*, 19, 526–531.

Reynolds, C., & Kamphaus, R. (1992). *Behavior assessment system for children manual.* US: American Guidance Services.

Rigby, K. (2006). What we can learn from evaluated studies of school-based programs to reduce bullying in schools. In S. Jimerson & M. Furlong (Eds), *Handbook of school violence and school safety: From research to practice* (pp. 325–337). Mahwah, NJ: Erlbaum.

Roberts, B., Walton, K., & Viechtbauer, W. (2006). Patterns of mean-level change in personality traits across the life course: A meta-analysis of longitudinal studies. *Psychological Bulletin*, 132, 1–25.

Roberts, T., Auinger, P., & Klein, J. (2006). Predictors of partner abuse in a nationally representative sample of adolescents involved in heterosexual dating relationships. *Violence and Victims*, 21, 81–89.

Robins, R., Caspi, A., & Moffitt, T. (2002). It's not just who you're with, it's who you are: Personality and relationship experiences across multiple relationships. *Journal of Personality*, 70, 925–964.

Robinson, T., Smith, S., Miller, M., & Brownell, M. (1999). Cognitive behavior modification of hyperactivity-impulsivity and aggression: A meta-analysis of school-based studies. *Journal of Educational Psychology*, 91, 195–203.

Roeser, R., Eccles, J., & Sameroff, A. (1998). Academic and emotional functioning in early adolescence: Longitudinal relations, patterns, and prediction by experience in middle school. *Development and Psychopathology*, 10, 321–352.

Rohde, P., Lewinsohn, P., & Seeley, J. (1991). Comorbidity of unipolar depression: II. Comorbidity with other mental disorders in adolescents and adults. *Journal of Abnormal Psychology*, 100, 214–222.

Rokach, A. (1987). Anger and aggression control training: Replacing attack with interaction. *Psychotherapy: Theory, Research, Practice, Training*, 24, 353–362.

Rose, A., & Rudolph, K (2006). A review of sex differences in peer relationship processes: Potential trade-offs for the emotional and behavioral development of girls and boys. *Psychological Bulletin*, 132, 98–131.

Rossow, I., Pape, H., & Wichstrom, L. (1999). Young, wet & wild? Associations between alcohol intoxication and violent behaviour in adolescence. *Addiction*, 94, 1017–1031.

Rotenberg, K. (1985). Causes, intensity, motives, and consequences of children's anger from self-reports. *Journal of Genetic Psychology*, 146, 101–106.

Rubin, K., Bukowski, W., & Parker, J. (1998). Peer interaction, relationships, and groups. In W. Damon & N. Eisenberg (Eds). *Handbook of child psychology, 5th ed.: Vol. 3. Social, emotional, and personality development* (pp. 619–700). New York: Wiley.

Rudolph, U., Roesch, S., Greitmeyer, T., & Weiner, B. (2004). A meta-analytic review of help giving and aggression from an attributional perspective: Contributions to a general theory of motivation. *Cognition & Emotion*, 18, 815–848.

Russell, J., & Fehr, B. (1994). Fuzzy concepts in a fuzzy hierarchy: Varieties of anger. *Journal of Personality and Social Psychology*, 67, 186–205.

Schaeffer, C., & Borduin, C. (2005). Long-term follow-up to a randomized clinical trial of multisystemic therapy with serious and violent juvenile offenders. *Journal of Consulting and Clinical Psychology*, 73, 445–453.

Schafer, M., Korn, S., Brodbeck, F., Wolke, D., & Schulz, H. (2005). Bullying roles in changing contexts: The stability of victim and bully roles from primary to secondary school. *International Journal of Behavioral Development*, 29, 323–335.

Schniering, C., & Rapee, R. (2004). The relationship between automatic thoughts and negative emotions in children and adolescents: A test of the cognitive content-specificity hypothesis. *Journal of Abnormal Psychology*, 113, 464–470.

Schultz, D., Izard, C., & Bear, G. (2004). Children's emotional processing: Relations to emotionality and aggression. *Development and Psychopathology*, 16, 371–387.

Shapiro, J., Dorman, R., Burkey, W., Welker, C., & Clough, J. (1997). Development and factor analysis of a measure of youth attitudes toward guns and violence. *Journal of Clinical Child Psychology*, 26, 311–320.

Shure, M. (2001). I can problem solve (ICPS): An interpersonal cognitive problem solving program for children. *Residential Treatment for Child & Youth*, 18, 3–14.

Siegel, O. (1982). Personality development in adolescence. In B. Wolman (Ed) *Handbook of Developmental Psychology* (pp. 537–548), Englewood Cliffs, NJ: Prentice Hall.

Sigelman, C., & Rider, E. (2003). *Life-span human development*. Belmont, CA: Wasdsworth.

Simmons, R., & Blyth, D. (1987). *Moving into adolescence: The impact of pubertal change and school context*. NY: Aldine de Gruyter.

Slep, A., Cascardi, M., Avery-Leaf, S., & O'Leary, K. (2001). Two new measures of attitudes about the acceptability of teen dating aggression. *Psychological Assessment*, 13, 306–318.

Smith-Khuri, E., Iachan, R., Scheidt, P., Overpeck, M., Gabhaim, S. Pickett, W., & Harrell, V. (2004). A cross-national study of violence-related behaviors in adolescents. *Archives of Pediatric and Adolescent Medicine*, 158, 539–544.

Snyder, J. N. (2004). Juvenile arrests 2002. *Office of Juvenile Justice Bulletin*, Washington, DC: Office of Juvenile Justice and Delinquency Prevention

Snyder, H., & Sickmund, M. (1999). *Juvenile offenders and victims: 1999 national report*. Washington, DC: Office of Juvenile Justice and Delinquency Prevention.

Spielberger, C. (1988). *Manual for the State-Trait Anger Expression Inventory*. Odessa, FL: Psychological Assessment Resources.

Spielberger, C. (1999). *STAXI-2 State-Trait Expression Inventory-2: Professional Manual*. Lutz, FL: Psychological Assessment Resources, Inc.

Stattin, H., & Magnusson, D. (1989). The role of early aggressive behavior in the frequency, seriousness, and types of later crime. *Journal of Consulting and Clinical Psychology*, 57, 710–718.

Straus, M. A. (1979). Measuring intrafamily conflict and violence. *Journal of Marriage and the Family*, 36, 13–29.

Straus, M. A., Hamby, S. L., Boney-McCoy, S., & Sugarman, D. B. (1996). The Revised Conflict Tactics Scale (CTS2): Developmental and preliminary psychometric data. *Journal of Family Issues*. 17, 283–316.

Stephens, R. (1998). Safe school planning. In D. Elliott, B. Hamburg, & K. Williams (Eds.) *Violence in American Schools* (pp. 253–289). New York: Cambridge University Press.

Sugarman, D., & Hotaling, G. (1989). Dating violence: Prevalence, context, and risk markers. In M. Perog-Good & J. Stets (Eds.), *Violence in dating relationships: Emerging social issues* (pp. 3–32). New York: Praeger.

Swaffer, T., & Epps, K. (1999). The psychometric assessment of anger in male and female adolescents resident at a secure youth treatment centre. *Journal of Adolescence*, 22, 419–422.

Swahn, M., Simon, T., Hammig, B., & Guerrero, J. (2004). Alcohol-consumption behaviors and risk for physical fighting and injuries among adolescent drinkers. *Addictive Behaviors*, 29, 959–963.

Swaim, R., Deffenbacher, J., & Wayman, J. (2004). Concurrent and prospective effects of multi-dimensional aggression and anger on adolescent alcohol use. *Aggressive Behavior*, 30, 356–372.

Swett, B., Marcus, R., & Reio, T. (2005). An introduction to "fight-seeking," and its role in peer-to-peer violence on college campuses. *Personality and Individual Differences* 38, 953–962.

Tangney, J., Wagner, P., Hill-Barlow, D., Marschall, D., & Gramzow, R., (1996). Relation of shame and guilt to constructive versus destructive responses to anger across the lifespan. *Journal of Personality and Social Psychology*, 70, 797–809.

Tangney, J., Hill-Barlow, D., Wagner, P., Marschall, D., Borenstein, J., Sanftner, J., Mohr, T., & Gramzow, R. (1996). Assessing individual differences in constructive versus destructive responses to anger across the lifespan. *Journal of Personality and Social Psychology*, 70, 780–796.

Tanner, J. M. (1970). Physical Growth. In P. Mussen (Ed.). *Carmichael's manual of child psychology* (3rd ed.) (pp. 77–155). New York: Wiley.

Tate, D., Repucci, N., & Mulvey, E. (1995). Violent juvenile delinquents: Treatment effectiveness and implications for future action. *American Psychologist*, 50, 777–781.

Tedeschi, J., & Felson, R. (1994). *Violence, aggression, and coercive actions*. Washington, DC: American Psychological Association.

Tobin, T., & Sugai, G. (1999). Using sixth-grade school records to predict school violence, chronic discipline problems, and high school outcomes. *Journal of Emotional and Behavioral Disorders*, 7, 40–53.

Toch, H. (1992). *Violent men*. Washington, DC: American Psychological Association.

Tolan, P. (1987). Implications of age of onset for delinquency risk Identification. *Journal of Abnormal Child Psychology*, 15, 47–65.

Tolan, P., & Gorman-Smith, D. (1999). Development of serious and violent offending careers. In R. Loeber & D. Farrington (Eds.). *Serious and violent juvenile offenders* (pp. 68–85). Thousand Oaks, CA: Sage.

Tolan, P., & Thomas, P. (1995). The implications of age of onset for delinquency risk II: Longitudinal data. *Journal of Abnormal Child Psychology*, 23, 157–181.

Tolmas, H. C. (1998). Violence among youth: A major epidemic in America. *International Journal of Adolescent Medicine and Health*, 10, 243–259.

Tracy, P. E., Wolfgang, M. E., & Figlio, R. M. (1990). *Delinquency careers in two birth cohorts*. New York: Plenum.

Tremblay, R. (2006). Prevention of youth violence: Why not start at the beginning? *Journal of Abnormal Child Psychology*, 34, 481–487.

Tuma, F., Loeber, R., & Lochman, J. (2006). Introduction to special section on the National Institutes of Health State of the Science Report on violence prevention. *Journal of Abnormal Child Psychology*, 34, 451–456.

Unnever, J. (2005). Bullies, aggressive victims, and victims: Are they distinct groups? *Aggressive Behavior*, 31, 153–171.

U.S. Department of Health and Human Services. (1997). *Morbidity and Mortality Weekly Report*, 46(5), Atlanta, GA: Centers for Disease Control and Prevention.

U.S. Department of Health and Human Services. (2001). *Youth violence: A report of the surgeon general*. Rockville, MD: U. S. Government Printing Office.

U.S. Department of Health and Human Services, Centers for Disease Control and Prevention. (2004). Violence-related behaviors among high school students-United States, 1991–2003. *Morbidity and Mortality Weekly Report*, 53, 651–655.

U.S. Department of Health and Human Services, Centers for Disease Control and Prevention. (2006a). *Morbidity and Mortality Weekly Report*. 55(SS05), Atlanta, GS: Centers for Disease Control and Prevention, 1–108.

U.S. Department of Health and Human Services, Centers for Disease Control and Prevention. (2006b) Youth Risk Behavior Survey: 1993–2005 on line at www.cdc.gov/YRBSS.

U.S. Department of Justice, Federal Bureau of Investigation (2002). *Crime in the United States*, 2001. Washington, DC: U.S. Government Printing Office.

U.S. Department of Justice. (2006). Synopsis of crime in schools and colleges: A study of the National Incident-based Reporting System(NIBRS) data, Federal Bureau of Investigation, www.fbi.gov/ucr/ucr.htm.

U.S. News and World Report (1993). When killers come to class: Violence in schools. November 8, pp. 31–36.

VandenBos, G. R. (2007). *APA Dictionary of Psychology*. Washington, DC: American Psychological Association.

Van Schoiack-Edstrom, L., Frey, K., & Beland, K. (2002). Changing adolescents' attitudes about relational and physical aggression: An early evaluation of a school-based intervention. *School Psychology Review*, 31, 201–216.

Vermeiren, R., Schwab-Stone, M., Ruchkin, V., King, R., Van Heeringen, C., & Debouette, D. (2003). Suicidal behavior and violence in male adolescents: A school-based study. *Journal of the American Academy of Child & Adolescent Psychiatry*, 42, 41–48.

Villani, S., & Sharfstein, S. (1999). Clinical case conference: Evaluating and treating violent adolescents in the managed care era. *American Journal of Psychiatry*, 156, 458–464.

von Collani, G. T., & Werner, R. (2005) Self-related and motivational constructs as determinants of aggression. An analysis and validation of a German version of the Buss-Perry Aggression Questionnaire. *Personality and Individual Differences*, 38, 1631–1643.

Waters, J. R., Hyder, A. A., Rajkotia, Y., Basu, S., & Butchart, A. (2005). The costs of interpersonal violence- an international review. *Health Policy*, 73, 303–315.

Webster's Contemporary American Dictionary of the English Language. (1979). New York: Houghton Mifflin.

Wechsler, D. (2003). *Wechsler Intelligence Scale for Children-Fourth Edition, Administration and Scoring Manual*. San Antonio, TX: Psychological Corporation.

Weissberg, R. (2005). Social and emotional learning for school and life success. Paper presented at the Annual Convention of the American Psychological Association, Washington, August.

Wekerle, C., & Wolfe, D. (1999). Dating violence in mid-adolescence: Theory, significance, and emerging prevention initiatives. *Clinical Psychology Review*, 19, 435–456.

White, R., Bates, H., & Buyske, S. (2001). Adolescent-limited versus persistent delinquency: Extending Moffitt's hypothesis into adulthood. *Journal of Abnormal Psychology*, 110, 600–609.

White, H., Brick, J., & Hansell, S. (1993). A longitudinal investigation of alcohol use and aggression in adolescence. *Journal of Studies Alcohol Supplement*, 11, 62–77.

White, H., & Hansell, S. (1998). Acute and long-term effects of drug use on aggression from adolescence into adulthood. *Journal of Drug Issues*, 28, 837–859.

Wiesner, M. (2003). A longitudinal latent variable analysis of reciprocal relations between depressive symptoms and delinquency during adolescence. *Journal of Abnormal Psychology*, 112, 633–645.

Wigfield, A., & Eccles, J. (1994). Children's competence beliefs, achievement values, and general self-esteem: Change across elementary and middle school. *Journal of Early Adolescence*, 14, 107–138.

Willoughby, T., Chalmers, H., & Busseri, M. A. (2004). Where is the syndrome? Examining co-occurrence among multiple problem behaviors in adolescence. *Journal of Consulting and Clinical Psychology*, 72, 1022–1037.

Wilson, S., Lipsey, M., & Derzon, J. (2003). The effects of school-based intervention programs on aggressive behavior: A meta-analysis. *Journal of Consulting and Clinical Psychology*, 71, 136–149.

Wolfe, D., Scott, K., Reitzel-Joffe, D., Wekerle, C., Grasley, C., & Straatman, A. (2001). Development and validation of the Conflict in Adolescent Dating Relationships Inventory. *Psychological Assessment*, 13, 277–293.

Wolfe, D., Wekerle, C., Reitzel-Jaffe, D., & Lefebvre, L. (1998). Factors associated with abusive relationships among maltreated and nonmaltreated youth. *Development and Psychopathology*, 10, 61–85.

Wolfe, D., Wekerle, C., Scott, K., Straatman, A., & Grasley, C. (2004). Predicting abuse in adolescent dating relationships over 1 year: The role of child maltreatment and trauma. *Journal of Abnormal Psychology*, 113, 406–415.

Wolman, B. (1982). *Handbook of developmental psychology*. Englewood Cliffs, NJ: Prentice Hall.

Zimmer-Gembeck, M. (2002). The development of romantic relationships and adaptations in the system of peer relationships. *Journal of Adolescent Health*, 31(Supplement 6), 216–225.

Zuckerman, M. (1994). *Behavioral expressions and biosocial bases of sensation seeking*. New York: Cambridge University Press.

Zuckerman, M., Kuhlman, D., Joireman, J., Teta, P., & Kraft, M. (1993). A comparison of three structural models for personality: The Big Three, the Big Five, and the Alternative Five. *Journal of Personality and Social Psychology*, 65, 757–768.

Index